THE SECRETS OF PROFESSIONAL CARTOONING!

KEN MUSE

PRENTICE-HALL, INC.
ENGLEWOOD CLIFFS, N.J. 07632

Library of Congress Cataloging in Publication Data

Muse, Ken, date
    The secrets of professional cartooning.

    Includes index.
    1. Cartooning.   I. Title.
NC1320.M86   741.5   80-15940
ISBN 0-13-798140-6
ISBN 0-13-798132-5 (pbk.)

Editorial/production supervision by Ros Herion
Cover design by Ken Muse
Manufacturing buyer: Joyce Levatino

Printed in the United States of America

10 9 8 7 6 5 4 3 2 1

PRENTICE-HALL INTERNATIONAL, INC., London
PRENTICE-HALL OF AUSTRALIA PTY. LIMITED, Sydney
PRENTICE-HALL OF CANADA, LTD., Toronto
PRENTICE-HALL OF INDIA PRIVATE LIMITED, New Delhi
PRENTICE-HALL OF JAPAN, INC., Tokyo
PRENTICE-HALL OF SOUTHEAST ASIA PTE. LTD., Singapore
WHITEHALL BOOKS LIMITED, Wellington, New Zealand

THIS BOOK IS
DEDICATED TO
THE FIRE INSIDE
THOSE FEW
PEOPLE WHO
HAVE NO CHOICE
BUT TO BE A
CARTOONIST.

CARTOON: GILLOTT 1290 / ACTUAL SIZE   LETTERING: GILLOTT 1290

CONTENTS

IN HAPPIER MOMENT

HI, I'M BACK HERE
*AGAIN. MY NAME IS
KEN MUSE, AND
ALL MY EXPERIENCE
AS A PROFESSIONAL
SYNDICATED
CARTOONIST IS
AT YOUR DISPOSAL!

FOR 5 YEARS I
LABORED ON MY
OWN STRIP, NAMED
WAYOUT,
FOR McNAUGHT
SYNDICATE, WRITING
THE GAGS AND
DOING THE DRAWING.
BEING A MEMBER
OF THE NATIONAL
CARTOONIST SOCIETY
PUT ME IN CONTACT
WITH ALL THOSE
CRAZY PEOPLE WHO
DREW THE OTHER
STRIPS.
IF IT WEREN'T FOR
THOSE GREAT PEOPLE
THIS BOOK WOULDN'T
HAVE BEEN POSSIBLE!

THERE'S A LOT
OF INFORMATION
IN THESE PAGES
YOU WON'T GET
ANYWHERE ELSE,
GATHERED FROM
PROFESSIONALS
WHO KNOW
WHAT
THEY'RE
TALKING
ABOUT!

* "PHOTO ONE" AND "PHOTO TWO"

THE SECRETS OF PROFESSIONAL CARTOONING!

NOT ONLY THAT... THEY'RE JUST NOT READING NEWS-PAPERS, MAGAZINES, WATCHING TV, OR NOT DOING MUCH OF ANYTHING!

SOME OF THE FIELDS OPEN TO A GOOD CARTOONIST ARE:

- DIRECT MAIL
- NEWSPAPERS
- MAGAZINES
- SMALL BUSINESS
- TELEVISION
- GREETING CARDS
- POSTERS
- PRINTERS
- SYNDICATES
- PUBLISHERS
- AD AGENCIES
- ART STUDIOS
- PRIVATE PARTIES

THERE'S A BETTER CHANCE FOR A CARTOONIST IN THE ART FIELD THAN ANY OTHER TYPE OF ARTIST! PEOPLE WHO TELL YOU OTHER-WISE, JUST AREN'T PAYING ATTENTION ABOUT WHAT'S GOING ON AROUND THEM.

IN LEARNING TO CARTOON, IT IS IMPORTANT TO SEE FIRST HAND

JUST HOW A PRO CARTOONIST "BEGINS" HIS DRAWING!

THE OBJECT OF THIS BOOK IS TO LET YOU SEE HOW IT'S DONE. I HAVE ALSO INCLUDED THE ACTUAL SIZE THE CARTOONIST DOES HIS DRAWING, SO YOU CAN STUDY THE PEN AND BRUSH STROKES.

STUDY THE PAGES AND MEMORIZE! DRAW AND REDRAW, BECAUSE THIS IS THE SAME WAY YOU LEARNED YOUR ABC'S AND HANDWRITING.

MUSIC IS THE SAME WAY... PRACTICE OTHER MUSICIAN'S MUSIC UNTIL YOU DEVELOP YOUR OWN STYLE.... THEN YOU CAN ORIGINATE YOUR OWN THING.

REMEMBER... I CAN GIVE YOU GOOD POINTERS ON THE SECRETS OF CARTOONING, BUT I CAN'T GIVE YOU ORIGINAL IDEAS, AND IT'S THE ORIGINAL IDEAS THAT SELL THE CARTOONS!

AND ANOTHER THING.... YOU HAVE TO WANT TO BE A CARTOONIST!

THE BASIC ART MATERIALS FOR CARTOONING ARE:

A BOTTLE OF INK,
A BRUSH OR PEN,
PAPER OR BRISTOL,
A PENCIL & ERASER,
AND AN IDEA !

BUT... IF YOUR'E REALLY SERIOUS ABOUT BECOMING A PROFESSIONAL CARTOONIST, YOU'LL NEED THIS:

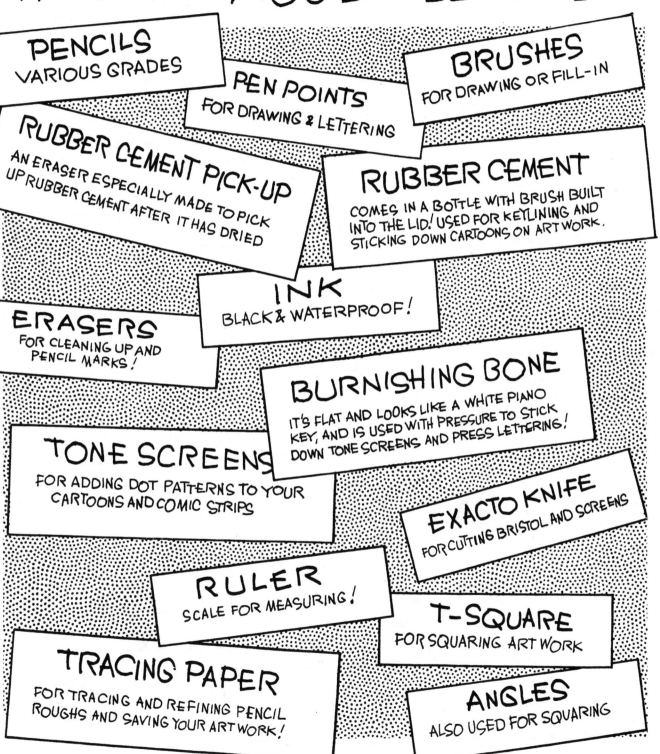

PENCILS
VARIOUS GRADES

PEN POINTS
FOR DRAWING & LETTERING

BRUSHES
FOR DRAWING OR FILL-IN

RUBBER CEMENT PICK-UP
AN ERASER ESPECIALLY MADE TO PICK UP RUBBER CEMENT AFTER IT HAS DRIED

RUBBER CEMENT
COMES IN A BOTTLE WITH BRUSH BUILT INTO THE LID! USED FOR KETLINING AND STICKING DOWN CARTOONS ON ARTWORK.

INK
BLACK & WATERPROOF!

ERASERS
FOR CLEANING UP AND PENCIL MARKS!

BURNISHING BONE
IT'S FLAT AND LOOKS LIKE A WHITE PIANO KEY, AND IS USED WITH PRESSURE TO STICK DOWN TONE SCREENS AND PRESS LETTERING!

TONE SCREENS
FOR ADDING DOT PATTERNS TO YOUR CARTOONS AND COMIC STRIPS

EXACTO KNIFE
FOR CUTTING BRISTOL AND SCREENS

RULER
SCALE FOR MEASURING!

T-SQUARE
FOR SQUARING ART WORK

TRACING PAPER
FOR TRACING AND REFINING PENCIL ROUGHS AND SAVING YOUR ART WORK!

ANGLES
ALSO USED FOR SQUARING

BESTINE
A THINNER FOR RUBBER CEMENT. WILL ALLOW THINGS CEMENTED TO BE TAKEN UP WITHOUT TEARING ARTWORK!

PRO WHITE
THIS IS USED TO COVER UP MISTAKES IN INK DRAWINGS. COMES IN SMALL BOTTLE!

CHAIR
SOFT, WITH BACK, AND WHEELS!

DRAWING ROOM
WHERE EVERYTHING IS KEPT!

MORGUE
A COLLECTION OF PHOTOS AND ART FOR REFERENCE, IN ALPHABETICAL ORDER!

LETTERING BOOK
WE ALL NEED REFERENCE!

FLUORESCENT LAMP
ADJUSTABLE. CLAMPS ON DRAWING BOARD

BRISTOL BOARD
COMES IN ONE, TWO, AND THREE PLY, AND SMOOTH OR MEDIUM SURFACE. THE MAJORITY OF CARTOONISTS USE IT EXCLUSIVELY!

PENCIL SHARPENER
ELECTRIC OR OTHERWISE...

CARTOONING BOOK
I HAVE DOZENS..THEY GIVE YOU INSPIRATION AND ALLOW YOU TO SEE HOW PROFESSIONAL CARTOONISTS DO THEIR STUFF. THIS IS GOOD!

LIGHT BOX
FLUORESCENT LIGHT UNDER FROSTED GLASS, ALLOWS CARTOONIST TO TRACE THROUGH BRISTOL FROM TRACING PAPER DRAWING. TERRIFIC!

I'M JUST SMILING AT WHAT ALL THIS IS GOING TO COST!

DRAWING BOARD
A GOOD ONE, NICE AND STURDY, THAT WON'T VIBRATE EVERYTIME YOU DRAW!

TABORET
A LITTLE TABLE NEXT TO YOUR DRAWING BOARD TO HOLD YOUR INK, PENS, PENCILS, BRISTOL, BRUSHES, COFFEE, ETC.

FINE ART

AND

COMMERCIAL ART

WHAT'S THE DIFFERENCE?

FINE ART-COMMERCIAL ART-WHAT IS THE REAL DIFFERENCE? IF YOU'RE LOOKING AT JUST THE ART WORK, THERE *IS* NO DIFFERENCE.

THERE IS ONLY GOOD ART AND BAD ART

THE DIFFERENCE IS *GOAL AND DISCIPLINE*

LET'S GIVE AN EXAMPLE: THE FINE ARTIST IS DRAWING AND PAINTING FOR HIS OWN ENJOYMENT, WHAT EVER HE OR SHE DESIRES.....AND AT HIS OWN *PACE*. THERE ARE FEW, IF ANY, RESTRICTIONS ON HIS TIME OR END RESULT. HIS FIRST CONCERN IS PLEASING HIMSELF. THE FINE ARTIST, IF HE WISHES, CAN LEAVE HIS WORK *UNFINISHED... AND HE OFTEN DOES*. IF THE FINE ARTIST DECLARES HIS WORK GREAT, WHO ARE WE TO DISAGREE. *IT COULD BE BAD ART!*

SO WHAT ABOUT THE COMMERCIAL ARTIST?

THE COMMERCIAL ARTIST DOES THE ART WORK THE WAY HIS "CLIENT".....THE ONE WHO IS PAYING HIM, WANTS IT DONE...BUT...HE ALSO WANTS THE COMMERCIAL ARTIST'S STYLE... *AND HE WANTS ALL THIS AT A CERTAIN TIME.*

THE COMMERCIAL ARTIST...... HAS DISCIPLINED HIMSELF TO WORK TO DEADLINES. HE WORKS IN HIS OWN TECHNIQUES, WHICH HE HAS MASTERED. THEY ARE HIS IDENTITY. THE ART WORK MUST BE "REALISTIC" AND *MUST BE COMPLETED!*

THE CLIENT WILL NOT ACCEPT ART WORK THAT DOES NOT REPRESENT HIS PRODUCT.

.....AND FINALLY, THE COMMERCIAL ARTIST DOES THIS FOR A SPECIFIED AMOUNT OF MONEY.

AND FINALLY.....IF THE COMMERCIAL ARTIST DOES'NT DELIVER ON ALL THESE COUNTS.. *HE'S HAD IT!*

THE FINE ARTIST DOES NOT WANT ALL OF THESE RESTRICTIONS.

BUT THEY'RE NOT RESTRICTIONS,

THEY'RE DISCIPLINES.

IT'S OBVIOUS THAT BOTH ENJOY THEIR PROFESSIONS, AND BOTH TURN OUT GOOD AND BAD ART.

THE SAD PART IS COMMERCIAL ARTISTS CAN'T SURVIVE ON POOR ARTWORK,

THE DRAWINGS WERE DONE WITH A DAMAGED NO. 64 QUILL PEN, USING ALL UP-STROKES

TO GO ON DEFINING THIS DIFFERENCE BETWEEN COMMERCIAL ART AND FINE ART WOULD SERVE NO PURPOSE. BUT SIMPLY PUT: "COMMERCIAL ART IS ART FOR COMMERCE."

FINE ART IS NOT!
BUT IT CAN BE.

WHEN A FINE ARTIST IS COMMISSIONED TO DO A PAINTING OR SCULPTOR FOR A CLIENT, FOR A SPECIFIED AMOUNT OF MONEY, AND TO BE DONE OVER A CERTAIN PERIOD OF TIME—

THAT'S COMMERCIAL ART!

THE FINE ARTIST CAN SAY ANYTHING HE WANTS...BUT IF HE WALKS LIKE A DUCK, AND QUACKS LIKE A DUCK, HE'S A DUCK!

REMEMBER—THE ACTUAL ART WORK HAS NOTHING TO DO WITH IT....

EDUCATION AND EXPERIENCE

THE IDEAL EDUCATION FOR COMMERCIAL ART IS TO WORK IN AN ART STUDIO LEARNING THE BUSINESS, RIGHT FROM THE ARTISTS THEMSELVES.

MANY COMMERCIAL ARTISTS HAVE STARTED OUT IN THIS WAY...... BEGINNING AS APPRENTICES, SO TO SPEAK, CUTTING MATS, FLAPPING ART WORK, RUNNING FOR STATS OR COFFEE, DELIVERING ART WORK, GETTING THE ART SUPPLIES, ETC., ETC...... AND OCCASIONALLY WORKING ON THE BOARD WHEN THERE'S TIME.

SIX MONTHS WORKING IN THIS CAPACITY FOR AN ART STUDIO, EXPOSED TO EVERY TYPE OF PROFESSIONAL ARTIST, IS BETTER THAN TWO YEARS IN ANY ART SCHOOL. YOU'LL LEARN ALL THE TRICKS OF THE TRADE.

AND RIGHT FROM THE PROS TOO!

13

HOWEVER—YOU'RE CHANCES OF LANDING SUCH AN OPPORTUNITY WILL DEPEND ON MANY FACTORS. JUST LIKE ANYTHING IN LIFE... IF YOUR FATHER OR A RELATIVE OWN THE BUSINESS AND YOU ARE A PRETTY GOOD ARTIST, THEN YOU'LL GET YOUR BIG CHANCE. OF COURSE, IT IS EXPECTED YOU WOULD HAVE A LIKING FOR THE COMMERCIAL ART BUSINESS.

REMEMBER-NO ONE WILL CARRY YOU... YOU WILL HAVE TO BE CREATIVE AND DRAW REALISTICALLY.

I HOPE YOU HAVEN'T DECIDED TO BE AN ARTIST FOR THE MONEY! *GOD FORBID!* THAT'S PICKING A CAREER FOR THE WRONG REASON!!

DON'T MISUNDERSTAND ME......THERE ARE LOTS OF WEALTHY COMMERCIAL ARTISTS, *BUT THEY WANTED TO BE ARTISTS.*
WHY IN THE WORLD WOULD YOU WANT TO BE STUCK WITH A JOB YOU DON'T LIKE ALL YOUR LIFE?

THERE ARE ENOUGH PEOPLE AROUND LIKE THAT.*/*

THERE IS ANOTHER WAY. A WAY THAT I RECOMMEND, AND THAT IS AN *ART SCHOOL!* A COMMERCIAL ART SCHOOL. AND THERE ARE SOME GOOD ONES! MOST GIVE DEGREES IN ART. BUT PLEASE KEEP THIS IN MIND:

A DEGREE DOES NOT MAKE YOU AN ARTIST!

IF I COULD HAVE A CENTER-FOLD IN THIS BOOK, THAT IS WHAT I WOULD PRINT.... IN BIG TYPE. NICE AND BIG! AFTER ALL, YOU COULD VERY WELL ATTEND AN ART SCHOOL OR COLLEGE AND GET "C's" ALL THE WAY THROUGH AND GRADUATE WITH A DEGREE, RIGHT? AND SOMEONE ELSE COULD GET ALL "A's" AND YET BOTH HAVE A DEGREE IN ART.

OF COURSE, A FOUR YEAR ART SCHOOL IS EXPENSIVE... NOT TO MENTION LIVING EXPENSES AND ART SUPPLIES, AND IT IS USUALLY FAR AWAY. ANOTHER GOOD CHOICE WOULD BE A COMMUNITY COLLEGE, SINCE WE ALL HAVE ONE CLOSE ENOUGH BY TO COMMUTE, BESIDES THE FACT THEY ARE RELATIVELY INEXPEN-SIVE AND HAVE INSTRUCTORS ON STAFF WHO ARE WORKING PROFESSIONAL ARTISTS..... *AND THAT'S WHAT YOU NEED!*

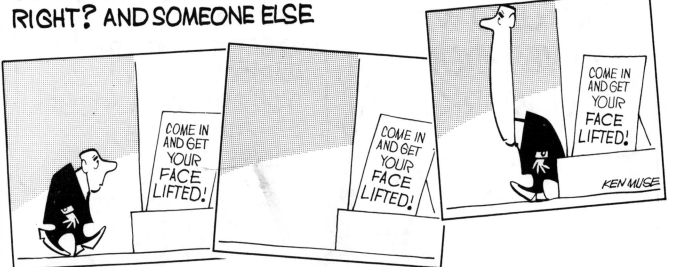

TO BE A COMMERCIAL ARTIST YOU MUST BE WARY OF FINE ARTS COURSES... AND THE REASON IS SIMPLE:

YOUR PORTFOLIO WILL NOT HAVE COMMERCIAL ART SAMPLES!

NOTICE I DIDN'T SAY YOUR PORTFOLIO WILL HAVE POOR ART WORK!

A WORKING PROFESSIONAL WHO TEACHES COMMERCIAL ART KNOWS WHAT IS NEEDED IN A PORTFOLIO TO GET YOU INTO THE JOB MARKET.... AND ONCE YOU BREAK-IN ON YOUR FIRST JOB, YOU'RE ON THE WAY....

ART SUPPLIES

ACTUALLY, WHEN IT COMES TO ART SUPPLIES, THE CARTOONIST HAS IT MADE, BECAUSE MUCH OF THE MATERIALS CAN BE PURCHASED AT AN ORDINARY STATIONARY STORE.

LET'S BEGIN WITH THE PENCIL!

MOST PROFESSIONAL ARTISTS AND CARTOONISTS I HAVE KNOWN USE PLAIN OLE ORDINARY NO.2 SCHOOL PENCILS, AS I CALL THEM....THE ONES WITH THE ERASERS ON THE END! THEY LOOK LIKE THIS:

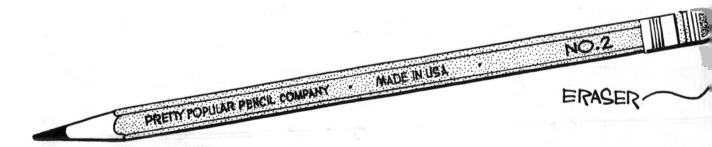

PRETTY POPULAR PENCIL COMPANY · MADE IN USA · NO.2 ERASER

I BUY MINE IN THE SUPERMARKET, AND THEY'RE GREAT FOR WORKING ON TYPING PAPER.... IN FACT THEY ARE THE ONLY PENCIL I USE FOR CARTOONING!

"ART SUPPLIES" LETTERING: SPEEDBALL FLICKER PEN FB5

PENCIL: GILLOTT NO. 1290

18

I WILL ADMIT THOUGH, THE SUPERMARKET PENCILS DO BREAK EASIER AND DON'T STAND UP TOO WELL TO AN ELECTRIC PENCIL SHARPENER.

I SOMETIMES USE ANOTHER MORE EXPENSIVE PENCIL, LIKE OTHER CARTOONISTS, BECAUSE THEY HOLD THE POINT LONGER AND YOU DON'T HAVE TO SHARPEN THEM AS MUCH!

THEY LOOK LIKE THIS:

NO ERASER

HB 100

HB

PRETTY EXPENSIVE PENCIL COMPANY .

MAYBE THE CHART ON THE NEXT PAGE WILL HELP!

YOU'RE BEST BET, AS A CARTOONIST, IS TO GO WITH THE NO. 2 OR HB LEAD. THIS IS BECAUSE IT'S SOFT ENOUGH TO WORK RIGHT ON YOUR BRISTOL BOARD WITHOUT MAKING AN ETCHING, AND IT'S EASY TO ERASE! YOU'LL FIND ALSO THAT THE HB WORKS WELL ON TRACING PAPER WITHOUT LOSING ITS POINT QUICKLY! IF YOU'RE USED TO WORKING WITH ANOTHER GRADE, THEN DON'T STOP. THESE ARE ONLY SUGGESTIONS BASED ON MY EXPERIENCES!

BALLOON LETTERING: HUNT QUILL PEN NO. 107   PENCIL, CARTOON, AND LARGE LETTERS: GILLOTT 1290

8B	TOO SOFT	H	SECOND CHOICE
7B	TOO SOFT	2H	FOR TRACING PAPER
6B	NOT PRACTICAL	3H	FOR TRACING PAPER
5B	NOT PRACTICAL	4H	KEEPS GOOD POINT
4B	NOT PRACTICAL	5H	TOO HARD
3B	NOT PRACTICAL	6H	TOO HARD
2B	SOMETIMES	7H	TOO HARD
B	FOR SKETCHING	8H	TOO HARD
HB	EXCELLENT	9H	FORGET IT
F	EXCELLENT	10H	IT WILL CUT PAPER

ALL THE PENCILS LISTED
ABOVE HAVE FOUR IMPORTANT
QUALITIES FOR DRAWING, BUT
NOT NECESSARILY FOR CARTOONING.
THEY ARE:
DURABILITY → LINES OF UNIFORMITY
NEEDLE POINT → STRENGTH FOR STAMINA
SMOOTHNESS → FAST WORK, LESS EFFORT
OPACITY → SHARPNESS AND VIVID CONTRAST

CARTOON: HUNT QUILL NO. 107

LETTERTONE PATTERN NO. LT 904

THERE ARE MANY OTHER
PENCILS MADE FOR SPECIAL
EFFECTS THAT ARE USED
BY EDITORIAL CARTOONISTS!
PENCILS LIKE THE NO. 60
FLEXICOLOR, AND
PRISMACOLOR NO. 935!
SO, WHEN THE OCCASION
ARISES DURING THE
INSTRUCTION IN THE BOOK,
I'LL DISCUSS THEM!

EXTRA SPECIAL PENCIL CO.

OK, NOW LET'S TALK PENPOINTS!

PENPOINTS

MY GOSH! THERE ARE A BUNCH OF PENPOINT COMPANIES, BUT THE CHOICE FOR THE CARTOONIST CAN BE NARROWED DOWN TO A FEW BASIC ONES. FOR EXAMPLE, THE BIG LETTERING AT THE TOP OF THIS PAGE, THE PENPOINTS, AND THE LITTLE GUY, WERE DRAWN WITH A HUNT CROWQUILL 107. THIS LETTERING WAS DONE WITH A SPEEDBALL A5 FLICKER PEN, MY FAVORITE LETTERING PEN, AND A LOT OF OTHER CARTOONISTS TOO.

WHEN I WAS IN ART SCHOOL I USED TO SPEND HOURS IN LEWIS ART SUPPLY, IN DETROIT, TRYING TO FIND A MAGIC PEN POINT. AS A MATTER OF FACT, I WAS ALSO LOOKING FOR A MAGIC BRUSH, MAGIC INK, MAGIC PAPER, OR *MAGIC ANYTHING!*

THE FACT IS, WHAT EVER PENPOINT YOU USE THAT MAKES YOU HAPPY AND GIVES YOU TERRIFIC PEN LINES, FOR GOODNESS SAKES DRAW WITH IT!

MORE ADVICE: DROP IN YOUR ART STORE AND GET DIFFERENT ONES!

Gillott's 1290 brush pen

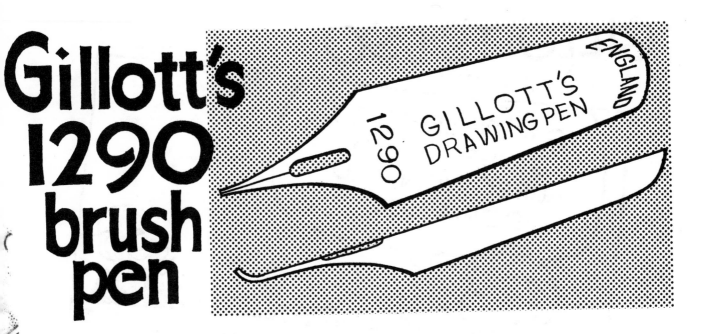

THIS WILL BE, WITHOUT A DOUBT, ONE OF THE MOST AMAZING PEN POINTS YOU WILL EVER USE! IT'S CALLED A BRUSH PEN BECAUSE YOUR CARTOON LOOKS LIKE IT WAS INKED WITH A BRUSH. THIS AMAZING PEN CAN ALSO PRODUCE A TYPICAL PEN LINE! YOU SEE, IT DEPENDS UPON THE AMOUNT OF PRESSURE YOU PUT ON IT... **BEAR DOWN AND YOU HAVE A BRUSH LINE**... LET UP AND YOU HAVE A PEN LINE. IT'S A DIFFICULT PEN TO MASTER BECAUSE OF THE SENSITIVE POINT, BUT ONCE YOU DO, YOU'LL NEVER GO BACK TO YOUR OLD PEN POINT!

EVERYTHING ON THIS PAGE: GILLOTT 1290

GILLOTT'S 1290

ACTUAL SIZE

NOTICE THE VARIATION OF VERY THICK AND VERY THIN LINES?

THIS WHOLE PANEL WAS DRAWN WITH THE 1290, EXCEPT THE LETTERING, WHICH WAS AN A5 FLICKER!

24% REDUCTION

64% REDUCTION

24

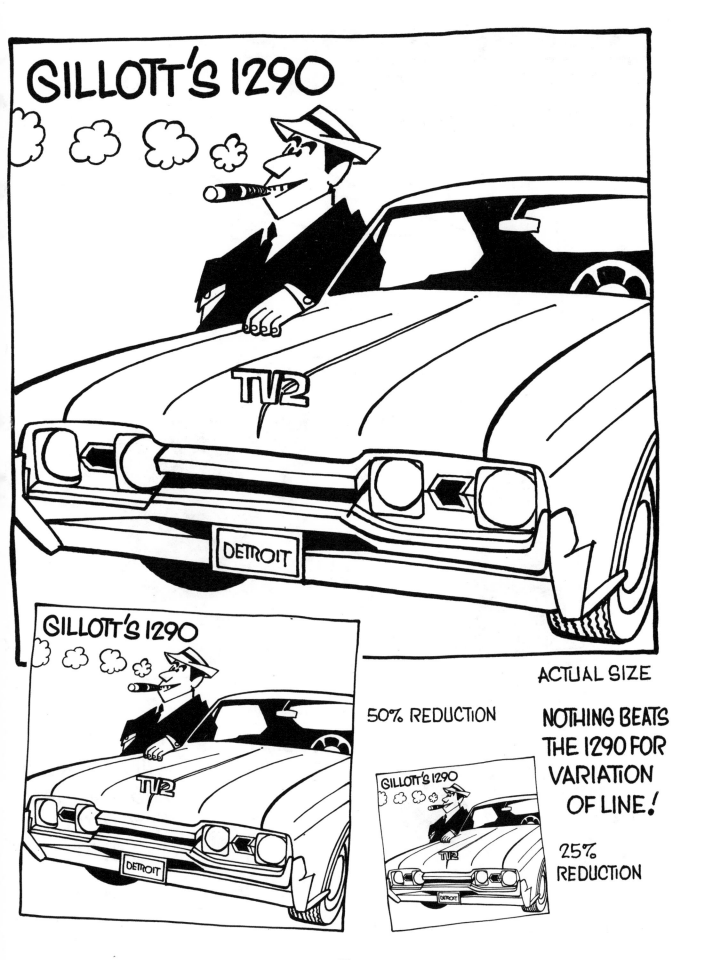

HUNT 513EF

ACTUAL SIZE

REJECTIONS

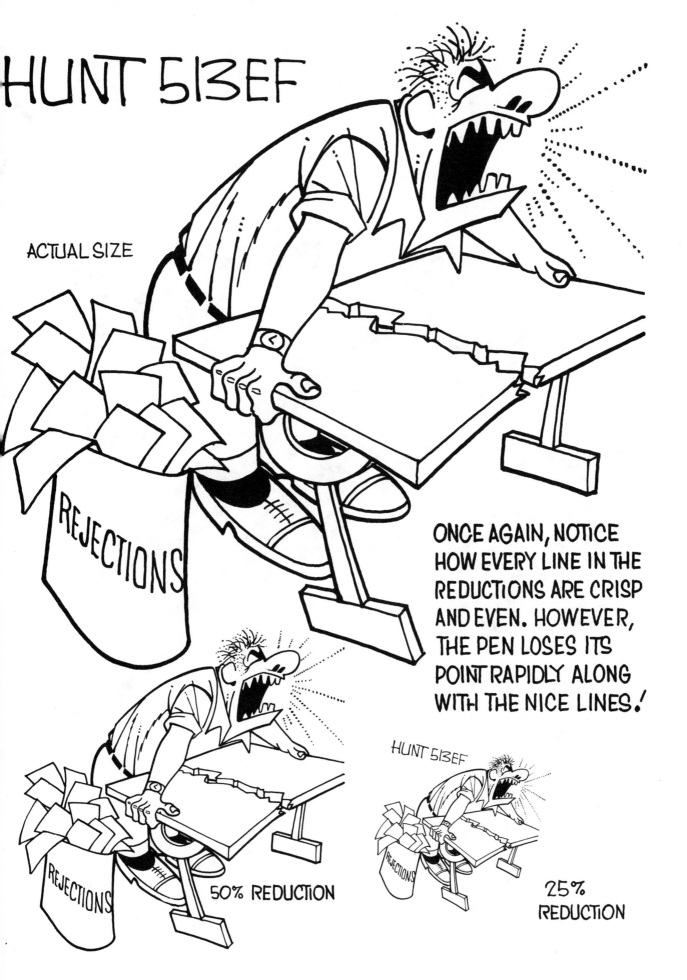

ONCE AGAIN, NOTICE HOW EVERY LINE IN THE REDUCTIONS ARE CRISP AND EVEN. HOWEVER, THE PEN LOSES ITS POINT RAPIDLY ALONG WITH THE NICE LINES!

50% REDUCTION

HUNT 513EF

25% REDUCTION

GILLOTT'S 659

HUNT'S 107

QUILL
PENS

HOLE

TWO POINTS THAT
MIGHT TURN YOU
ON, AND MAYBE NOT.
THEY SORT OF DIG
INTO THE PAPER
WHEN YOU'RE TRYING
TO MAKE A WIDE
LINE!
YOU MIGHT TRY
BOTH OF THEM AND
DISCOVER YOUR
FAVORITE.
OF COURSE, UNLIKE
THE OTHER PEN POINTS
THEY NEED A SMALL
SPECIAL PEN HOLDER
WITH A ROUND HOLE!

THIS IS THE ONLY
HOLDER THAT WILL
FIT THE QUILL PENS!

GILLOTT'S 659 QUILL

ACTUAL SIZE

65%
REDUCTION

33% REDUCTION

HUNT 107 QUILL

ACTUAL SIZE

33% REDUCTION

65% REDUCTION

GILLOTT'S 170

JOSEPH GILLOTT'S WARRANTED
ENGLAND
170

THE GILLOTT 170 AND 290 ARE WHAT MOST CARTOONISTS USE WHEN IT COMES TO PEN POINTS..... *OTHER THAN A BRUSH!* THIS IS A FLEXIBLE POINT, AND WILL MAKE JUST ABOUT ANY KIND OF LINE YOU WANT.
ONE THING ABOUT THESE FLEXIBLE PEN POINTS IS **THEY WEAR DOWN** AND LOSE THE ABILITY TO FLOW THE INK SMOOTHLY.

WHEN YOU FIRST TRY THIS PEN, IT BLOBS-UP ON YOU! THIS IS A HARD ONE TO CONTROL, AND IT WILL TAKE PRACTICE.

YOU'LL HAVE TO TRY EVERY ONE YOU GET YOUR HANDS ON SO YOU CAN DECIDE YOUR FAVORITE!

GILLOTT'S 170

ACTUAL SIZE

33% REDUCTION

65% REDUCTION

GILLOTT'S 290
LITHOGRAPHIC PEN

THE GILLOTT 290 IS PROBABLY THE MOST POPULAR PEN POINT FOR CARTOONISTS! THIS ONE IS MORE *FLEXIBLE* THAN THE 170, *IF THAT SEEMS POSSIBLE!* THIS ONE YOU'VE GOT TO TRY!

THIS PEN COULD GIVE YOU TROUBLE! SOME OF THE LINES IT MAKES COULD BE TOO FINE FOR THE REDUCTION. BUT IF YOU PRACTICE A LOT YOU CAN MASTER IT.

CHECK THE NEXT PAGE AND SEE WHAT I MEAN.

IF YOU'RE NOT CONFUSED YOU JUST DON'T UNDERSTAND THE SITUATION!

GILLOTT'S 290

ACTUAL SIZE

65% REDUCTION

33% REDUCTION

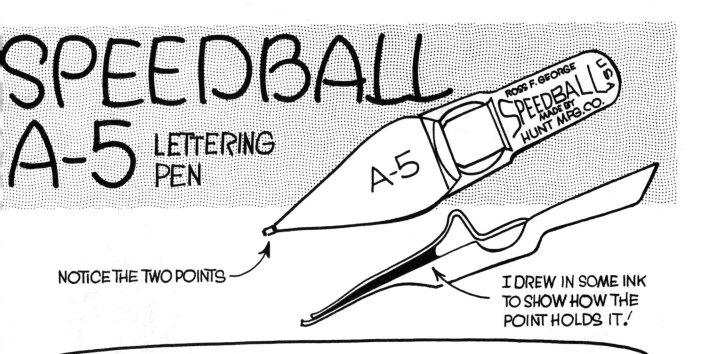

SPEEDBALL A-5 LETTERING PEN

A-5

ROSS F. GEORGE
SPEEDBALL
MADE BY
HUNT MFG. CO.
USA

NOTICE THE TWO POINTS

I DREW IN SOME INK TO SHOW HOW THE POINT HOLDS IT!

MOST OF THIS BOOK HAS BEEN DONE WITH AN A5 SPEEDBALL PEN POINT! THE POINTS STORE A LOT OF INK AND WILL LAST A LONG TIME BETWEEN DIPS IN THE INK BOTTLE. THE NICE THING ABOUT THE LINE THEY MAKE IS THAT IT TAKES A BIG REDUCTION!

INK

ACTUAL SIZE

33% REDUCTION

65% REDUCTION

ESTERBROOK 509

LETTERING PEN

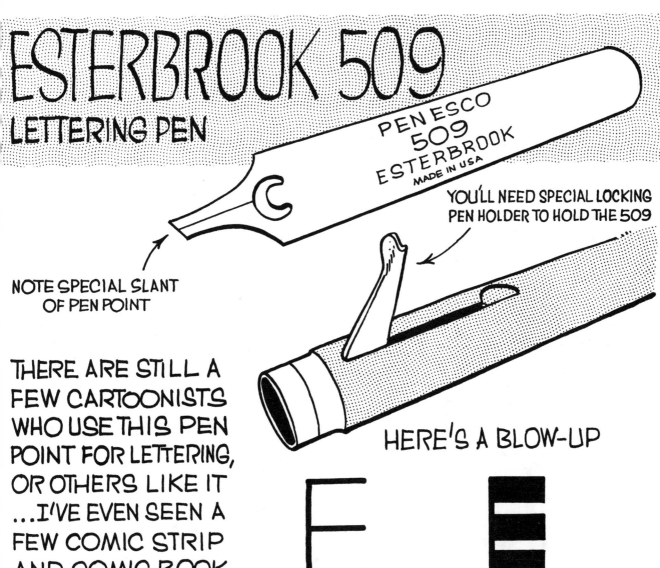

PEN ESCO
509
ESTERBROOK
MADE IN USA

NOTE SPECIAL SLANT
OF PEN POINT

YOU'LL NEED SPECIAL LOCKING
PEN HOLDER TO HOLD THE 509

HERE'S A BLOW-UP

THERE ARE STILL A FEW CARTOONISTS WHO USE THIS PEN POINT FOR LETTERING, OR OTHERS LIKE IT ...I'VE EVEN SEEN A FEW COMIC STRIP AND COMIC BOOK LETTERERS *FILE DOWN* OTHER POINTS WITH EMERY STONES AND MAKE THEIR OWN FLAT POINTS, LIKE THE ESTERBROOK 509.'

THE 509 WORKS BEST ON A MEDIUM SURFACE BRISTOL, RATHER THAN A SMOOTH GLOSSY ONE.

A5 SPEEDBALL   ESTERBROOK 509

COMPARE THIS LETTERING WITH THE OTHER LETTERING ON THIS PAGE, AND NOTICE THE CARTOON FEELING THE ESTERBROOK 509 BRINGS TO THE PRINTING.'

ESTERBROOK 509

THE ESTERBROOK 509 IS AN EXTREMELY DIFFICULT PEN TO USE AND MASTER. IT IS A PEN YOU WILL LOVE OR HATE, AND THAT IS BECAUSE IT NEEDS THE RIGHT TEXTURE OF PAPER. NOTICE HOW THE DOWNSTROKES ARE THIN AND THE SIDE-STROKES ARE THICK? THAT'S CHARACTER!

LIKE THIS

A HIGH SURFACE BRISTOL BOARD IS A TOTAL DISASTER FOR THE ESTERBROOK 509 BECAUSE IT MAKES ALL LINES ABOUT THE SAME THICKNESS!

IT'S HARD TO KEEP JUST THE RIGHT AMOUNT OF INK IN THE 509 TO KEEP THE DOWNSTROKES THIN AND SIDESTROKES THICK

HERE'S AN EXAMPLE OF WHAT A HIGH, OR SMOOTH SURFACE PAPER DOES TO THE ESTERBROOK 509

HERE IS A SENTENCE PRINTED WITH THE 509 ON SMOOTH, HIGH SURFACE BRISTOL BOARD

HIGH SURFACE PAPER IS A DISASTER!

AND HERE'S A 200% BLOW-UP

HIGH SURFACE PAPER IS A DISASTER!

THE SAME MESSAGE PRINTED WITH THE 509 ON A MEDIUM SURFACE BRISTOL BOARD

HIGH SURFACE PAPER IS A DISASTER!

AND THE 200% BLOW-UP

HIGH SURFACE PAPER IS A DISASTER!

NOTICE IN THE EXAMPLE AT TOP HOW THE HIGH SURFACE PAPER THICKENS THE DOWN STROKES IN THE WORDS "HIGH SURFACE", AND AS THE POINT GETS LOWER ON INK, AS IN "DISASTER", THE DOWN STROKES GET THINNER!

THIS 400% BLOW-UP REALLY SHOWS HOW THE PAPER SURFACE CONTROLS THE PEN INK LINE!

THICK SIDE STROKES! AND THEY ARE SUPPOSED TO BE THIN.

ALL THE SAME THICKNESS.

THINNER STROKES BECAUSE PEN IS GETTING LOW ON INK!

HIGH SURFACE

ESTERBROOK 509 · SMOOTH SURFACE BRISTOL

THIN DOWN STROKES

THIS IS THE WAY IT IS SUPPOSED TO BE!

THICK SIDE STROKES

HIGH SURFACE

ESTERBROOK 509 · MEDIUM SURFACE BRISTOL

WHAT I'M REALLY TRYING TO SHOW YOU IS THAT THE PAPER SURFACE IS ALSO A TOOL, JUST LIKE THE PEN OR BRUSH! ON THE HIGH SURFACE, THE 509 "BLOBS!" ON THE MEDIUM SURFACE, THE DOWN STROKES ARE THIN, REGARDLESS OF THE INK FLOW!

the BRUSH

IF YOU CAN'T BUY THE BEST.... DON'T BUY ANY!

IT'S EASY TO TELL A GOOD BRUSH FROM A BAD ONE ... A GOOD BRUSH KEEPS ITS POINT, AND IT WILL DO SO FOR THE LIFE OF THE BRUSH.

BASED ON MY EXPERIENCE, AND OTHER CARTOONISTS I KNOW, YOU WON'T GO WRONG WITH A WINSOR-NEWTON SERIES 7, WATER COLOR BRUSH. THEY USE ONLY THE FINEST SABLE HAIR!

BRUSHES COME IN ALL SIZES!

CHECK THE CHART ON PAGE 44!

NOTICE THE NICE CONSISTENT LINE A BRUSH PUTS OUT!

43

THE BRUSH GAME

#00 JUST A FEW HAIRS IN THIS ONE! WILL MAKE A LINE FINER THAN A PENPOINT.

#0 THIS IS ANOTHER GOOD ONE FOR DRAWING POSTAGE STAMPS. GOOD FOR REAL FINE STUFF.

#1 PRETTY GOOD FOR CARTOONS.

#2 MY FAVORITE. EVEN MAKES REAL FINE LINES!

#3 AN ALL AROUND GOOD BRUSH. FILLS IN BLACKS!

#4 GOOD CHOICE FOR ALL AROUND EVERYTHING.

#5 THIS ONE WILL HOLD A LOT OF INK.

#6 I USE THIS FOR LETTERING SIGNS.

#7 TOO BIG FOR ORDINARY SIZE CARTOONS!

#8 IF I'M GOING THIS BIG I'D RATHER HAVE A NO.12!

#9 RATHER HAVE A NO.12.

#10 RATHER HAVE A NO.12.

#11 RATHER HAVE A NO.12.

#12 I COULD ONLY AFFORD ONE OF THESE WHEN I WAS IN ART SCHOOL AND IT WAS TERRIFIC FOR LARGE SIGNS, POSTERS, ETC, ETC, AND FILLING IN BIG AREAS!

SECRETS OF USING THE BRUSH

PRACTICE WITH DIFFERENT SIZE BRUSHES TO FIND THE ONE YOU'RE COMFORTABLE WITH.

WHEN FINISHED INKING, USE WARM WATER AND A MILD SOAP AND PULL THE BRUSH OVER YOUR FINGER DURING CLEANING.... DON'T PUSH! YOU WILL JUST FORCE THE INK BACK UP INTO THE BRUSH.

BRUSHS NEED BETTER CLEANING THAN PEN POINTS. ANY INK LEFT ON THE BRUSH WILL EAT AWAY THE HAIRS AND POINT!

BRUSH LINES DRY FASTER THAN PEN LINES, SO YOU CAN USUALLY INK IN ANY DIRECTION THAT DRIES FIRST.

A BRUSH, LIKE A PEN, IS PULLED DURING INKING, NEVER PUSHED. IF YOU DON'T BELIEVE IT, TRY IT YOURSELF.

A BRUSH, UNLIKE A PEN, DOES NOT HAVE TO BE BROKEN-IN!

WATERPROOF INK IS THE WORSE THING YOU CAN STICK YOUR BRUSH INTO — BUT WE HAVE NO CHOICE. THAT'S WHY IT'S SO IMPORTANT TO KEEP THEM CLEAN!

ERASING PENCIL MARKS AFTER INKING SHOULD BE DONE GENTLY. IF NOT, BRUSH LINES WILL GRAY-DOWN. THE ERASER FOR THIS PURPOSE IS A "KNEADED-RUBBER".

SAVE YOUR MONEY AND BUY THE BEST BRUSHES MADE.!!!

SOME MORE SECRETS ON DRAWING WITH A BRUSH

YOU'LL DO BETTER ON A BRISTOL BOARD WITH SOME "TOOTH" IN IT, LIKE A MEDIUM SURFACE COLD PRESSED.

DON'T DIP AND COVER ALL THE HAIRS OF THE BRUSH WITH INK, ONLY ABOUT THREE QUARTERS OF THE WAY IN.

AFTER DIPPING, MAKE A POINT ON THE BRUSH BY PULLING THE HAIRS OVER THE OPENING OF THE INK BOTTLE!

TURN YOUR PAPER DURING INKING!

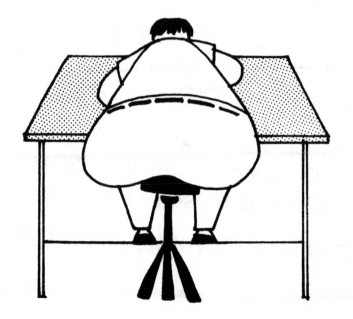

CARTOON: MAGIC MARKER

LETTERING: GILLOTT 1066

SECRETS OF USING A PEN!

IF YOU WANT VARIETY OF LINE, LIKE THICK AND THIN STROKES LIKE THIS: YOU'LL HAVE MORE SUCCESS WITH A SMOOTH, HIGH SURFACE, COLD PRESSED BRISTOL BOARD.

A PEN POINT, UNLIKE A BRUSH, HAS TO BE "BROKEN-IN", AND IT GETS TO THAT CONDITION BY A LOT OF USE. A PEN POINT USED FOR THE FIRST TIME WILL USUALLY *BLOB-OUT* INK ONTO YOUR CARTOON. I USUALLY SUCK AWHILE ON THE NEW POINT TO GET THE OIL OFF, BUT I'VE SEEN SOME CARTOONISTS HOLD A MATCH TO THEM.

ANOTHER WAY TO BREAK-IN THE POINT IS TO SPEND FIVE TO TEN MINUTES MAKING LOTS OF PEN LINES! WHEN CARTOONISTS BREAK-IN A PEN POINT THEY CHERISH THEM AND USE THEM AS LONG AS POSSIBLE.

LIKE A BRUSH, DON'T MAKE *UP STROKES*. MAKE *SIDE* AND *DOWN* STROKES.

DON'T DIP THE POINT TOO DEEP IN THE INK. TOO MUCH INK ON THE POINT AND YOU LOSE CONTROL.

MOST CARTOONISTS ARE CONSTANTLY LOOKING FOR THE PERFECT PEN POINT. SOMETIMES THEY THINK THEY FIND IT, BUT IT'S A DELUSION!

HERE ARE SOME MORE SECRETS ON USING PEN POINTS

WHEN YOU'RE FINISHED, CLEAN THEM UP! USE A PEN CLEANING FLUID IF NECESSARY.

TURN YOUR CARTOON WHEN INKING.

TRY TO INK FROM TOP LEFT TO BOTTOM RIGHT.

A PEN, LIKE A BRUSH, IS PULLED NOT PUSHED.

A PEN NEEDS MORE PRESSURE THAN A BRUSH.

INK LINES TAKE LONGER TO DRY THAN BRUSH LINES!

AND REMEMBER...

WORK ON A SMOOTH SURFA

CARTOON: NO.2 BRUSH

DRAWING SURFACES

WHEN I WAS A KID, I DREW ALL MY CARTOONS ON ANYTHING I COULD GET MY HANDS ON, AND THAT INCLUDED SHIRTBOARDS, CORRUGATED CARD-BOARD, WRAPPING PAPER, BUTCHER PAPER, GIFT BOXES, OLD GREETING CARDS, AND VARIOUS GRADES OF TYPING PAPER. I COULD NOT AFFORD EXPENSIVE BRISTOL BOARD!

PROFESSIONAL CARTOONISTS INK ON THE FOLLOWING SURFACES:

STRATHMORE BRISTOL	ILLUSTRATION BOARD	BOND TYPING PAPER
ONE PLY IS A LITTLE TOO THIN. MOST WORK ON A 2 PLY. 3 PLY IS EXPENSIVE!	GOOD IF YOU'RE WORKING IN WATERCOLOR OR WASH! TOO EXPENSIVE FOR JUST INK.	GAG CARTOONISTS USE THIS FOR FINAL ART. TERRIFIC FOR PRACTICING INK LINES.

LIKE ALL LITTLE GOOD CARTOONISTS, DRAW ON WHAT EVER GIVES YOU A GOOD LINE. I KNOW ONE CARTOONIST, TOM RYAN, WHO DRAWS "TUMBLE WEEDS", DOES HIS STRIP WITH A BRUSH ON MOUNT BOARD.

SOME WORDS ABOUT BRISTOL BOARD

MOST CARTOONISTS WORK ON 2 PLY BRISTOL BOARD. AT LEAST MOST OF THE COMIC STRIP ARTISTS!

ALL OF THE COMIC STRIPS, EXCEPT A RARE FEW, ARE DRAWN ON SMOOTH SURFACE BRISTOL BOARD, WITH PENS!

COMIC STRIPS DRAWN WITH BRUSH ARE DONE ON MEDIUM SURFACE BRISTOL!

YOU SHOULD TRY THESE SURFACES AND FIND OUT FOR YOURSELF WHY THIS IS SO! THAT'S THE BEST WAY TO LEARN.

WHEN USING THE LESSONS IN THIS BOOK, THE BEST WAY TO GO IS 100% RAG CONTENT 8½ X 11 BOND TYPING PAPER!

NOT ONLY IS IT GOOD FOR PENCIL, BUT IT'S TERRIFIC FOR INK!

IT WILL TAKE ALL KINDS OF PEN LINES, AND YOU'LL GET LOTS OF PAPER FOR YOUR MONEY!

AND IT'S ALSO GOOD FOR DRAWING WITH A BRUSH!

THE MAGIC MARKER!

OK, SO WHY DON'T CARTOONISTS USE MARKERS?

THEY DO! FOR MAKING OUT CHECKS, WRITING LETTERS, TAKING NOTES, SKETCHING, SIGNING CHRISTMAS CARDS, ADDRESSING ENVELOPES, SIGNING AUTOGRAPHS, ETC., ETC.

HOW ABOUT FOR FINISHED INKING?

NOT ME!

WHY?

THE POINTS WEAR DOWN AND THE LINES GET THICKER AND THICKER... AND THAT MEANS YOU LOSE CONTROL!

THEY SMEAR! (WHY TAKE A CHANCE?)

IT TAKES NO SKILL BECAUSE THERE IS NO LINE VARIATION!

NO THANKS... WHEN I DO MY FINAL INKING I WANT SOMETHING MORE PERMANENT!

YOU CAN DRAW YOUR CARTOONS WITH MARKERS ON TYPING PAPER, CUT THEM OUT, AND CEMENT THEM DOWN ON BRISTOL BOARD!

MAGIC MARKERS ARE GREAT FOR EXPRESSING YOUR FREEDOM IN CARTOONS, BUT WHEN YOU ARE DOING A TIGHT PENCIL DRAWING, AND IT HAS TO BE INKED, THE MARKER DOES NOT LEND ITSELF TO A TIGHT INK DRAWING – IT'S TOO FREE A MEDIUM FOR THAT!

SINCE CARTOONS ARE DRAWN IN PENCIL FIRST BEFORE INKING, DRAWING DIRECTLY IN MAGIC MARKER CAN PRODUCE SOME PRETTY WILD CARTOONS! SINCE THERE ARE LOTS OF DIFFERENT NIBS ON MARKERS, YOU CAN REALLY HAVE FUN!

INK

ONE THING YOU HAVE TO REMEMBER ABOUT INK WHEN YOU'RE DRAWING CARTOONS: *IT HAS TO BE WATER-PROOF!* OTHERWISE YOUR ART WORK ISN'T PERMANENT!

FOUNTAIN PEN INK WILL DISSOLVE IN WATER AND RUN OFF THE BRISTOL BOARD! IT ALSO HAS A TENDENCY TO SMUDGE WHEN ERASED!

YOU HEAR A LOT ABOUT "HIGGINS" WATERPROOF DRAWING INK BECAUSE IT HAS BEEN AROUND THE LONGEST, AND BE-CAUSE MOST CARTOONISTS USE IT. BUT OF COURSE THERE ARE OTHER FINE WATERPROOF DRAWING INKS.

FOR FIVE YEARS I DREW MY NATIONALLY SYNDICATED COMIC STRIP WITH "ARTONE" EXTRA DENSE BLACK. I LIKED IT BECAUSE I DIDN'T HAVE TO GIVE MY BLACK AREAS AN EXTRA COAT...THE STUFF IS REALLY BLACK!

CHECK THE NEXT PAGE FOR A LIST OF INKS!

HERE'S SOMETHING YOU CAN MAKE OUT OF A SMALL PIECE OF POSTER BOARD!

SOONER OR LATER YOUR BOTTLE OF INK IS GOING TO TIP OVER AND RUN DOWN INTO YOUR LAP AND ONTO THE FLOOR!

CUT OUT SQUARE PIECE AND TRACE AROUND BOTTOM OF INK BOTTLE LIKE THIS

CUT-OUT THIS WAY AND BEND BACK THE SECTIONS LIKE THIS!

THEN INSERT BOTTLE LIKE THIS

NO ONE KNOWS WHO INVENTED THIS, BUT IT'S BEEN AROUND A LONG TIME, WITH VARIATIONS!

EVER SINCE I WAS A LITTLE KID I'VE DRAWN CARTOONS WITH HIGGINS INK. YOU CAN EVEN BUY IT IN DRUG STORES! HIGGINS NOW HAS A TERRIFIC INK CALLED "BLACK MAGIC!"

THERE ARE ALSO OTHER BRANDS THAT ARE ALSO EXCELLENT INKS FOR CARTOONING! A FEW I'M FAMILIAR WITH:

HIGGINS BLACK MAGIC

PELIKAN

WINSOR AND NEWTON

KOH-I NOOR RAPID-OGRAPH BLACK DRAWING INK

AND MY FAVORITE: "ARTONE EXTRA DENSE BLACK"!

ERASERS

TALKING ABOUT ERASERS, AS IF THEY'RE IMPORTANT, SOUNDS LIKE A LOT OF NONSENSE DOESN'T IT? THAT'S WHAT I SAID WHEN I WAS IN ART SCHOOL, BECAUSE I DIDN'T KNOW ANY BETTER! BUT NOW I KNOW IT <u>DOES</u> MAKE SENSE.

IF EACH ERASER DIDN'T HAVE ITS SPECIAL FUNCTION, THERE WOULDN'T BE SO MANY DIFFERENT KINDS! *JUST LIKE PEN POINTS!*

SO WHAT DOES THIS ALL MEAN? IT MEANS THE BULK OF ALL THE CARTOONISTS HAVE THEIR FAVORITE, BUT THEY STICK PRETTY CLOSE TO SOME BASIC ONES. I REMEMBER WHEN I SWITCHED FROM AN EBERHARD "PINK PEARL" TO AN EBERHARD "RUB KLEEN" AFTER 6 YEARS BECAUSE THE RUB-KLEEN DIDN'T LEAVE AS MANY ERASER CRUMBS. FINALLY, I DISCOVERED THE EBERHARD "KNEADED RUBBER" DIDN'T DROP *ANY ERASER CRUMBS! ERASER CRUMBS GET EVERYWHERE. ALL OVER YOUR DESK, IN YOUR POCKETS, IN YOUR COFFEE, IN YOUR ASHTRAY, ON YOUR GLASSES…. AND ON THE FLOOR! EVERYTIME I FINISHED 12 STRIPS, I'D VACUUM DOWN THE RUG!*

THE ERASER STORY

3ERHARD FABER NEADED RUBBER ERASER

MAKES HIGHLIGHTS IN CHARCOAL AND NU PASTELS!

IT'S PLASTIC THAT CAN BE KNEADED INTO ANY SHAPE.

WILL NOT LEAVE A FILM ON YOUR PAPER, OR SMUDGE.

AND NO ERASER CRUMBS

MARS PLASTIC ERASER

DRAFTING ERASER FOR USE ON DRAFTING FILM, TRACING CLOTH OR PAPER.

CONTAINS NO ABRASIVES, AND WILL NOT HARM THE DRAWING SURFACE.

ART GUM ERASER

ONLY ONE THAT WILL TAKE PENCIL OFF POSTER BOARD. GOOD FOR ANYTHING!

LEAVES ERASER CRUMBS!

USED BY ARCHITECTS, HOMES, AND SCHOOLS.

SED BY OTS OF RTISTS!

PINK PEARL ERASER

SELF CLEANING, SMUDGE FREE AND PLIABLE.

GOOD QUALITY.

WILL TAKE SHEEN OFF BRISTOL BOARD AND LEAVE ERASER CRUMBS.

RACE KLEEN ERASER

BEVELED AT BOTH ENDS AND DESIGNED FOR DRAFTSMEN FOR USE ON VELLUM, MYLAR OR PAPER.

WILL LEAVE ERASER CRUMBS.

BUY ONE OF EACH, THEN PICK YOUR FAVORITE!

AND MORE...

RUBKLEEN EBERHARD FABER ERASER 6002

GOOD FOR CLEANING BOOKS, DRAWING BOARDS, TRACING CLOTH, LEATHER, WOOD, WALLPAPER, AND WILL LEAVE ERASER CRUMBS!

WILL NOT WEAKEN LINES!

GREEN, SOFT, AND IS BLOCK SHAPE.

CHARTPAK NO. PTO35 G

MAGIC RUB ERASER

THIS ONE IS VINYL AND ERASES QUICKLY.

WILL NOT SMUDGE OR SMEAR, AND IS GOOD FOR ERASING OVER TRANSFER LETTERING.

NOT BAD FOR CRUMBS.

CHARTPAK NO. PTO33 G

VAN DYKE SOFT ERASER 6500

PINK, SOFT, AND WILL REMOVE INK!

ALSO WORKS WITH PENCIL ON TRACING CLOTH.....

WITHOUT DAMAGE!

CHARTPAK NO. PTO92 G

RUBY ERASER

A NICE FIRM RED PENCIL ERASER.

VERY PRACTICAL!

IS DURABLE AND ECONOMICAL FOR GENERAL PENCIL WORK!

LETRATONE NO. 904

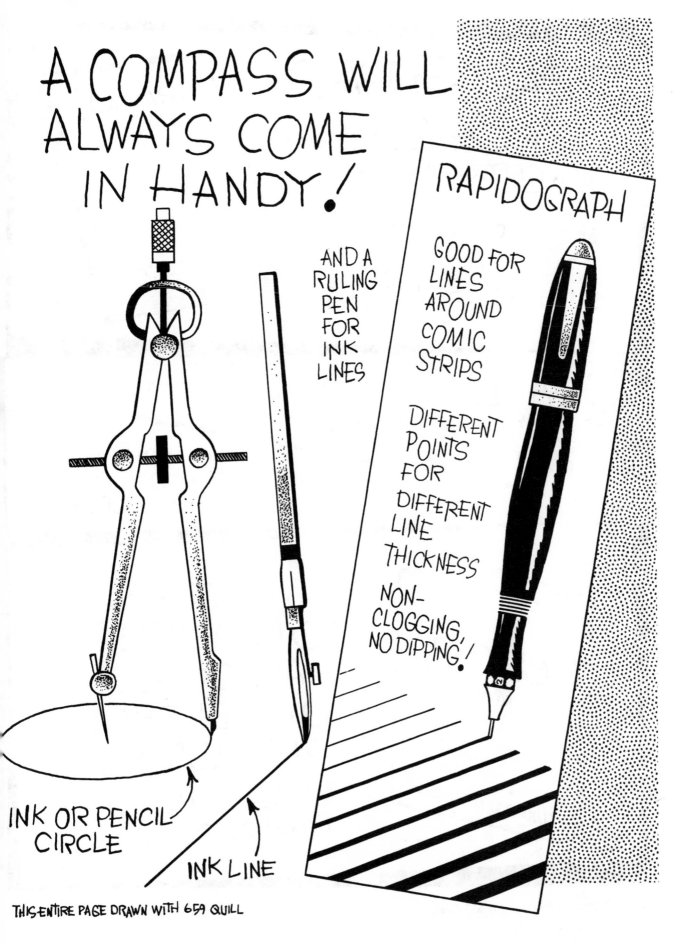

A COMPASS WILL ALWAYS COME IN HANDY!

AND A RULING PEN FOR INK LINES

INK OR PENCIL CIRCLE

INK LINE

RAPIDOGRAPH

GOOD FOR LINES AROUND COMIC STRIPS

DIFFERENT POINTS FOR DIFFERENT LINE THICKNESS

NON-CLOGGING, NO DIPPING!

THIS ENTIRE PAGE DRAWN WITH 659 QUILL

TRACING PAD

THIS IS JUST AS IMPORTANT TO A CARTOONIST AS HIS BREATHING!

ALSO IMPORTANT FOR TRACING ART AND CLEANING UP THE LINES!

TRACING PAD

9X12   100 SHEETS

SCALE
24 INCHES

HOW CAN YOU MAKE ART WORK THE RIGHT SIZE WITHOUT ONE?

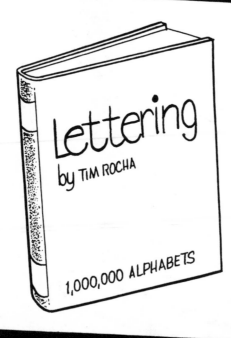

Lettering
by TIM ROCHA

1,000,000 ALPHABETS

IT'S IMPOSSIBLE TO REMEMBER ALL OF THE DIFFERENT ALPHABETS!

BESIDES, YOU CAN TRACE OUT OF IT!

THIS ENTIRE PAGE DRAWN WITH 659 QUILL

EXACTO KNIFE

BLADE CAN BE CHANGED

YOU'LL NEED THIS FOR CUTTING BRISTOL, PATTERN SCREENS, PRESS LETTERING, AND CARDBOARD!

A SPECIAL LIQUID PAPER CEMENT!

USED FOR CEMENTING CARTOONS AND ART WORK.

GET A PLASTIC BOTTLE.

RUBBER CEMENT

ANGLES

THEY HELP SQUARE-UP ART WORK.

AND GET A TINY ONE!

METAL CAN!

BESTINE

THIS IS A THINNER FOR RUBBER CEMENT, SO CEMENTED MISTAKES CAN BE TAKEN-UP!

PRO WHITE

LIQUID WHITE FOR COVERING MISTAKES!

THIS WHOLE PAGE DRAWN WITH 659 QUILL

T-SQUARE
24 INCHES

GET A METAL ONE IF YOU CAN, BECAUSE YOU CAN USE IT FOR A STRAIGHT EDGE TO CUT WITH! YOU NEED ONE ALSO FOR SQUARING-UP STRIPS.

GET AS MANY CARTOONING BOOKS AS YOU CAN AFFORD!

THEY HAVE A LOT OF GOOD POINTERS FROM PROS!

THEY'LL SAVE YOU LOTS OF TIME!

HOW TO DRAW CARTOONS

AND STAY NORMAL

CHECK THE LIBRARY FOR SOME GOOD ONES!

BURNISHER
THE PLASTIC ONES ARE GOOD, BUT THERE ARE OTHER KINDS!

THEY ARE USED FOR BURNISHING-DOWN PATTERN SCREENS AND INSTANT LETTERING!

THIS ONE IS ACTUAL SIZE!

THIS WHOLE PAGE DRAWN WITH 659 QUILL

HERE'S A QUICK WAY TO MAKE STRAIGHT INK LINES...

GET A WOODEN 18 INCH RULER, LIKE THIS, AND USE THE PEN AGAINST THE BACK OF THE RULER...

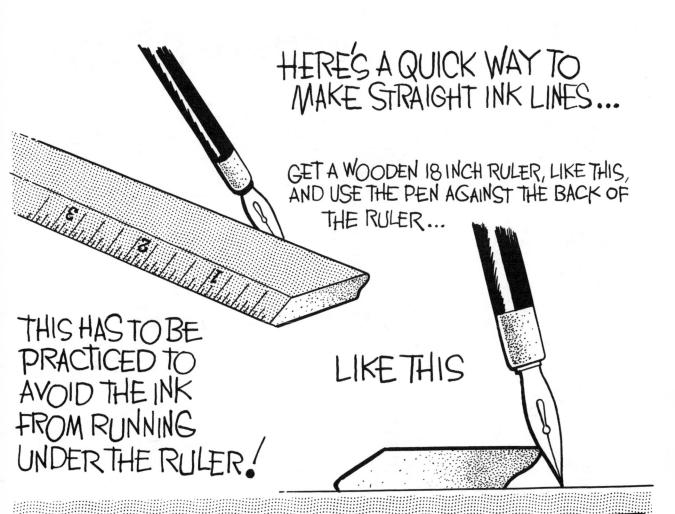

THIS HAS TO BE PRACTICED TO AVOID THE INK FROM RUNNING UNDER THE RULER!

LIKE THIS

A FINAL NOTE ON ART SUPPLIES — MOST PROFESSIONAL CAR—TOONISTS HAVE EXTENSIVE BACKGROUNDS IN NEWSPAPERS, TELEVISION, ADVERTISING AGENCIES, ETC., ETC., AND SOME ARE ACCOMPLISHED ILLUSTRATORS. MANY DO FREE-LANCE WORK, BESIDES THEIR STRIP OR PANEL. IF YOU WERE TO VISIT A PROFESSIONAL CARTOONIST, YOU WOULD BE SURPRISED TO SEE A WELL *EQUIPPED* STUDIO, NOT FOR JUST THE DRAWING OF CARTOONS, BUT COMMERCIAL ART ALSO!!

CHECK THE NEXT PAGE FOR A TYPICAL ARTIST'S STUDIO...

SETTING UP YOUR STUDIO
PLATE 60 LESSON 24

1 DRAWING TABLE
2 BOOK SHELVES
3 2 DRAWER FILE CABINET
4 RADIO
5 CALENDAR PAD
6 METAL CHEST of DRAWERS FOR SMALL ITEMS
7 WATER FOR WASHING BRUSHES
8 ADJUSTABLE CHAIR
9 TABOURET
10 CUTTING BOARD
11 TABLE with LARGE DRAWERS
12 SAMPLE PORTFOLIO
13 WASTE PAPER CAN
14 CLOTH FOR WIPING PENS
15 ADJUSTABLE LAMP
16 MASKING TAPE
17 TELEPHONE

FOR STORAGE OF LARGE MATERIALS

WHITE FORMICA TOP

STORAGE SPACE FOR TRACING PADS, etc.

SLIDING SHELF

CASTERS

CartoonErama

A PAGE FROM LEO STOUTSENBERGER'S "CARTOONERAMA", A CORRESPONDENCE COURSE. THIS WOULD BE A TYPICAL ART STUDIO OF A CARTOONIST OR COMMERCIAL ARTIST!

THE LIGHT BOX

OTHER NAMES FOR THE LIGHT BOX ARE: *STUDIO TRACING BOX*, *LIGHT TABLE*, AND *PORTA-TRACE*!
THE MORE ELABORATE ONES ARE MADE INTO TABLES THAT CAN BE TILTED LIKE DRAWING TABLES.

THERE IS A *FLUORESCENT* LIGHT UNDER A SMOOTH WORKING GLASS SURFACE. THE UNDERSIDE OF THE GLASS IS SANDBLASTED TO CREATE A DIFFUSED LIGHTING EFFECT. THIS CUTS DOWN GLARE AND ALSO PRODUCES ALL-OVER *EVEN* ILLUMINATION!

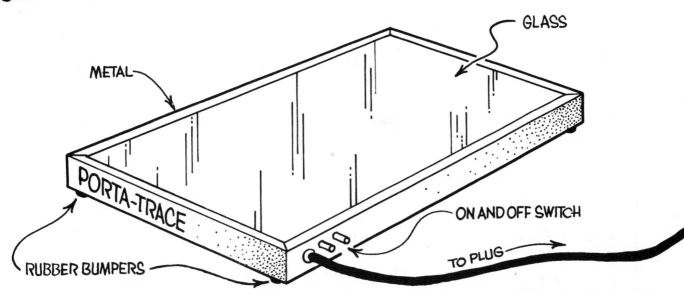

GLASS

METAL

PORTA-TRACE

RUBBER BUMPERS

ON AND OFF SWITCH

TO PLUG

THERE ARE ALSO RUBBER BUMPERS ON THE BOTTOM OF THE LIGHT BOX FOR NO-SLIP AND TO PREVENT MARRING! WHEN YOU LAY DOWN A PENCIL DRAWING ON BOND OR TRACING PAPER ON THE GLASS, AND A PIECE OF BRISTOL OVER IT, YOU CAN SEE YOUR PENCIL LINES SHINING THROUGH. YOU CAN THEN DRAW OVER THEM IN PENCIL, OR DIRECTLY IN INK, IF YOU'RE BRAVE!

OBVIOUSLY, THE BRISTOL BOARD CAN BE MOVED TO ANY POSITION FOR THE BEST COMPOSITION, THUS SAVING ALL THAT TIME ERASING IF YOU HAD JUST DRAWN IT STRAIGHT ON TO THE BRISTOL IN THE WRONG POSITION!

BESIDES THAT, YOU CAN MAKE ADDITIONS OR CORRECTIONS FROM YOUR ORIGINAL PENCIL TRACINGS!

LOOK AT IT FROM THE CARTOONIST'S POINT OF VIEW!

YOU CAN, OVER A PERIOD OF TIME, MAKE MANY, MANY DRAWINGS OF YOUR MAIN CHARACTER, AND OTHERS, IN YOUR STRIP OR PANEL, ON TRACING PAPER! THESE CAN BE FILED AWAY AND RETRACED AGAIN IN NEW STRIPS... THUS SAVING YOU TIME! ANOTHER ADVANTAGE IS YOU CAN RETAIN THE TRUE CHARACTER OF YOUR DRAWING **OVER AND OVER AGAIN!**

HERE'S ANOTHER IDEA WHERE THE LIGHT-BOX CAN MAKE YOU A MORE VERSATILE CARTOONIST: BELOW IS THE ALPHABET I PUT ON TRACING PAPER! NOTHING SPECIAL ABOUT IT...JUST A FUNNY CARTOON LETTERING STYLE. JUST MAKE UP ANYTHING!

BE SURE TO ADD GUIDE LINES!

A B C D E F G H I J K L M N O P Q
R S T U V W X Y Z · 1 2 3 4 5 6 7 8 9

THEN THE LETTERS ARE TRACED ON TO BRISTOL AND INKED!

THERE IS ONE TERRIFIC BENEFIT TO ALL THIS... YOU HAVE ALL THE CARTOONS YOU EVER DREW *ON TRACING PAPER!* SOME OF MY WORK GOES BACK OVER THIRTY YEARS. *AND YOU CAN DRAW THEM AGAIN!*

THIS CARTOON WAS DRAWN 12 YEARS AGO AND RETRACED ON BRISTOL, WITH CHANGES!

HERE'S SOME LIGHT-BOX MAGIC! THE FIRST GUY WAS THE ORIGINAL TRACING... AND THE REST ARE CHANGES RIGHT ON TO THE BRISTOL!

NOTICE THAT THE CHARACTER OF THE CARTOON STAYS THE SAME? THE LIGHT-BOX IS REALLY A TIME SAVER!

FOR THOSE **STRUGGLING** CARTOONISTS WHO WANT THE **ADVANTAGES** OF A LIGHT-BOX BUT CAN'T **AFFORD ONE,** THERE ARE TWO WAYS TO GO!

WE'LL ELIMINATE YOUR WINDOW BECAUSE IT ONLY WORKS DURING THE DAY! BESIDES, YOU'LL GET ARTHRITIS!

IMPROVISE YOUR OWN LIGHTBOX!

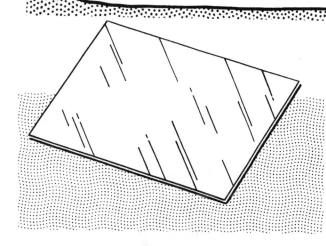

DASH OVER TO THE HARDWARE STORE AND GET A PIECE OF DOUBLE THICKNESS GLASS!

GET IT AT LEAST 16X18 INCHES AND NOT TOO THIN BECAUSE IT WILL CRACK EASILY.

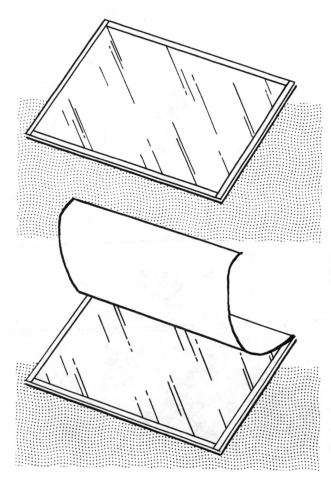

PUT MASKING TAPE AROUND ALL THE EDGES SO YOU CAN'T CUT YOURSELF.

DO IT CAREFULLY!

THEN TAKE SOME TRACING PAPER AND TAPE IT OVER ONE COMPLETE SIDE.

LAYOUT PAPER IS BETTER.

THEN YOU HAVE YOURSELF A PIECE OF HOME-MADE FROSTED GLASS, GREAT FOR TRACING!

THEN BEND YOUR DESK LIGHT DOWN LIKE THIS UNDER THE GLASS AND YOU'LL BE ABLE TO SEE THROUGH YOUR BRISTOL BOARD FOR TRACING!

OF COURSE YOU'LL HAVE TO BUY THIS TYPE OF LAMP

ADVANTAGES OF LIGHTBOXES

YOU ONLY HAVE TO MAKE ONE BASIC DRAWING.

YOU CAN CHANGE, ADD, CORRECT, OR
REDRAW FROM YOUR BASIC ART.

YOU CAN MOVE THE TRACING AROUND
FOR THE BEST POSITION!

YOU'LL ALWAYS HAVE YOUR ORIGINAL WORK, CLEAN!

NO-LIGHT / LIGHT-BOX

THIS IS ANOTHER SOLUTION FOR THOSE WHO CAN'T DISH-OUT THE MONEY FOR A "LIGHT" LIGHT BOX!

HERE'S THE DESCRIPTION:

MINI-LUX IS A PORTABLE, ADJUSTABLE, TABLE-TOP TRACING UNIT OFFERED AS AN ALTERNATIVE TO THE HIGHER PRICED LIGHT-BOX. IT IS ACTUALLY A LIGHTLESS UNIT DESIGNED TO BE USED BY LOCATING A DESK OR DRAFTING LAMP BEHIND THE HARD TRANSLUCENT PLEXIBOARD SURFACE. MEASURING 60 X 80 CMS, IT IS MOUNTED WITH A SEVEN-STAGE RATCHET STAND ALLOWING FLAT TO NEAR-VERTICAL ADJUSTMENT OF THE WORK SURFACE. IT IS CONSTRUCTED OF DURABLE PLASTIC WITH METAL FRAMING AND FOLDS FLAT OFFERING A CON-VENIENT HANDLE FOR PORTABILITY!

IT LOOKS SOMETHING LIKE THIS!

LIGHT SHINES IN HERE

MANY CARTOONISTS AND COMMERCIAL ARTISTS WORK ON ILLUSTRATION BOARD INSTEAD OF BRISTOL BOARD, WHICH MEANS A LIGHT-BOX WON'T WORK! OBVIOUSLY, LIGHT CAN'T SHINE THROUGH ILLUSTRATION BOARD. SO THE PROCESS OF GETTING THAT CARTOON OFF THE TRACING PAPER AND ON TO THE ILLUSTRATION BOARD, OR BRISTOL, IS A SIMPLE ONE!

FIRST-

GET YOUR CLEANED-UP CARTOON ON TO THE TRACING PAPER!

AN HB PENCIL DOES THIS VERY WELL!

SECOND-

TURN THE TRACING OVER AND RUB THE SIDE OF THE LEAD OF THE HB PENCIL ON THE BACK OF THE DRAWING!

(DON'T USE CARBON PAPER, IT'S TOO GREASY)

BE SURE THE PENCIL SHADING COVERS-UP THE TOTAL DRAWING!

THIRD-

TAPE THE TWO TOP CORNERS OF THE TRACING PAPER TO THE ILLUSTRATION BOARD. THIS WILL ALLOW YOU TO CHECK THE DRAWING AS YOU GO ALONG!

FOURTH-

TRACE THE CARTOON WITH A 2H PENCIL

FIFTH-

TAKE OFF THE TRACING PAPER AND INK THE PENCIL LINES!

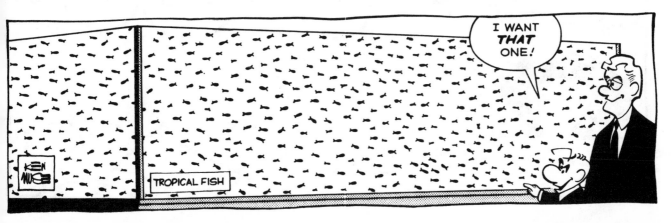

THE MORGUE

DON'T GET EXCITED! THE MORGUE IS JUST YOUR COLLECTION OF PHOTOGRAPHS, CARTOONS, AND ILLUSTRATIONS YOU HAVE CUT-OUT OF VARIOUS NEWSPAPERS AND MAGAZINES TO USE DURING DRAWING FOR REFERENCE.

NOTICE I SAID REFERENCE!

NEVER TRACE OR COPY OTHER ARTISTS' WORK! IF YOU DO, YOU'LL BE IN BIG TROUBLE.

AFTER ALL, YOU SHOULD TAKE PRIDE IN YOUR OWN ART.

HOW TO SET-UP A MORGUE......

DID YOU EVER TRY TO DRAW AN ELEPHANT RUNNING? A PANDA BEAR WALKING TOWARDS YOU? A CAT CHASING A DOG? HOW ABOUT A KANGAROO JUMPING?

HOW ABOUT A RUSSIAN RIFLE? AN F-104 JET? A 1939 PONTIAC? A 6 INCH REFLECTOR TELESCOPE? A COLT 45? BINOCULARS? THE UNDERSIDE OF A CAR? A SAXOPHONE? A SPEED BOAT?

NOT MANY CARTOONISTS, OR COMMERCIAL ARTISTS CAN DRAW ALL THESE THINGS WITHOUT SOME KIND OF REFERENCE... AND WOULDN'T EVEN TRY!

DON'T KID YOURSELF, YOU CAN'T FAKE IT.... FOR EVERYTHING YOU TRY TO FAKE, THERE ARE A HUNDRED PEOPLE OUT THERE WHO KNOW WHAT IT REALLY LOOKS LIKE, AND THEY'LL WRITE AND TELL YOU SO.
GOOD MAGAZINES FOR CUTTING-UP ARE:
LIFE, TIME, LOOK, FAN, AUTOMOTIVE, CAMPING, PHOTOGRAPHY, TRAVEL, ETC, ETC, ETC, ETC, ETC, START CUTTING!

ART DIRECTORS, ARTISTS, LETTERING MEN, KEYLINERS, WRITERS, LAYOUT—ARTISTS, PHOTOGRAPHERS, PRINTERS, AND ANYONE ELSE IN THE BUSINESS KNOWS ABOUT PHOTO-STATS!

BUT REMEMBER—USUALLY THE "STATS" ARE DONE BY OTHER THAN THE ARTIST. THE CREATIVE PEOPLE ARE TOO BUSY AT THE BOARD. MOST OF THE TIME THEY'RE SENT TO A "STAT HOUSE!
OK! NOW LET'S SEE HOW IT'S DONE:

WHAT ARE PHOTO STATS

PHOTO-STATS, OR "STATS", AS THEY ARE CALLED IN THE BUSINESS, ARE PHOTOGRAPHS. BUT INSTEAD OF USING FILM LIKE YOU WOULD IN A CAMERA, PAPER IS USED.

AS A RESULT, THE NEGATIVE, INSTEAD OF BEING ON FILM IS ON PAPER.... IN OTHER WORDS YOU HAVE A NEGATIVE PRINT WHERE BLACK AND WHITE ARE REVERSED.

FOR EXAMPLE:

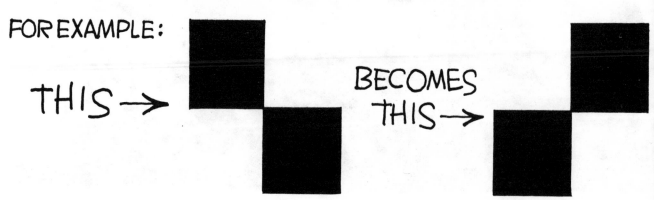

THIS →   BECOMES THIS →

THIS IS HOW THE LAST PAGE WOULD LOOK ON THE NEGATIVE STAT. YOU COULD CORRECT, ADD, OR TAKE AWAY ANYTHING WITHOUT AFFECTING THE ORIGINAL.

HERE'S THE ORIGINAL
SIZE HAND LETTERING

30 years
Together

THEN A NEGATIVE
PHOTO STAT IS
MADE A LITTLE
SMALLER.

LIKE THIS!

THEN A POSITIVE IS MADE
SMALLER FROM THE
NEGATIVE...LIKE THIS!

.....AND SMALLER!

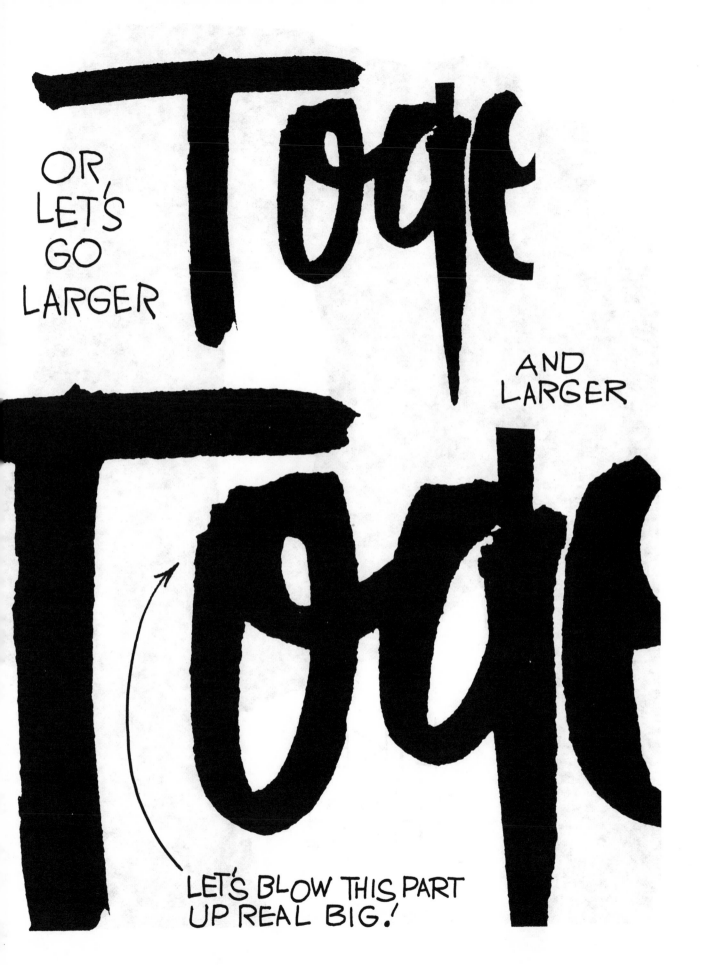

OR
LET'S
GO
LARGER

AND
LARGER

LET'S BLOW THIS PART
UP REAL BIG!

HERE'S A STANDARD CONTINOUS TONE PRINT OF
A BUILDING IN DOWNTOWN DETROIT, MICHIGAN...

....AND THIS IS WHAT HAPPENS WHEN A PHOTO-
STAT IS MADE FROM IT. NOTICE HOW THE TONE
DISAPPEARS AND SHADOWS "BLOCK-UP."

LET'S TAKE AN ORIGINAL STRIP, AND WITH THE STATMASTER WE REDUCE IT DOWN TO 3 COLUMN.

THIS IS WHAT THE NEGATIVE STAT LOOKS LIKE!

THEN FROM THE NEGATIVE STAT WE REDUCE THE STRIP DOWN TO 2 7/16" SO YOU CAN SEE HOW THE LINES HOLD UP!

THEN, JUST FOR FUN, LET'S BRING IT DOWN TO 3/4 OF AN INCH!

BUT WAIT... LET'S GO THE OTHER WAY! LET'S KEEP DOUBLING THE SIZE AND SEE WHAT THE LINES DO!

WAIT! DO YOU HAVE A PERMIT TO CARRY THAT GUN?

GREAT GOING O'SHAUGHNESS THAT WAS THE PASSWORD

NOTICE THE DOT SCREEN AND HOW STRONG IT'S GETTING!

IT'S NOT A GOOD IDEA TO DRAW SMALL AND THEN BLOW UP LARGE FOR REPRODUCTION. AFTER A POINT THE LINES BECOME UNEVEN BECAUSE OF THE SURFACE OF THE BRISTOL BOARD!

BLOWING-UP CARTOONS *BIG* LIKE THIS WOULD BE GREAT FOR POSTERS! NOTICE THE IMPACT BIG CARTOONS HAVE!

AND BIGGER, THE LINES BECOME VERY WAVY!

IT'S PROBABLY BIG ENOUGH NOW FOR A BILLBOARD.

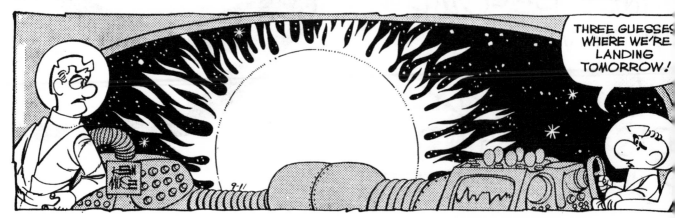

THE COMIC STRIP

WHO DRAWS THEM?

WHAT INK DO THEY USE?

WHAT DO THEY DRAW ON?

HIGH BIG ARE THEY?

WHAT KINDS OF PENS DO THEY USE?

WHO BUYS THEM?

HOW MANY SHOULD I SEND?

ETC, ETC, ETC, ETC.

ORIGINAL SIZE: 21¾" X 6¾"

ACTUAL NEWSPAPER SIZE

PRINTED WITH PERMISSION FROM MILTON CANIFF & FIELD NEWSPAPER SYN

ACTUAL SIZE

FROM AUTHOR'S PRIVATE COLLECTION

STEVE CANYON

by

MILTON CANIFF

ONE OF THE GREATEST
GUYS IN THE BUSINESS
AND CERTAINLY ONE
OF THE BETTER ARTIST
CLEAN SNAPPY BRUSH
STROKES, WELL THOUGH
OUT BLACKS, MILT IS
A TRUE PRO! HE HAS
BEEN DRAWING STEVE
CANYON FOR 32 YEAR

ACTUAL SIZE

FROM AUTHOR'S PRIVATE COLLECTION

NAME: *MILTON CANIFF* **ART SCHOOL:** *FINE ARTS, OHIO STATE U.*

INK: *HIGGINS* **BRISTOL:** *STRATHMORE 3 PLY KID* **PENCIL:** *2H VENUS*

LETTERING PEN: *ESTERBROOK BANK #303* **ZIP SCREEN:** *NONE*

DRAWING PEN: *GILLOTT'S #659* **BRUSH:** *WINSOR-NEWTON #3 SERIES 7*

ERASER: *EBERHARD PINK 101*

METHOD OF WORKING: *MILT WORKS DIRECTLY ON BRISTOL WITH PENCIL, THEN TIGHTENS-UP LINES BEFORE INKING.! (THE HARD WAY)*

BEETLE BAILEY

by MORT WALKER

NEWSPAPER SIZE, JUNE 10, 1961

IT SEEMS LIKE EVERYTIME YOU PICK-UP A BOOK ON THE COMICS, YOU SEE MORT WALKER'S, BEETLE BAILEY! THAT'S BECAUSE THE GUY IS SUCH A PRO. MORT PRODUCES TWO OTHER STRIPS WITH A COMBINED 1,966 NEWSPAPERS

ANOTHER GREAT GUY IN THE COMIC STRIP BUSINESS

MORT'S ASSISTANT IS EX-DETROITER, JERRY DUMAS

BEETLE BAILEY by MORT WALKER

EVERYTHING SEEMS SO SIMPLE NOW. I KNOW EXACTLY HOW TO SOLVE ALL MY PROBLEMS

FROM AUTHOR'S PRIVATE COLLECTION

6-10

PERMISSION OF KING FEATURES SYNDICATE

ORIGINAL SIZE: 18⅛ X 5¼

NAME: MORT WALKER **COLLEGE:** MISSOURI UNIV. **INK:** HIGGINS

BRISTOL: 3 PLY STRATHMORE **PEN FOR DRAWING:** GILLOTT NO. 170

PEN POINT FOR LETTERING: SPEEDBALL A5 **ERASER:** KNEADED

BRUSH: WINDSOR-NEWTON #2 FOR BLACKS **PENCIL:** VARIOUS NO. 2's

ZIP: STOPPED USING!

METHOD OF WORKING:

MORT SKETCHES ON THE BRISTOL, TIGHTENS THE SKETCH IN PENCIL, THEN INKS! THE LETTERING IS INKED FIRST—MANY, MANY, HOURS!!

HI and LOIS by MORT WALKER and DIK BROWNE

SUNDAY PAGE, FEBRUARY 7, 1965

PERMISSON OF KING FEATURES SYNDICATE

NAME: *DIK BROWNE* ART SCHOOL: *COOPER UNION* INK: *HIGGINS*

BRISTOL: *3 PLY STRATHMORE, PLATE* PEN POINT: *GILLOTT #170*

PEN FOR LETTERING: *SPEEDBALL B6* ERASER: *EBERHARD KNEADED*

BRUSH: *NO. 1 FOR WHITES, NO. 2 FOR BLACKS* PENCIL: *2B LEADS*

METHOD OF WORKING:

DIK ROUGHS ON BOND PAPER, CLEANS-UP ON TRACING PAPER, THEN TRACES THROUGH TO BRISTOL, USING A LIGHT-BOX!

ORIGINAL SIZE: 18⅝ X 12⅝

YOU CAN TELL IMMEDIATLY THAT DIK HAS WORKED IN ADVERTISING! HIS WORK HAS THAT POLISHED COMMERICAL LOOK...CLEAN, WELL DRAWN, AND SIMPLE! HI AND LOIS, AS FAR AS I'M CONCERNED, IS THE MOST CAREFULLY PLANNED AND EXCECUTED STRIP I'VE EVER SEEN...GOOD ENOUGH TO BE AN AD!

PEANUTS

by CHARLES SCHULZ

NEWSPAPER SIZE, DECEMBER 13, 1960

© 1960 UNITED FEATURE SYNDICATE, INC.

"PEANUTS" IS *TRULY* THE SUPER STAR OF COMIC STRIPS, AND CHARLES SCHULZ DOES HIS OWN GAGS... AND DRAWINGS!

PEANUTS by CHARLES SCHULZ

ORIGINAL SIZE: 27½ X 5½

NAME: *CHARLES M. SCHULZ* ART SCHOOL: *ART INSTRUCTION SCHOOLS*
COLLEGE: *NONE* INK: *HIGGINS* BRISTOL: *STRATHMORE 3 PLY PLATE*
PEN POINT FOR DRAWING: *C-5* PEN POINT FOR LETTERING: *C-5*
BRUSH: *NONE* PENCIL: *NO. 2* ERASER: *EBERHARD KNEADED*
METHOD OF WORKING:
*SCHULZ WORKS DIRECTLY ON THE BRISTOL, ROUGHING IN PENCIL,
TIGHTENING-UP THE LINES, THEN INKING! LOTS OF WORK!*

MUTT & JEFF

by AL SMITH

NEWSPAPER SIZE

REPRINTED BY PERMISSION OF THE McNAUGHT SYNDICATE

*ACCORDING TO CARTOONIST-HISTORIAN COULTON WAUGH, THE FIRST COMIC STRIP EVER PRINTED RAN ACROSS THE TOP OF AN ORDINARY EDITORIAL PAGE!

THE STRIP WAS CALLED "A. PIKER CLERK", AND WAS DRAWN BY CLARE BRIGGS. IT RAN IN THE *CHICAGO AMERICAN* IN 1904 AND WAS THE INVENTION OF MOSES KOENIGSBERG, THE EDITOR!

BUT THE FIRST COMIC STRIP TO RUN ON A DAILY BASIS WAS MUTT & JEFF, DRAWN BY BUD FISHER, A CHICAGO SPORTS CARTOONIST. IT FIRST APPEARED IN THE *SAN FRANCISCO CHRONICLE* IN 1907.

BUD FISHER DREW THE STRIP FOR 25 YEARS, AND WHEN HE DIED, AL SMITH, HIS ASSISTANT, CONTINUED ON! AL HAS BEEN DRAWING MUTT & JEFF NOW FOR OVER 40 YEARS!

*THE PENGUIN BOOK OF COMICS, PAGE 96, 1971 EDITION

MUTT & JEFF
BY AL SMITH

NED DOWN BECAUSE N'T S?

YEH, JULIUS, AND I HAVE A LIVING ARRANGEMENT!

HE GETS PAID ON FRIDAYS AND HE'S BROKE ON TUESDAYS, THEN HE BORROWS FROM ME!

12-1-61

FROM THE AUTHOR'S PRIVATE COLLECTION

GINAL SIZE 5X17

L WORKS DIRECTLY ON BRISTOL WITH PENCIL, THEN INKING-IN AKING SLIGHT CHANGES AS HE GOES! HIS CORRECTIONS ARE ADE BY PASTING-DOWN OFF-SET PAPER AND RE-DRAWING OVER IT.

NAME: *ALBERT SMITH*   ART SCHOOL: *NONE*   COLLEGE: *NONE*

INK: *HIGGINS*   BRISTOL: *BAINBRIDGE AND STRATHMORE, 3 PLY*

DRAWING PEN: *GILLOTT'S 290 & 170*   LETTERING: *SPEEDBALL #5*

BRUSH: *NO. 2 & 3, FOR FILL-IN*   PENCIL: *NONE NAMED*

ZIP SCREEN: *STOPPED USING*   ERASER: *EBERHARD FABER*

BRINGING UP FATHER

BY GEORGE McMANUS

JUNE 7, 1930

PERMISSION OF KING FEATURES SYNDICATE

BRINGING UP FATHER IS TRULY A STRIP FROM THE PAST THAT HAS SURVIVED TO THE PRESENT DAY!

FROM AUTHOR'S PRIVATE COLLECTI

PERMISSION OF KING FEATURES SYNDIC

THE EDITOR AND PUBLISHER SYNDICATE DIRECTORY LISTS KAVANAGH-FLETCHER-CAMP, AS THE CREATIVE PEOPLE NOW PRODUCING THE STRIP, SINCE GEORGE McMANUS, ORIGINAL ARTIST, DIED IN 1954!

BRINGING UP FATHER
GEORGE McMANUS

> T SO TIGHT-
> LIKE TO BE
> LE TO
> WALLOW
> LITTLE.

> YOU MUST LOOK IN THE BOOK OF ETIQUETTE AND LEARN HOW TO ADDRESS A JUDGE.

> I'LL JUST ASK YOUR BROTHER- HE CERTAINLY KNOWS HOW TO TALK TO A JUDGE.

6·7

PERMISSION OF KING FEATURES SYNDICATE

ORIGINAL SIZE: 17 X 4⅛

IF ANY STRIP WAS THE WAY THINGS WERE BACK IN THE 1920'S, "BRINGING UP FATHER" WAS JUST THAT... THE CLOTHES, THE HOME FURNISHINGS.. EVERYTHING!

BRINGING UP FATHER, LIKE POLLY AND HER PALS, USED TO FILL-UP THE WHOLE FRONT PAGE OF THE SUNDAY PAPER... AND THE DAILY RAN THE ENTIRE WIDTH OF THE PAGE.... A REAL THRILL TO BEHOLD!

I HAVE NO INFORMATION ON GEORGE'S METHOD OF WORKING, OR HIS TOOLS, HOWEVER, HIS DRAWING PEN MUST HAVE BEEN VERY FINE AND VERY FLEXIBLE! EVERYTHING WAS FREE-HAND, AND IT LOOKS, FROM THE ORIGINAL, HE LETTERED WITH THE SAME PEN POINT AS HE DREW!

BACK IN THE 1930'S AND 40'S, WHEN I WAS GROWING UP, POLLY AND HER PALS WAS IN FULL GLORY, IN BOTH DAILY AND SUNDAY PAPERS. CLIFF'S HANDLING OF BLACK WAS A WORK OF PURE DESIGN! THE PLACEMENT OF BLACKS WERE WELL THOUGHT-OUT... NO OTHER CARTOONIST WAS ANYWHERE NEAR CLIFF IN SHEER DRAWING STYLE! SINCE CLIFF'S NO LONGER WITH US, I DON'T HAVE INFORMATION ON HIS WORKING TOOLS OR METHODS.. BUT FROM STUDYING THE ORIGINAL, HIS DRAWING PEN WAS VERY *FLEXIBLE!* THE LETTERING APPEARS TO BE DONE IN SOME TYPE OF SPEEDBALL, AT LEAST THE BOLD WORDS!

WAYOUT

by KEN MUSE

I JUST GOT PAID TODAY!

WHAT DO YOU HAVE THAT'S *REAL* EXPENSIVE?

HOW ABOUT CLAMS STUFFED WITH $20 BILLS!

I'LL HAVE THAT AND A *DOUBLE* ORDER OF THAT STUFFING!

REPRINTED WITH PERMISSION OF ME, KEN MUSE

NEWSPAPER SIZE

HEY, IT'S ME! I WAS BORN AND RAISED ON THE EAST SIDE OF DETROIT, AND AS FAR BACK AS I CAN REMEMBER I'VE WANTED TO BE A CARTOONIST, AND STARTED DRAWING WHEN I WAS FIVE... AT SEVEN I BECAME SERIOUS!

THE COMIC STRIPS WERE MY FAVORITES, AND I HAD MY IDOL THEN... IT WAS AL CAPP'S, "L'IL ABNER"

"WAYOUT" WAS SOLD TO McNAUGHT SYNDICATE IN 1964, AFTER 4 YEARS AND A DOZEN DIFFERENT STRIPS LATER! IT WAS *AFTER* I SOLD THE STRIP, AND IT WAS SEEN IN ABOUT 120 NEWSPAPERS, THAT I DISCOVERED IT WAS HARD WORK!

THE CARTOONS WERE EASY... IT WAS THE GAGS!

IN ANY EVENT, AFTER FIVE YEARS AND 3500 STRIPS LATER, EVERY TIME I LOOKED IN THE MIRROR I LOOKED LIKE "WAYOUT."... SO I RESIGNED THE STRIP TO TEACH COMMERCIAL ART IN COLLEGE AND HAVE BEEN HAPPY EVER SINCE! *COMIC STRIPS ARE STILL IN MY BLOOD*

WAYOUT
KEN MUSE

ACTUAL SIZE: 4⅞ X 17

NAME: *KEN MUSE*   ART SCHOOL: *MEINZINGER, DET.*   INK: *ARTONE*

BRISTOL: *2 PLY PLATE STRATHMORE*   PEN FOR LETTERING: *SPEEDBALL A5*

PEN FOR DRAWING: *GILLOTT'S 1290*   BRUSH: *ANY SIZE THAT WORKS*

PENCIL: *HB*   ZIP SCREEN: *FORMATT #7211*   ERASER: *KNEADED*

METHOD OF WORKING: *I DO ROUGHS ON BOND PAPER THEN CLEAN THEM UP ON TRACING PAPER. THEN USE A LIGHT-BOX AND TRACE THROUGH THE BACK OF THE BRISTOL! I INK THE LETTERING FIRST THEN INK OVER PENCIL LINES! A LOT OF HARD WORK!*

111

WAYOUT by KEN MUSE

NEWSPAPER SIZE

OCCASIONALLY, SO I WOULDN'T GO OUT OF MY MIND, I'D SWITCH PEN POINTS! HERE, THE DRAWING OF THE BIG GUY WAS AN FB5 FLICKER, AND WAYOUT AND THE LETTERING WAS AN A5! BIG PRINTING WAS AN A4

B.C.
by JOHNNY HART

CONGRATULATIONS MEN, YOU'VE STRUCK INK!

NEWSPAPER SIZE

B.C. BY PERMISSION OF JOHNNY HART AND FIELD ENTERPRISES, INC.

JOHNNY HART HAS A FREE STYLE OF DRAWING THAT YOU HAVE TO ADMIRE. THE ORIGINALS ARE A WORK OF ART... AND THE GAGS AS WELL! BELIEVE ME, A LOT OF WORK GOES INTO THIS COMIC STRIP, AND I HOPE IT IS AROUND A LONG TIME!

B.C. WAS LAUNCHED IN 1964.

MR. HART LISTS HIS HOBBYS AS "WORKING ON WEEKENDS," AND HIS GOALS: "NOT WORKING ON WEEKENDS."

THE ORIGINAL STRIP MEASURES 17$\frac{9}{16}$" X 4"$\frac{11}{16}$"

B.C. by JOHNNY HART

3·25

B.C. BY PERMISSION OF JOHNNY HART AND FIELD ENTERPRISES, INC.

NAME: JOHNNY HART   **ART SCHOOL:** NONE   **COLLEGE:** NONE
INK: HIGGINS   **BRISTOL:** STRATHMORE/GRUMBACHER
PEN FOR LETTERING: OVAL (SIMILAR TO HUNT-GLOBE)
PEN FOR DRAWING: OVAL   **BRUSH:** NONE   **PENCIL GRADE:** #2
ZIP SCREEN: 32 LINE   **ERASER:** KNEADED

METHOD OF WORKING:
MR. HART DRAWS DIRECTLY ON THE BRISTOL, ROUGHING-IN
THE CARTOON, THEN TIGHTENING-UP THE PENCIL LINES AND
THEN INKING. FOLLOWED BY CLEANING-UP THE PENCIL LINES.

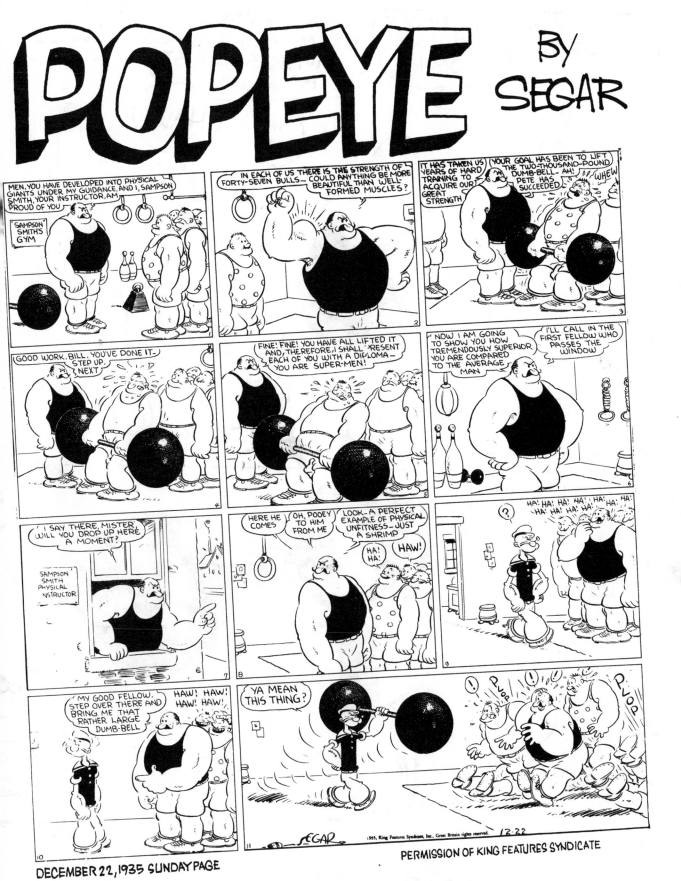

DECEMBER 22, 1935 SUNDAY PAGE

POPEYE, BY ELZIE SEGAR, WAS ANOTHER STRIP THAT GREW OUT
OF THE 1930's! IT ALSO FILLED THE ENTIRE SUNDAY PAGE!

SEGAR

ORIGINAL SIZE: 18¾ X 18⅝

MANY CARTOONISTS IN THOSE DAYS LETTERED WITH THE SAME PEN POINT THEY DREW WITH!

POPEYE

by BUD SAGENDORF

Panel 1: YA BLASTID MONARCH! IF YA WAS A GOOD KING YA WOULD **DO** SUMPIN' ABOUT THEM JAY BIRDS!

Panel 2: A KING IS SUSPOSED TA PROTECK HIS PEOPLES FROM MONSKERS AN' ANY OTHER TROUBLES!

Panel 3: BLOW ME DOWN! I BETCHA IF **I** WAS A KING, I WOULD KNOW HOW TA DEAL WIT' 'EM THIEVIN' JAY BIRDS!

NEWSPAPER SIZE

PERMISSION OF KING FEATURES SYNDICATE

BUD SAGENDORF IS THE THIRD ARTIST TO DRAW "POPEYE"! AFTER SEGAR'S DEATH, BILL ZABOLY TOOK OVER THE DRAWING OF THE STRIP FOR SOME 20 YEARS! *BILL IS RETIRED AND LIVING IN CLEVELAND.*

YOU CAN SEE THE EXCELLENT JOB, BUD SAGENDORF DOES ON THE STRIP... IT'S HARD TO TELL THE DIFFERENCE

BUD DOES ALL HIS OWN GAGS, WITH THE HELP OF HIS FAMILY. HIS STRIPS ARE NOT DRAWN TOO FAR AHEAD... ONLY A WEEK AT A TIME!

BUD HAS A DIFFICULT TIME STICKING TO A WORKING SCHEDULE! SOMETHING LIKE BOWLING OR GOLF CAN DRAG HIM FROM THE DRAWING BOARD!

HE DOES ADMIT HOWEVER, HE CAN DO HIS BEST WORK WHEN HIS DEADLINE IS DUE, AND HIS BACK IS AGAINST THE WALL!

POPEYE by BUD SAGENDORF

ORIGINAL SIZE: 17¾ X 5⅛

NAME: *BUD SAGENDORF*   ART SCHOOL: *NONE*   COLLEGE: *NONE*

INK: *PELIKAN*   BRISTOL: *3 PLY STRATHMORE - HIGH SURFACE*

PEN FOR DRAWING: *GILLOTT 170 - 290 - 303*   BRUSH: *ANY SIZE*

PEN FOR LETTERING: *SPEEDBALL A5*   PENCIL: *TURQUOISE HB*

ERASER: *KNEADED*   HOW DO YOU WORK? *ALL THE TIME*

METHOD OF WORKING:

BUD ROUGHS-IN ON THE BRISTOL, THEN TIGHTENS-UP THE PENCIL, AND THEN INKS THE FINAL RESULT... *A LOT OF HARD DRAWING!*

HERE'S THE INFORMATION SHEET BUD SAGENDORF, THE CARTOONIST OF POPEYE, SENDS TO ASPIRING CARTOONISTS WHO WRITE HIM FOR ADVICE ON BREAKING INTO THE FIELD!

TIPS FOR THE BEGINNING CARTOONIST

The most important thing for the budding cartoonist to remember is that he or she is first a writer and second an artist. A beautiful drawing seldom sells a weak idea, but many times a strong idea will sell a poor drawing.

You only learn to draw by drawing. Take all of the art classes you can in school, and spend as much time as possible practicing your craft at home. Because you are going to be a writer, too, you must not forget those English and literature classes. READ! Read anything and everything.

Don't be afraid to pick out a cartoonist you admire and copy his work. We all learn by copying. After you have mastered the use of the tools of your trade, your own style will develop.

MATERIALS ...

Cartoons are drawn with pen or brush--using a black, waterproof drawing ink.

Cartoons are nearly always drawn in black and white on white paper or board. Paper is flexible. Board is paper--mounted on a heavy backing--and is stiff. Color is added afterward by the engraver. If an editor wants a full-color drawing, he will tell you so.

PENCILS ...

You pencil in your cartoon first--then ink it. Any good drawing pencil will do. Most cartoonists like to use HB pencils. Don't use too soft a pencil-- remember after you finish inking the drawing, you will want to erase the pencil, and a soft pencil makes it difficult to finish with a clean drawing.

PENS ...

Any pen you can draw with is a good pen for you. The favorites are the GILLOTT pens, numbers: 170, 290, and 303.

BRUSHES ...

Brushes are expensive, but don't buy cheap ones. Winsor and Newton sable brushes are the best. Choose by the number, the size you like.

THERE'S MORE

BUD SAGENDORF
POPEYE

PAPER ...

    A good quality of drawing paper or board is important. The standard for years has been the Strathmore papers. Most cartoonists use a two or three ply paper for their work. (The more plys--the thicker the paper.) For brush, use a board with a rough surface. It is called KID FINISH. It will work for pen, too. For pen drawings, most artists use the smooth or HIGH SURFACE board.

SIZE ...

    Comic strips as well as single panel cartoons are usually drawn larger than the size they are to be reproduced. Here again, it is up to the individual. The average is from a third to twice size.

IDEAS ...

    Creating funny ideas is habit, just like learning anything else. When you are practicing your drawings, practice your idea creating, too. Have some kind of an idea for every practice drawing you make. Read and study the work of other cartoonists and humor writers. They studied the men that went before them.

GETTING STARTED ...

    Selling that first drawing is the big hurdle. Luckily, today, most local newspapers are printed by the offset process. This cuts the odds in your favor. Unlike the older letterpress printing, with offset, there is no engraving cost to the paper for a line drawing. Try doing a local strip or single panel. A lot of today's pros started this way. Local advertisers are another good bet. They love to have spot drawings to illustrate their business. The main thing is to get get in print! Future buyers of your work will want to see samples of your

in print! Future buyers of your work will want to see samples of your published work, so even if you have to give it away or take a chicken in trade--get your stuff into print!

                          Bud Sagendorf (POPEYE)

THE COMIC STRIP CARTOONISTS RECEIVE MUCH MAIL FROM FANS, AND IT'S NOT *UNUSUAL* TO GET CARTOONS FROM OTHER ASPIRING CARTOONISTS WHO WANT ADVICE. RATHER THAN SEND OUT PERSONALLY TYPED ADVICE OVER AND OVER AGAIN, THE BEST WAY IS A XEROXED COPY. I USED TO SEND A SIMILAR ONE MYSELF!

BLONDIE

by CHIC YOUNG

NEWSPAPER SIZE DAILY, JULY 23, 1951

PERMISSION OF KING FEATURES SYNDICATE

BLONDIE MADE ITS APPEARANCE IN 1930, IN THE NEW YORK AMERICAN, AND WAS THE MOST POPULAR STRIP IN THE HISTORY OF THE COMICS! BY THE MIDDLE OF THE 50'S, BLONDIE WAS APPEARING IN 1,300 NEWSPAPERS...AND IN THE 40'S, THERE WAS A LONG SERIES OF FILMS ABOUT THE BUMSTEAD FAMILY! *IT WAS ALSO ON RADIO!*

CHIC DID ANOTHER STRIP BEFORE BLONDIE, CALLED DUMB DORA, WHICH RAN FROM 1921 TO 1931!

CHIC YOUNG IS NO LONGER WITH US, AND THE STRIP IS NOW PRODUCED BY TWO CAPABLE AND TALENTED GENTLEMEN: *DEAN YOUNG*, HIS SON, WHO WRITES THE STRIP, AND *JIM RAYMOND*, WHO DRAWS IT!

THIS WAS ANOTHER COMIC STRIP I GREW-UP WITH IN THE 30'S! NOTICE THE RATIO SIZE THEN WAS DIFFERENT!

BLONDIE by CHIC YOUNG

ORIGINAL SIZE: 17½ X 5 5/16

I HAVE NO INFORMATION ON CHIC YOUNG'S METHOD OF WORKING, HOWEVER, MUCH CAN BE LEARNED BY STUDYING THE ORIGINAL STRIP!

HIS PEN POINT WAS VERY *FLEXIBLE*, PROBABLY A GILLOTT 170 OR 290, AND HIS LETTERING PEN WAS PROBABLY THE SAME! GREAT CARE WAS TAKEN WITH THE LETTERING... REAL PROFESSIONAL... NICELY SPACED!

SOME OF THE PEN LINES ARE VERY THIN... THIS, ALONG WITH THE THICK ONES, CREATE A VERY SLICK COMIC STRIP! *BLONDIE WAS A SUPER-STRIP!*

DEAN YOUNG AND JIM RAYMOND, CREATORS OF "BLONDIE" HAVE SOME ADVICE!

THE COMIC STRIP "BLONDIE" WITH A FEW COMMENTS ON IT AND CARTOONING IN GENERAL
BY DEAN YOUNG

The comic strip "BLONDIE" was created by my father Chic Young in the year 1930. Blondie at the inception of the strip was still single but was soon to be married to one Dagwood Bumstead. Incidentally, Blondie's maiden name was Miss Blondie Boopadoop.

Blondie and Dagwood were actually married in the comic strip on February 13, 1933. The marriage was a very happy one and a complete success. Today, almost a half century later, the two continue to perform in blissful togetherness in over 1,800 United States and foreign newspapers...translated into 24 different languages and read by over 80 million people daily. To "localize" in foreign countries, the names of the character are changed; for instance, in Spanish-speaking countries, Blondie is known as "Pepita" and Dagwood as "Lorenzo". In France, Dagwood is "Emile" and in Sweden he is "Dagobert".

My father's first attempt at drawing was art in its simplest form...making "hop skotch" panels on the pavement with white chalk for the little girls of his neighborhood. That paid off only in happy smiles and "thank yous" from the little girls. He soon found out, however, that if you worked humorous little ideas into similar panels, it was called a comic strip and that newspapers, bless their little hearts, paid you money for it. Now in spite of all the mean things they say about money, my father had always found it pleasant stuff to have around, so he turned professional comic strip artist. Thus, the beginning history and a comic strip called "BLONDIE".

Today, some 16,000 comic strips later, the institution of "BLONDIE" is carried on by two of my father's long-time collaborators...me, his son, and Jim Raymond. I supply the story line continuity while Jim supplies the artistic accoutrements. The two of us work in close harmony and warm mutual respect to carry on the tradition of our "BLONDIE" heritage.

ADVICE, QUESTIONS, AND ANSWERS FOR ASPIRING YOUNG COMIC ARTISTS

I believe the popularity of "BLONDIE" lies in its simplicity to humorously depict the four basic projects which all of us are involved with at one time or another in our lives--eating, sleeping, making money, and the business of raising children. The question most folks ask me is: "Do I get my ideas from my own home life?" The answer is No because no family group could turn up enough situations to maintain a comic strip every day for years on end. Most of the material I use has to be dreamed up. All in all, drawing a comic strip is fun and interesting in a monotonous sort of way.

AND MORE

DEAN YOUNG / JIM RAYMOND
BLONDIE

The biggest problem is drawing an entertaining strip every day. When you break down into smaller specific problems, you find that the "restrictions" and "don'ts" afford the most trouble. A comic strip of world circulation must fit into a certain groove to entertain the greatest number of people and offend no one.

A comic strip should not lend itself to propaganda, its sole purpose being the amusement of the reader. Politics, religion, and racial subjects should be avoided for obvious reasons.

The comic strip is a medium that goes right into the home, and its contents should be of the most wholesome nature. The so-called comic artist who does not consider this will not make it "big", and he hurts the conscientious artist who is trying to give newspaper readers good, clean entertainment.

Reference to liquor should be avoided...the characters in "BLONDIE" do not use cigarettes. Divorce, infirmities of the body, sickness, and other such unpleasant subjects do not lend themselves to satisfactory humor for comic strips and should not be used.

The material used should not be localized. Remember, when it is snowing in New York, people are swimming in Florida and California. Jokes about U.S. holidays are meaningless in Europe and South America. If your strip is translated for foreign papers, the text should be such that it will not lose its meaning in translation.

Pages could be written on what to do or not do; those listed above are only a few of the more important ones. Broadly speaking, it is up to the careful comic artist to ensure that he offends no one, steps on no toes, hurts no group, and that his strip is all in good, clean fun.

BLONDIE IS WITHOUT A DOUBT THE KING OF COMIC STRIPS! IT IS IN MORE NEWSPAPERS THAN ANY OTHER COMIC STRIP IN THE WORLD!

CARTOONISTS WOULD DO WELL TO STUDY DEAN YOUNG'S STYLE OF HUMOR, AMOUNG OTHER GREATS! AFTER ALL, REACHING THE GREATEST AUDIENCE IS THE SECRET TO A SUCCESSFUL COMIC STRIP!

"Why do you peel the bread when you
make sandwiches for your club?"

ORIGINAL SIZE: 6⅞ X 6⅞

COURTESY THE REGISTER AND TRIBUNE SYNDICATE, INC.

ORIGINAL SIZE: 27½ X 12½

WHEN YOU'RE VISITING BIL KEANE, AT HIS HOME, IN SCOTTSDALE, ARIZONA, YOU HAVE TO KEEP ON YOUR TOES! HE'S A VERY SHARP AND HUMOROUS CARTOONIST. BILL WORKED ON THE PHILLY BULLETIN AS ARTIST FOR 15 YEARS.

BIL'S PHILOSOPHY: "I USUALLY WORK BETWEEN TENNIS GAMES. WHEN THE WORK BEGINS TO INTERFERE WITH THE TENNIS, THE WORK HAS TO GO!"

BUT NOTICE HOW SKILLFULLY BIL KEANE WORKS HIS PEN LINES!

FAMILY CIRCUS
BY BIL KEANE

SUNDAY PAGE, AUGUST 8, 1965

COURTESY THE REGISTER AND TRIBUNE SYNDICATE, INC.

NAME: *BIL KEANE* ART SCHOOL: *NONE (SELF-TAUGHT)*

COLLEGE: *NONE (RIGHT INTO ARMY FROM HIGHSCHOOL)*

INK: *HIGGINS OR PELIKAN* BRISTOL: *2 PLY STRATHMORE, PLATE*

PEN POINT FOR DRAWING: *HUNT CROWQUILL 107* ERASER: *PLASTIC*

PEN POINT FOR LETTERING: *B6 OR B5½ SPEEDBALL*

BRUSH: *#2 WINSOR-NEWTON SABLE - HEAVY LINES & BLACKS*

PENCIL: *VENUS 3H & H* ZIP: *GRAFIX BOARD 26 LINE SCREEN*

METHOD OF WORKING: *BIL WORKS DIRECTLY ON BRISTOL, SKETCH-ING, AND THEN CLEANING-UP BEFORE INKING! OCCASIONALLY USES LIGHTBOX FOR RE-DOING CARTOON NOT SATISFIED WITH!*

MiCKEY FiNN

by LANK LEONARD

NEWSPAPER SIZE

REPRINTED BY PERMISSION OF THE McNAUGHT SYNDICATE

SUNDAY PAGE

REPRINTED BY PERMISSION OF THE McNAUGHT SYNDICATE

THE CREATOR OF MICKEY FINN, LANK LEONARD, IS NOW DECEASED. HIS ASSISTANT, MORRIS WEISS, NOW DRAWS THE COMIC STRIP!

MICKEY FINN BY LANK LEONARD

FEATURING
DIAVALO
THE WORLD'S
GREATEST
MAGICIAN

TEN OTHER
STAR ACTS

—THERE'S
—N A MAGICIAN
—R AS THIS
—AN!

BAH! EVERYBODY
HAS SEEN THAT
KIND OF STUFF!

GRENADIER
GOAT HILL
LODGE

DIAVALO
WORLD FAMOUS
MAGICIAN

LOOK! WE CAN'T CANCEL
HIM NOW—HE'S ALREADY
IN TOWN!

WHERE'S
HE STAYING
AT WHAT
HOTEL?

—MAKIN'
—S DISAPPEAR
—O STUFF!

WELL, I DO OTHER
THINGS, TOO! JUST
BE PATIENT!

I TRUST I HAVE
CONVINCED YOU,
SHERIFF!

I'VE GOT NEWS FOR
YOU! YOU DEFINITE—
HAVE **NOT**!

633

FROM THE AUTHOR'S PRIVATE COLLECTION

**THIS IS A SECTION OF A SUNDAY ORIGINAL ACTU—
SIZE MEASURING 12 BY 17¾ INCHES!**

MICKEY FINN
BY LANK LEONARD

ACTUAL SIZE 5 X 16½

FROM THE AUTHOR'S PRIVATE COLLECTION

NAME: *LANK LEONARD* ART SCHOOL: *ART STUDENT'S LEAGUE &*
CORRESPONDENCE SCHOOL COLLEGE: *NONE* INK *ART TONE*
BRISTOL: *3 PLY STRATHMORE* LETTERING PEN: *FLICKER A5*
BRUSH: *#1 FOR BLACKS* PENCIL GRADE: *SOFT MEDIUM*
ZIP SCREEN: *CRAFT-TINT BOARD* ERASER: *RUB-KLEEN*
METHOD OF WORKING: *LANK DREW DIRECTLY ON BRISTOL BOARD*
AFTER TALKING OVER STORY WITH MORRIS WEISS, THEN MORRIS
INKED LETTERING. LANK PENCILED TIGHT, (ALL BUT WOMEN),
AND THEN MORRIS INKED FINAL ART.

MICKEY FINN

BY MORRIS WEISS

NEWSPAPER SIZE

REPRINTED WITH PERMISSION OF McNAUGHT SYNDICATE

ACTUAL SIZE: 16½ X 4⅞

FROM AUTHOR'S PRIVATE COLLECTION

A SKILLFULLY RENDERED AND WELL WRITTEN, MICKEY FINN, BY MORRIS WEISS. "MANNY," BEARS A CLOSE RESEMBLANCE TO LANK LEONARD!

PENCIL ROUGH OF MICKEY FINN, ON REVERSE OF BRISTOL, BY MORRIS WEISS

FROM AUTHOR'S PRIVATE COLLECTION

REPRINTED WITH PERMISSION OF McNAUGHT SYNDICATE

NAME: *MORRIS WEISS* **ART SCHOOL:** *ART STUDENT'S LEAGUE*

COLLEGE: *NONE* **INK:** *ART TONE* **BRISTOL:** *2 PLY STRATHMORE*

DRAWING PEN: *DIETZGEN* **LETTERING PEN:** *A5 FLICKER*

BRUSH: *#1* **PENCIL:** *REGULAR- NOT TOO SOFT* **ERASER:** *RUB KLEEN*

METHOD OF WORKING:

MORRIS FIRST WRITES THE SCRIPT, THEN RULES THE LINES! WHEN PENCILLING, HE USES A LIGHT-BOX TO REVERSE THE PAPER. MOST OF HIS STRIPS ARE PENCILLED ON REVERSE SIDE.

LI'L ABNER

by AL CAPP

TELEGRAM

A. YOKUM
DOGPATCH, U.S.A.

COME TO NEW YORK CITY
IMMEDIATELY AND DON'T
FORGET TO BRING YOUR UN-
WASHED BACK.

ARCHIBALD McFLEECE
ATTORNEY
715 PARK AVE, N.Y.

(-"THEY BETTER NOT TAKE
TOO LONG SETTLIN' THET
WILL!! AH BRUNG HIM UP
TO WASH HIS BACK
EV'RY SATTIDY
NIGHT-RAIN
OR SHINE!!-")

(-"COME **NEXT** SATTIDY
NIGHT— **SWISH!!**—HE'LL
WASH IT!! —HE JEST
CAIN'T HELP IT!!-")

NEWSPAPER SIZE

REPRINTED WITH PERMISSON OF CAPP ENTERPRISES, INC.

THERE IS NO DOUBT, AL CAPP'S *LI'L ABNER*, WAS A SUPER STAR IN THE COMIC STRIP BUSINESS, AMOUNG A FEW OTHERS. THE STRIP WAS MADE INTO A BROADWAY MUSICAL, AND MOVIE, AND MUCH OF LI'L ABNER MADE ITS WAY TO OUR LANGUAGE, LIKE *SADIE HAWKINS DAY*, *KICKAPOO JOY JUICE, DAISY MAE, GENERAL BULL MOOSE, ETC.*

AL STARTED HIS CAREER AS AN ASSISTANT FOR HAM FISHER, WHO DREW "JOE PALOOKA", A COMIC STRIP ABOUT BOXING!

LI'L ABNER BECAME A COMIC STRIP IN 1934!

AL CAPP ATTENDED VARIOUS ART SCHOOLS IN BOSTON AND PHILADELPHIA, AND HIS FIRST BIG-TIME JOB WAS WITH A.P., DOING "COL. GILFEATHER."

LI'L ABNER WAS ANOTHER COMIC STRIP I GREW UP WITH! THE GREATEST.

LI'L ABNER by AL CAPP

ORIGINAL SIZE: 18⅞ X 5⁹⁄₁₆

I'M SORRY, BUT INFORMATION ON MR. CAPP'S TOOLS, AND METHOD OF WORKING WERE NOT AVAILABLE! FROM STUDYING THE ORIGINAL, THERE IS NO DOUBT AL USED SOME KIND OF VERY *FLEXIBLE* PEN POINT.... PROBABLY A QUILL OR GILLOTT 290! HIS LETTERING WAS WITH A DIFFERENT PEN POINT... ONE NOT SO *FLEXIBLE* ...LIKE A HUNT 513 E.F.

IT IS DOUBTFUL AL USED A LIGHTBOX, BUT DREW DIRECTLY ON THE BRISTOL, TIGHTENING-UP THEN INKING!

JEFF COBB

BY PETE HOFFMAN

NEWSPAPER SIZE

PRINTED WITH PERMISSION OF PETE HOFFMAN

PETE LIVES IN TOLEDO, OHIO, AND "JEFF COBB" HAS BEEN IN DOMESTIC SYNDICATION FOR 21 YEARS. THE STRIP IS NO LONGER SYNDICATED! I DON'T KNOW OF ANY OTHER CARTOONIST WHO SPENT MORE TIME DRAWING A STRIP THAN MR. HOFFMAN... A REAL PERFECTIONIST!

PETE, ALSO HAS BEEN DRAWING A PANEL SINCE 1950 CALLED "WHY WE SAY"!

ACTUALLY, LIKE MILTON CANIFF, PETE HOFFMAN IS LESS A CARTOONIST AND MORE AN ILLUSTRATOR! AFTER ALL, THE PEOPLE ARE LIFE-LIKE, AND THE STORY DOES FOLLOW A SERIOUS LINE!

NOTICE THE EFFORT PETE HAS TAKEN TO CONVEY THE WRINKLES AND SHADOWS! *BEAUTIFUL!*

136

JEFF COBB PETE HOFFMAN

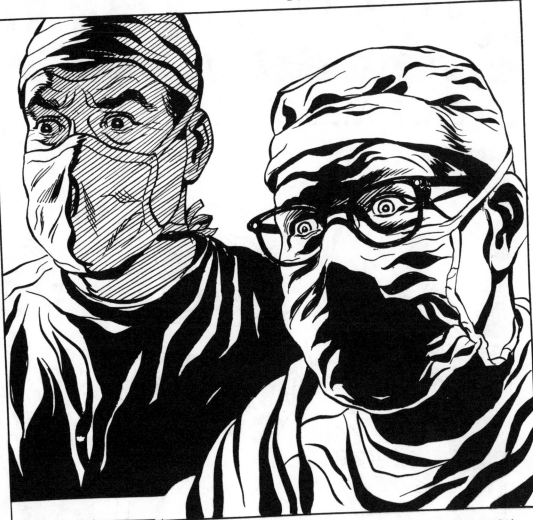

FROM THE AUTHOR'S PRIVATE COLLECTION

ACTUAL SIZE: 5⁹/₁₆ X 17¾

NAME: PETE HOFFMAN **ART SCHOOL:** NONE **INK:** HIGGINS/PELIKAN

COLLEGE: UNIV. OF TOLEDO (B.B.A.) **BRISTOL:** 2 PLY STRATHMORE

PEN FOR DRAWING: HUNT 108 **LETTERING PEN:** ESTERBROOK 314

PENCIL: 3H LEAD (KOH-I-NOOR) **ERASER:** EBERHARD FABER

METHOD OF WORKING: DRAWING IS PENCILED DIRECTLY ON THE STRATHMORE FROM WRITTEN CONTINUITY, THEN INKED! NO. 2 & 3 BRUSH SUPPLEMENTS BASIC PEN WORK-FOR CLOTHING, WRINKLES AND FOLDS, HAIR TREATMENT, SHADOWS, ETC., ETC.

BRENDA STARR

BY DALE MESSICK

NEWSPAPER SIZE: 43 PICAS (7 1/16")

ORIGINAL SIZE: 15 1/16 X 4 7/16

A SKILLFULLY DRAWN "BRENDA STARR" COMIC STRIP!
DALE MESSICK'S STRIP WAS FIRST PUBLISHED IN 1940.

138

BRENDA STARR by DALE MESSICK

OUT OF THOUSANDS OF CARTOONISTS, SINCE THE START OF COMICS IN THIS COUNTRY, THERE ARE FEWER THAN TWENTY WOMEN...DALE MESSICK IS ONE!

NAME: *DALE MESSICK* ART SCHOOL: *CHICAGO ART INSTITUTE & RAY-VOGUE* INK: *PELIKAN* BRISTOL: *STRATHMORE 2 PLY*
PEN FOR DRAWING: *CROW QUILL* PEN FOR LETTERING: *SAME*
BRUSH: *NO. 2 FOR ALL CHARACTERS* PENCIL GRADE: *NO. 3*
ERASER: *PINK PEARL & KNEEDED* LIGHTBOX: *OCCASIONALLY*
METHOD OF WORKING:

AFTER THE SCRIPT IS WRITTEN BY DALE MESSICK, HER ASSISTANT, JOHN OLSEN, LETTERS AND BLOCKS-IN THE ACTION. HE ALSO COMPLETES THE BACKGROUNDS AND INCIDENTAL CHARACTERS. DALE MESSICK THEN REFINES THE FACES AND FIGURES WITH PENCIL; THEN FINISHES ALL THE CHARACTERS WITH BRUSH!

L.P. and U.P.

BY CLIFF WIRTH

(LOWER PENINSULA AND UPPER PENINSULA)

8-22

U.P., WHAT DOES A **CONFIDENCE CRISIS** MEAN TO YOU?

SOO

HAVE YOU EVER WATCHED THE TIGERS TRY TO BRING A MAN HOME FROM SECOND?

REPRINTED BY PERMISSION OF CLIFF WIRTH

NEWSPAPER SIZE

WOULD YOU CASH THIS $1000. BILL?

LP

11-16

CERTAINLY DOCTOR!

BANK

I'M NOT A DOCTOR!

LP

- A T.V. REPAIRMAN THEN!

BANK

REPRINTED BY PERMISSION OF CLIFF WIRTH

NEWSPAPER SIZE

CLIFF WIRTH HAS SELF-SYNDICATED HIS OWN COMIC STRIP...ABOUT THE STATE OF MICHIGAN! HE XEROXES THE ORIGINALS DOWN TO ABOUT 55% AND SENDS OUT A MONTH'S SUPPLY TO HIS CLIENT NEWSPAPERS THROUGH-OUT MICHIGAN...IT'S MICHIGAN'S OWN COMIC STRIP!

IF THERE'S ANYTHING CLIFF HASN'T DOWN IN THE CARTOONING BUSINESS, I DON'T KNOW ABOUT IT!

L.P. AND U.P. by CLIFF WIRTH

WOULD YOU CASH THIS $1000. BILL?

11-16

CERTAINLY DOCTOR!

BANK

I'M NOT A DOCTOR!

ORIGINAL SIZE: 12¾ X 3¹⁵/₁₆

NAME: CLIFF WIRTH   ART SCHOOL: MEINZINGER, DETROIT
COLLEGE: MICHIGAN STATE   INK: HIGGINS   ZIP: 20% BENDAY
BRISTOL: STRATHMORE 3 PLY   PEN FOR DRAWING: A-5 & A-6
BRUSH: #3 FOR LARGE AREAS, SANFORD SHARPIE 59, SMALL AREAS
PENCIL: BLUE-NON REPRODUCING   ERASER: EBERHARD KNEADED
METHOD OF WORKING:

CLIFF DRAWS DIRECTLY ON THE BRISTOL WITH HIS BLUE NON-RE-
PRODUCING PENCIL, THEN INKS, THUS SAVING TIME BY NOT ERASING.......
HE THEN INKS OVER THE BLUE! SOMETIMES USES A LIGHTBOX WHEN
SPEED IS NEEDED! GETS IDEAS FROM READING, RADIO, TV, ETC., ETC.

NAPOLEON

BY FOSTER MOORE

NEWSPAPER SIZE

PERMISSION OF SMITH SERVICE

FROM AUTHOR'S PRIVATE COLLECTION

PERMISSION OF SMITH SERVICE

IN THE 1930'S, THE ORIGINAL ARTIST AND CREATOR WAS CLIFFORD McBRIDE, AND THE STRIP WAS CALLED "NAPOLEON AND UNCLE ELBY"... *NOW DRAWN BY MOORE!*

IF THAT DOG SO MUCH AS SNIFFS AT THIS NEW CEMENT BEFORE IT'S DRY I'LL BREAK HIS CONFOUNDED NECK!

FROM AUTHOR'S PRIVATE COLLECTION

NO BACKBONE!

PERMISSION FROM SMITH SERVICE

ANOTHER WELL EXECUTED DAILY NAPOLEON COMIC STRIP BY FOSTER MOORE- ORIGINAL STRIP IS DRAWN TO 14" X 4 1/8"!

NAPOLEON by FOSTER MOORE

ORIGINAL SIZE

WITH PERMISSION OF SMITH SERVICE

NAME: *FOSTER MOORE* ART SCHOOL: *PASADENA ART INSTITUTE*

COLLEGE: *UNIV. OF SOUTHERN CALIF.* INK: *PELIKAN (17 BLACK)*

BRISTOL: *STRATHMORE 2 PLY* PEN FOR DRAWING: *NONE*

PEN FOR LETTERING: *C-5 SPEEDBALL* PENCIL: *GRADE 4H*

BRUSH: *WINSOR-NEWTON, SERIES 7, NO.0, FOR ENTIRE DRAWING!*

ZIP: *RARELY USED* ERASER: *KNEADED* LIGHTBOX: *YES*

METHOD OF WORKING: *SCRATCH PAPER (TYPING) TO STRATHMORE VIA THE LIGHTBOX. THE ABOVE INFO APPLIES TO THE "NAPOLEON" STRIP. ON "GUM-DROPS" (UFS), I USE THE SAME INK & PAPER. HOWEVER, I USE A COMBIN-ATION BRUSH (SAME AS ABOVE) AND RAPIDOGRAPH PENS. LETTERING IS DONE WITH AN OSMIROID PEN AND ITALIC BROAD STRAIGHT NIB. SCREENING IS DONE WITH ZIP-A-TONE 275-10 (27½ LINE -10 PERCENT)!*

LITTLE FARMER
BY KERN PEDERSON

NEWSPAPER SIZE

PERMISSION OF SMITH SERVICE

ORIGINAL SIZE

FROM AUTHOR'S PRIVATE COLLECTION

KERN HAS BEEN DRAWING HIS STRIP FOR 30 YEARS, AND LOVES EVERY MINUTE OF IT! AT PRESENT, HE IS AN ART TEACHER IN NORTH ST. PAUL, MINNESOTA. HE BEGAN AS AN EDITORIAL AND SPORTS CARTOONIST!

LITTLE FARMER by KERN PEDERSON

ORIGINAL SIZE

NAME: KERN O. PEDERSON *ART SCHOOL:* UNIV. OF MINN., ALSO ART INSTRUCTION COURSE (MPLS. MINN.) *INK:* PELIKAN

BRISTOL: STRATHMORE 3 PLY *LETTERING PEN:* C5 & B6

DRAWING PEN: GILLOTT 170 AND B5 *PENCIL GRADE:* NO.3

BRUSH: NO.3 FOR FILLING IN BLACKS, AND NO.1 FOR USING WHITE FOR CORRECTIONS. *ZIP:* 27½ LINE -30%, SOMETIMES.

ERASER: LIGHT GREEN -PEDIGREE

METHOD OF WORKING: RULE STRIP, INK-IN, PUT ON LOGOS, ROUGH-SKETCH CHARACTERS AND LETTERING, IF ANY, THEN GO OVER ROUGH QUICK SKETCHES WITH NO.3 PENCIL, THEN INK STRIP. USE SOFT ERASER TO CLEAN-UP PENCIL LINES!

PARK AVE. BY PAUL GRINGLE

BUZZ OFF, MAN!... THIS IS 100% PURE TOBACCO!!

TAP! TAP!

KEEP OFF THE GRASS

PAUL GRINGLE

NEWSPAPER SIZE

PRINTED WITH PERMISSION OF PAUL GRINGLE

PAUL IS ANOTHER PERSONAL FRIEND OF MINE, NOW LIVING IN SAN DIEGO, CALIF. MR. GRINGLE DID CARTOONS FOR THE HOBO NEWS, A STRIP CALLED "RURAL DELIVERY", WAS ASSISTANT TO VING FULLER ON "DOC SYKE", AND RECENTLY DREW "OUT OUR WAY" FOR NEA! PAUL'S DONE GREETING CARDS AND ANIMATION.!

HE HAS ALSO TAUGHT CARTOONING AT ARIZONA ACAD. OF ARTS, AND IS DIRECTOR OF THE NATIONAL SCHOOL OF CARTOONING!
(A CORRESPONDENCE SCHOOL)

PAUL HAS A MODERN STYLE TO HIS CARTOONING, AND SPENDS HOURS AND HOURS ON HIS STRIPS...OFTEN REDRAWING OVER AND OVER UNTIL HE'S SATISFIED!

147

PARK AVE.
PAUL GRINGLE

ACTUAL SIZE 5⅛ X 18⅛

FROM AUTHOR'S PRIVATE COLLECTION

NAME: *PAUL GRINGLE* ART SCHOOL: *SCHOOL OF VISUAL ARTS* INK: *PELIKA*

COLLEGE: *BIARRITZ, PHOENIX C.C., PALOMAR* BRISTOL: *STRATHMORE 2 PL*

PEN FOR DRAWING: *HUNT #512, GILLOTT #170 & 290* PENCIL GRADE: *2H*

LETTERING PEN: *ESTERBROOK RELIEF #314* ERASER: *PINK PEARL*

METHOD OF WORKING: *PAUL DOES LOTS OF ROUGHS AND DOODLES ON BOND PAPER. HE THEN REFINES THEM ON TRACING PAPER, AND FROM THERE TO A LIGHTBOX, (ANIMATION SYSTEM), AND THEN ON TO THE STRATHMORE. LETTERING IS INKED FIRST. HE THEN INKS AND USES #2 OR #3 TO BEEF-UP OUTLINES, SLASH WRINKLES, DO BLAC*

FUN BUG by HOW'RANDS

NAME: *HOW'RANDS* ART SCHOOL: *ABBOTT & ART INSTITUTE*

INK: *PELIKAN* BRISTOL: *STRATHMORE 3 PLY* ZIP: *NONE*

PEN FOR DRAWING: *GILLOTT'S 290* FOR LETTERING: *SPEEDBALL B6*

BRUSH: *WINSOR-NEWTON #2 FOR THICK & THIN & BLACK AREAS*

ERASER: *EBERHARD RUBKLEEN 6002* LIGHTBOX: *NO*

METHOD OF WORKING: *DIRECTLY ON BRISTOL*

HOW' MAKES A PHOTO-COPY OF FIRST DRAWING AND THEN ADDS THE CHANGES TO IT FOR THE SECOND PICTURE!

FUN BUG by RANDS

HOW QUICKLY CAN YOU FIND SEVEN DIFFERENCES IN THE SECOND PICTURE?

3-4-76

ANSWERS: 1. BIRD, 2. CHIMNEY, 3. RABBIT, 4. BEAR PRINT, 5. BELT, 6. TURTLE, 7. RIFLE.

ORIGINAL SIZE

JOHN LaBRECQUE

REPRODUCTION SIZE

PERMISSION OF JOHN LABRECQUE

JOHN IS A TOTALLY COMMITTED *FREE LANCE CARTOONIST!* HE IS ABLE TO DRAW IN MANY STYLES – AN ADVANTAGE FOR HIS CLIENTS!

NAME: *JOHN LaBRECQUE* **ART SCHOOL:** *MEINZINGER, IN DETROIT, AND ALLEN AIRBRUSH INST.* **COLLEGE:** *MACALESTER, ST. PAUL, MINN.*

INK: *PELIKAN* **BRISTOL:** *STRATHMORE, 4 PLY* **ERASER:** *KNEADED*

DRAWING PEN: *PELIKAN GRAPHOS 04 & 08* **LETTERING:** *08 & FB5*

BRUSH: *WINSOR-NEWTON #2, SERIES 7, FOR DRAWING. #6 FOR FILL-IN*

PENCIL: *F GRADE, LIGHT TOUCH* **ZIP:** *WHATEVER JOB DICTATES*

METHOD OF WORKING: *I TRY TO AVOID ANY TYPE OF RE-DRAWING. I FIND MY FIRST IMPRESSIONS OF A SITUATION OR CARICATURE ARE THE MOST VIVID AND TO THE POINT... ANY COPYING-OVER SEEMS TO RUIN THE MOOD OF THE ART. I GO FROM PENCIL LAYOUT, RIGHT TO FINAL INK & RENDERING!*

JOHN LABRECQUE

ROY PAUL NELSON

"YOU KNOW THE RULES, MR. LORTON. NO DOGS IN THE CLASSROOM...."

PERMISSION OF ROY NELSON

PRINTED SIZE

NAME: ROY PAUL NELSON **ART SCHOOL:** ART CENTER, L.A.
COLLEGE: UNIV. OF OREGON & UNIV. OF SOUTHERN CALIF.
INK: HIGGINS...AND OTHERS. **BRISTOL:** WHAT EVER'S THERE.
PEN FOR DRAWING: ALL KINDS **ERASER:** ART GUM/PINK PEARL
PEN FOR LETTERING: OSMIROID AND SPEEDBALL, SOMETIMES
EVEN A BRUSH. **BRUSH:** NO. O FOR OUTLINING, AND THICKER
ONE FOR FILL-IN. **LIGHTBOX:** SOMETIMES!

METHOD OF WORKING: I HAVE NO SET PATTERNS. I USE WHATEVER IS
HANDY. I DON'T LIKE EXPENSIVE PAPER BECAUSE I TEND TO TIGHTEN-
UP ON IT. I SOMETIMES PATCH PIECES OF DRAWINGS TO BETTER
CONTROL COMPOSITION OR TO IMPROVE, SAY, A FACE. SOMETIMES I
DO A REALLY CRUDE ROUGH, THEN TRACE IT IN INK, CHANGING IT!

ROY PAUL NELSON

ORIGINAL SIZE

Magazine Article Writing

ROY PAUL

"YOU KNOW THE RULES, MR. LORTON. NO DOGS IN THE CLASSROOM.

ROY IS A PROFESSOR OF JOURNALISM AT THE UNIVERSITY OF OREGON, AND BESIDES HIS HUNDREDS OF ARTICLES, HE HAS THOUSANDS OF PUBLISHED CARTOONS TO HIS CREDIT. HERE IS A LIST OF SOME OF HIS BOOKS:

- CARTOONING • ARTICLES AND FEATURES • PUBLICATION DESIGN • THE DESIGN OF ADVERTISING • THE FOURTH ESTATE (WITH JOHN L. HULTENG)
- VISITS WITH 30 MAGAZINE ART DIRECTORS • FELL'S GUIDE TO COMMERCIAL ART DIRECTORS • FELL'S GUIDE TO THE ART OF CARTOONING • COMIC ART & CARICATURE • *PUBLISHED BY CONTEMPORARY BOOKS, CHICAGO.*

THE EDITORIAL CARTOON

DRAWN WITH A "SHARPIE" MAGIC MARKER ON BOND PAPER AND SHADED WITH AN EBONY 6325 PENCIL

THE EDITORIAL CARTOONIST

THE EDITORIAL, OR POLITICAL CARTOON IS A TOTALLY DIFFERENT BALL GAME THAN THE COMIC STRIP. EVEN THOUGH SOME COMIC STRIPS DO, AND HAVE INFRINGED ON THE POLITICAL CARTOON, THE ART IS DIFFERENT, AS YOU WILL SEE IN THIS CHAPTER! THE SPORTS CARTOON IS ALSO DRAWN IN THE SAME STYLE! THE POLITICAL CARTOONISTS ARE NEWSPAPER REPORTERS, AND THE ONLY DIFFERENCE IS THEY DRAW INSTEAD OF WRITE! IN MY OPINION, THE GREATEST POLITICAL CARTOONIST OF ALL TIMES WAS *HAL TALBURT!*

SORRY I COULDN'T INCLUDE MORE ON POLITICAL CARTOONS ... WILL DO SO IN MY NEXT CARTOONING BOOK!

HERE IS HAL TALBURT'S CREED FOR THE EDITORIAL CARTOONIST!

I BELIEVE A CARTOON SHOULD BE SIMPLE.

I BELIEVE A CARTOONIST SHOULD WORK ON ONE THOUGHT AT A TIME.

I BELIEVE A CARTOONIST SHOULD MINIMIZE DETAILS.

I BELIEVE THE IDEAL CARTOON WOULD BE DRAWN WITH ONE STROKE.

I BELIEVE A CARTOONIST SHOULD RESPECT HIS RESPONSIBILITY.

I BELIEVE A CARTOONIST SHOULD BELIEVE WHAT HIS PICTURE SAYS.

I BELIEVE A CARTOONIST IS A SALESMAN OF POLICY.

I BELIEVE A CARTOONIST IN A SMALL WAY ILLUS-TRATES HISTORY IN THE MAKING.

POLITICAL CARTOON TECHNIQUE

IN THIS EXCELLENT EXAMPLE OF EDITORIAL CARTOON TECHNIQUE BY LEO STOUTSENBERGER, WITH A DRAWING OF MIKE PYLE, RECENT YALE ALL AMERICAN FOOTBALL PLAYER, IS SHOWN THE LITHOGRAPHIC CRAYON ON COQUILLE BOARD APPROACH!

WHAT HAPPENS?

THE LITHOGRAPHIC CRAYON BRINGS OUT THE *TEXTURE* OF THE COQUILLE BOARD, ENABLING THE ARTIST TO SHADE THE DRAWING IN A LIFE-LIKE MANNER, AND THE PRINTER TO RUN THE PICTURE AS A STRAIGHT LINE-CUT, WITHOUT THE EXPENSIVE SCREENING!

BOB STEVENS

BOB DREW FOR THE STARS AND STRIPS, AND THE ARMY TIMES FOR 22 YEARS AND THEN GOT TIRED AND RETIRED!

BOB STEVENS FREELANCES EDITORIAL CARTOONS FOR 300 NEWSPAPERS!

REPRINTED WITH PERMISSION OF BOB STEVENS

NAME: *BOB STEVENS* COLLEGE: *SYRACUSE UNIVERSITY* INK: *PELIKAN*

BRISTOL: *STRATHMORE 2 PLY, COLD PRESSED, FOR EDITORIAL WORK*

PEN POINT FOR LETTERING: *505 STUB* PEN POINT FOR DRAWING: *NONE*

BRUSH: *#2 WINSOR-NEWTON SABLE FOR ALMOST ALL WORK*

PENCIL: *"B" DRAFTING LEAD* ERASER: *KNEADED* LIGHTBOX: *NO*

METHOD OF WORKING: *BOB WORKS DIRECTLY ON STRATHMORE, ALSO USES "UNISHADE" (CRAFTINT BOARD 26D)*

AMERICA

ROCKY

STAR SPANGLED IMAGE CO.

FROM AUTHOR'S PRIVATE COLLECTION

ORIGINAL SIZE: 11 X 13⅛

REPRINTED WITH PERMISSION OF BOB STEVENS

REG MANNING

REPRINTED WITH PERMISSION OF REG MANNING

REG WON THE 1951 PULITZER PRIZE FOR HIS EDITORIAL CARTOON CALLED "HATS."

HE WAS ALSO EDITORIAL CARTOONIST FOR THE ARIZONA REPUBLIC FOR 25 YEARS!

NAME: REGINALD (REG) MANNING ART SCHOOL: NONE COLLEGE: NONE

INK: PELIKAN FOR BRUSH, HIGGINS FOR PEN BRISTOL: BAINBRIDGE COQ-UILLE #2 COARSE, ALSO "GRAFIX" DUO-SHADE #242 FINE LINE

PEN FOR DRAWING: USE BRUSH PEN FOR LETTERING: USED TO USE BRUSH, NOW I USE HUNT "BOWL POINTED" STEEL PEN BRUSH: WINSOR-NEWTON #7

PENCIL: BLACK CHINA MARKING PENCIL, BLAISDELL #173T FOR SHADING ON CROWQUILL PAPER! ERASER: GREEN "RUB KLEEN" #6004

ORIGINAL: 10⅝ X 12¼

REG MANNING

REPRINTED WITH PERMISSION OF REG MANNIN

METHOD OF WORKING: *REG WORKS DIRECTLY ON BAINBRIDGE COQUILLE BRISTOL, MAKIN ROUGHS FIRST ON COPY PAPER FOR COMPOSITION, THEN PENCILS DIRECTLY ON DRAWING BOARD WITH "NO-PHOTO" BLUE PENCIL! HE THEN GOES OVER IT WITH #2 PENCIL, AND THEN FINISHES IT WITH INDIA INK AND SHADES IT. REG USES "PRO-WHITE" FOR THE WHITE LETTERING ON BLACK AREAS, AND FOR CORRECTING! SOMETIMES USES AN ORDINARY BALL POINT PEN FOR CORRECTIONS!*

THIS LETTERING WITH GILLOTTS REGISTRY PEN NO. 1066

CHUCK STILES

Occupational Safety & Health Administration does away with 1,100 nitpicking rules, including...

Acme & Naugahyde Toilet Seat Mfg. Corp.
Since 1898 — at the seat of things

TISSUES — PERFECT PERFORATIONS

CHUCK STILES, AL SMITH FEATURE SERVICE.

"HELLO, OSHA?... LISSEN, MY COMPANY JUST RETOOLED AND MANUFACTURED 1,377,000 TOILET SEATS TO CONFORM TO YOUR U-SHAPE STANDARDS..!"

PERMISSION FROM AL SMITH FEATURE SERVICE

NEWSPAPER SIZE

NAME: *CHUCK STILES* **ART SCHOOL:** *AMERICAN ACADEMY OF ART*

COLLEGE: *UNIV. OF CALIFORNIA, RIVERSIDE* **INK:** *PELIKAN*

BRISTOL: *STRATHMORE, KID FINISH, 3 PLY... ALSO GRAFIX DUO-TONE BOARD (THIS ONE LOOKS LIKE NO. 240 OR 242)*

PEN FOR LETTERING: *PENTELS / BRUSH* **LETTERING:** *PENTELS*

BRUSH: *NO.1 FOR DRAWING* **ZIP:** *ZIPATONE 32:5 LINE*

PENCIL: *(PROBABLY SKY BLUE 740½)* **LIGHTBOX:** *YES*

METHOD OF WORKING:

CHUCK DRAWS WITH PENTELS ON GOOD GRADE NEWSPRINT, AND COPYS TO ILLUSTRATION PAPER (OFTEN USE "NEW ITEM" TECHNIQUE AND SITUATIONS OUT OF THE MAINSTREAM OF NEWS & LESS LIKELY TO CHANGE BECAUSE OF ADVANCE DEADLINE REQUIRED FOR SUBSCRIBERS)

CHUCK STILES

News Item ▸ Occupational Safety & Health Administration does away with 1,100 nitpicking rules, including...

Acme & Naugahyde Toilet Seat MFG. Co.

Since 1888 ~ at the seat of things

TISSUES

PERFECT PERFORAT-IONS

"HELLO, OSHA?... LISSEN, MY COMPANY JUST RETOOLED AND MANUFACTURED 1,377,000 TOILET SEATS TO CONFORM TO YOUR U-SHAPE STANDARDS...!"

Chuck Stiles
AL SMITH FEATURE SERVICE

2-23-78

PERMISSION FROM AL SMITH FEATURE SERVICE

ORIGINAL SIZE

164

LEO STOUTSENBERGER

"WOW, DID YOU HEAR THAT JET?"

LEO, BESIDES BEING ONE OF MY PERSONAL FRIENDS, IS NOT ONLY AN EXCELLENT CARTOONIST, BUT A TERRIFIC WATERCOLORIST! MR. STOUTSENBERGER RUNS HIS OWN CORRESPONDENCE SCHOOL FOR ASPIRING CARTOONISTS (AND SOME PROS WHO LEARN FROM HIM)!

HIS COURSE IS CALLED "CFA", AND STANDS FOR "CARTOONS FOR ADVERTISING"! HIS SCHOOL IS IN BRANFORD, CONNECTICUT / BOX 263 / 06405!

YOU'LL SEE MORE OF HIS WORK, AND SOME OF HIS LESSON PLATES THROUGH-OUT THIS BOOK! NOTE HIS VERY CLEAN LINES!

"WOW, DID YOU HEAR THAT JET?"

NAME: LEO STOUTSENBERGER **ART SCHOOL:** YALE UNIVERSITY OF FINE ARTS
COLLEGE: GEORGE WASHINGTON UNIV., WASH., D.C. **PENCIL:** PLAIN #2 MEDIUM
INK: HIGGINS **BRISTOL:** 2 PLY STRATHMORE & 202 ILLUSTRATION BOARD
DRAWING PEN: NO SPECIAL ONE **LETTERING PEN:** PROBATE (THANXS, KEN)
BRUSH: #2, SERIES 7, WINSOR & NEWTON **ERASER:** KNEADED
MORE—

WITH PERMISSION FROM LEO STOLTSENBERGER

METHOD OF WORKING: *LEO PREFERS TO WORK ON THE TRACING PAPER AND TRACE THE DRAWING TO THE BRISTOL BOARD. HE THEN COVERS THE BACK OF THE SKETCH WITH GRAPHITE AND GOES OVER THE LINES OF THE DRAWING WITH A HARD SHARP PENCIL !*

HERE'S INFORMATION ON LEO'S CORRESPONDENCE COURSE!

LEO STOUTSENBERGER

There are **NO**

I B M MACHINES

at CFA

That's right...here at Cartoonerama headquarters the director, Leo Stoutsenberger personally criticizes every cartoon sent to us by our students. Unlike some cartooning and art courses on the market, we will never employ any mechanical devices for the instruction of those who enroll in our Course. Why do we insist upon this highly personal and individual attention to each student? Simply because we have learned through many years of experience in teaching, that a personal contact with each student is essential if the aim is to turn out competent, professional, and experienced cartoonists. And we assure you that this is our primary aim.

Automation has already ruled out the possibility of any personal contact in many businesses we could mention. If we were to employ such methods, we could easily process many more students than we now have. However, we would sacrifice our most precious commodity: individual service to our students.

Reproduced below, we show you an example of just how this service works. On the left is the student's drawing. This is one of four different drawings which he is told to work up for this lesson. The sixth lesson deals with cartoon action, and this assignment is an especially significant one because it combines the knowledge the student has gained from the previous five lessons: Media, Heads, Expression, Hands and Feet and The Cartoon Figure. This procedure is followed throughout the 24 lessons including 69 assignment drawings for criticism along with any additional cartoons that the student desires help with.

These assignment drawings which the student is asked to do are not copied but original cartoons. When he gets his criticized drawings back, each one has attached to it (directly over the student's drawing) the director's drawing. Pertinent comments and suggestions for changes along with complimentary remarks when the student has made progress since his previous lesson, accompany the director's drawings.

The director's drawing is made on a translucent sheet of paper so that the student can see his own drawing underneath and compare it at a glance with the corrected drawing.

Several different colors, as well as black drawing ink, are used by the director on his drawings for the student, in order to emphasize certain salient points. These drawings on the right are reproduced less than 1/2 the size that the actual drawings are made. The student draws his cartoons on 8-1/2" x 11" paper and the criticisms are made the same size as the students' work.

The student has no trouble carrying out the assignment cartoons because he is told in the text and shown on the plates exactly how to fulfill the requirements of the particular lesson he's working on at the time.

When the student's criticized drawings are returned to him, he re-draws his cartoon following the helpful comments and drawings of the director. It is only in this way that the student can put to good use what he has learned and then go on to the next lesson. When he gets through a certain number of lessons, he can always refer back to some of his earlier criticisms and note the improvement in his work that has taken place.

The Student's Drawing 〰

The Director's Criticism 〰

WILLIAM PETERSEN
WHARTON, OHIO
LESSON 6
ASSIGNMENT 4

GOOD INTERPRETATION OF THE ASSIGNMENT, BILL. NOTICE, THOUGH HOW I'VE EXAGGERATED THE ACTION, LEANING THE FIGURE FORWARD MORE.

HAND DRAWN AT ANGLE TO GIVE VARIETY AND INTEREST.

NOTE MORE VIOLENT ACTION IN THE ARMS.

BEGIN DRAWING BY USING THE TUBE AND SACK METHOD AS SHOWN ON PLATE 15. THIS WILL ENABLE YOU TO GET MORE ACTION BY EMPHASIZING THE FORESHORTENING.

SHADOW UNDER FIGURE GIVES HIM MORE LIFE!

YOUR LINE WORK COULD BE MORE EXCITING, BILL. NOTICE HOW I'VE VARIED THE WEIGHT OF THE LINE THROUGHOUT.

KEEP PRACTICING, BILL. YOU'RE DOING FINE!

Here's how Cartoonerama gives you

personal

criticism

A SAMPLE OF HOW LEO RUNS HIS CARTOONING CORRESPONDENCE COURSE!

THIS IS THE STUDENT'S DRAWING

THIS DRAWING WAS MADE BY THE DIRECTOR ON A SHEET OF PAPER DIRECTLY OVER THE STUDENT'S WORK.

Lesson #12
WALTER KELLY
E. AVE. "S"
PALMDALE, CAL

THIS IS A GREAT IMPROVEMENT, WALT — SINCE YOUR WORK ON LESSON 11. NOTICE THAT I'VE ELIMINATED MOST OF THE ZIP-A-TONE SCREEN. I FEEL THAT BY DOING THIS, THE ATTENTION IS FOCUSED MORE ON THE NEWSPAPER BECAUSE OF THE SCREEN BEING ISOLATED AT THIS POINT. THEN WE PICK UP THE SPOT OF BLACK ON THE GIRL.

LET UMBRELLA RUN OUT OF PICTURE.

NOTICE THAT I'VE GIVEN HER A SMILE AND SPRIGHTLY WALK.

CUT DOWN ON THE NUMBER OF BLACK AREAS!

DON'T LET THE BACKGROUND OBJECTS BECOME TOO PROMINENT.

This is a typical example of the kind of individual help the director gives each student. The assignment here called for a cartoon depicting a group at the seashore. The gag was to be supplied by the student. In this case there was no gag caption needed. This type of gag cartoon that needs no explanatory line of copy is the most difficult kind of a gag cartoon to work up.

The assignment drawing was made for Lesson 12 entitled Backgrounds, Details and Perspective. Notice that the assignment requirements are planned so as to include all of these elements.

FLATTEN OUT THE BLANKET. SEE HOW THE LINES CONVERGE ON HORIZON LINE...

H.L.

DRAW EYES LOWER ON HEAD.

KEEP UP THE FINE WORK, WALT. I'LL BE LOOKING FORWARD TO GOING OVER YOUR LESSON 13 ASSIGNMENTS...

CFA

CARTOONS FOR ADVERTISING

PRINTED WITH PERMISSION OF LEO STOUTSENBERGER

COLORING

THIS PAGE WAS DRAWN ON GRAFIX DUO-SHADE BOARD NO. 232. I SURE WOULDN'T WANT TO PUT THIS TOGETHER ON A STICK-DOWN SHADING SCREEN ... IT WOULD TAKE HOURS OF CUTTING !

THIS IS THE BASIC RAW CARTOON... FLAT AND UNINTERESTING! NO SINGLE PART CATCHES THE EYE. *IT NEEDS BLACKS!*

NOTICE HOW THE BLACKS HOLD THINGS TOGETHER? ADDING SHADING AT TOP, AND CHECKED SUIT, ADD MORE ZIP!

IN THIS COLORING APPROACH, THE BLACKS ARE SPOTTED ABOUT TO ALLOW THE EYE TO FOLLOW THROUGH THE CARTOON..DON'T OVERDO.!

TERRIBLE, TERRIBLE, THE WHOLE THING IS OVERDONE.!
...IF IN DOUBT, DO *NOTHING*.!

BASIC LINE DRAWING WITH HUNT QUILL PEN, NO. 107

THERE'S A DIFFERENCE BETWEEN A CARTOON DRAWN WITH A PEN, AND ONE DRAWN BY A BRUSH ... AS YOU CAN PLAINLY SEE!

THE HUNT QUILL NO. 107 CAN MAKE A PRETTY EVEN LINE WHEN A CONSTANT PRESSURE IS USED, MAKING THE CARTOON FIGURES BLEND INTO THE BACKGROUND!

WINSOR-NEWTON, SERIES 7, NO. 2 BRUSH

THE BRUSH, ON THE OTHER HAND, MAKES BOTH OF THE CARTOON CHARACTERS POP-OUT FROM THE BACKGROUND

THE BRUSH IS NOT USED IN COMIC STRIPS AS MUCH AS THE PEN! THE REASON BEING THE PEN IS FASTER, EASIER TO CONTROL, AND MUCH CHEAPER!

ALL OF THESE SIX CARTOONS ARE REDUCED 50%

GILLOTT'S 170   LETRATONE 909

HERE'S THE GILLOTT 170 PEN POINT IN ACTION... ONE OF THE PEN POINTS COMMONLY USED BY CARTOONISTS! THIS POINT ALSO POPS-OUT THE CARTOON FIGURES, BUT NOT AS GOOD AS THE BRUSH! HOWEVER, THE LETRATONE ZIP-SCREEN DID A GOOD JOB HELPING THE FIGURES STAND OUT!

THE GILLOTT 1290 IS THE CLOSEST THING YOU'LL GET TO A BRUSH!

GILLOTT'S 1290   FORMATT 7056   27.50 LINE   10-90%

FORMATT 7056 IS GREAT FOR CARTOONS. JUST LOOK AT THE WAY IT POPS THAT GUY RIGHT-OUT OF THE DOORWAY!

BUT DON'T OVERDO IT!

GILLOTT'S 1290   BEHIND MAN: LETRATONE 909, WOMAN: FORMATT 7002

A GOOD CARTOONIST KNOWS WHEN TO STOP. LOOK AT THIS MESS.

THIS IS WHAT YOU HAVE TO BE CAREFUL NOT TO DO! THE CHECKERBOARD ON THE MAN'S SUIT SHOULD CURVE TO HIS BODY LINES... LIKE THE SQUARES ON THE WOMEN'S DRESS... *SHAME!*

GILLOTT'S 1290   GRAFIX UNI-SHADE BOARD, PATTERN 320

THIS IS GRAFIX UNI-SHADE BOARD.

THE PATTERN IS ALREADY ON THE BOARD, AND IS BROUGHT OUT BY APPLYING A SINGLE TONE SOLUTION WITH A BRUSH!

IT'S FUN TO USE... BUT ONCE AGAIN, DON'T GET CARRIED AWAY!

NEXT → GRAFIX PATTERNS!

PATTERN SCREENS

WINSOR- NEWTON, SERIES 7, NO.2 BRUSH

I'M NOT ABOUT TO SHOW AN EXAMPLE OF EVERY POSSIBLE PATTERN SCREEN AVAILABLE TO CARTOONISTS, BECAUSE MANY WON'T TAKE THE RE-DUCTION OF AT LEAST 50%, WHICH CARTOONISTS DRAW! INSTEAD, I WILL SHOW THOSE THAT I HAVE HAD EXPERIENCE

50% REDUCTION

WITH, IN MY COMIC STRIP. I HAVEN'T TRIED THEM ALL! OTHERS WORK TOO.

FORMATT 7000 27.50 LINE 10%

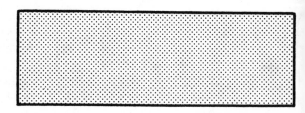

NO..NO..NO..! JUST LOOK AT IT...IT'S ALMOST GONE IN THE 50% REDUCTION.! THINK REDUCTION . . . .

ZIP-A-TONE 106, BY PARATONE, 36 LINE, 20%

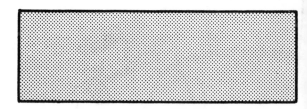

TOO FINE. USE THIS SCREEN FOR CARTOONS THAT WILL NOT BE REDUCED MORE THAN 75% ... TERRIBLE!

CHARTPAK PT033 STIPPLE

THE STIPPLE IS TOO FINE IN THIS ONE ...USE THIS FOR CARTOONS NOT REDUCED MORE THAN 75% !

FORMATT 7081   THE HOLE: FORMATT 7205

THIS IS A FUN SCREEN THAT WILL TAKE A 20% TO 30% REDUCTION. NICE TO USE FOR DRAWING A LOT OF ATTENTION!

FORMATT BRICK 7084   THE HOLE: FORMATT 7002

THINK HOW LONG IT WOULD TAKE TO DRAW ALL OF THOSE BRICKS! AT A 30% REDUCTION THE PATTERN GOES BLACK!

YOU CAN USE THE PATTERNS I'VE SUGGESTED, OR TRY OTHERS...THE ART STORES HAVE PLENTY! I HAVEN'T HAD MUCH LUCK WITH PATTERN SCREENS THAT DRY-TRANSFER TO THE CARTOONS BECAUSE OF THE WAXY SURFACE THEY CREATE. I CAN'T DRAW ON WAX....AND IF YOU WANT TO REMOVE ONE PATTERN ALREADY ON THE CARTOON, OR REPLACE IT WITH ANOTHER......IT'S DIFFICULT...BUT WITH THE CUT-OUT SCREENS YOU CAN! I'D RATHER SPEND THE TIME DRAWING!

SKY: FORMATT 7000   GROUND: LETRATONE :904   HOLE: FORMATT 7205

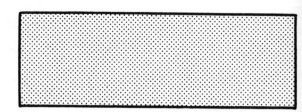

MY FAVORITE FOR TONING MY COMIC STRIPS. THIS IS A 50% REDUCTION, BUT IT WILL TAKE ALL THE WAY DOWN TO 40%

FORMATT 7002   27.50 LINE   30%

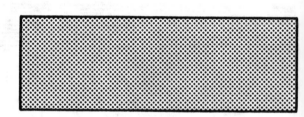

THIS PATTERN IS A LITTLE TIGHT, BUT SHOULD TAKE A 40% REDUCTION IF IT'S ALL YOU HAVE AVAILABLE!

FORMATT 7205

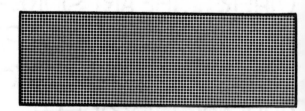

YOU COULD SQUEAK-BY WITH THIS ONE, BUT NOT FOR 40%, I WOULDN'T GO MORE THAN A 75% REDUCTION ON THIS ONE!

ETRASET 904

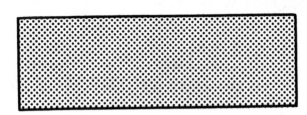

THIS WOULD BE MY SECOND
CHOICE FOR COMIC STRIPS OR
CARTOON PANELS. I ALWAYS
HAVE LOTS OF THIS, AND 7000

LETRASET 909

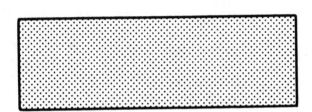

THIS MIGHT DISAPPEAR IN A
40% REDUCTION. I WOULDN'T
TAKE THE CHANCE. IF YOU'RE
NOT SURE, GET SOME STATS!

CHARTPAK PT 035

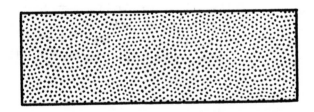

A TERRIFIC STIPPLE SCREEN.
THESE ALWAYS SEEM TO
MAKE YOUR CARTOONS ALOT
FUNNIER. IT'LL TAKE A 40%

HOW to APPLY SHADING FILM to YOUR CARTOONS

1
Choose the screen pattern desired from the many patterns available. The cartoon should have all the inking-in completed and be cleaned of smudges and pencil marks.

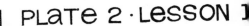

2
Place entire sheet over the cartoon to determine the area needed. With a <u>sharp</u> blade, cut out the screen a quarter of an inch or so larger all around than the area to be covered. Use just enough pressure to cut the top sheet only-leaving the backing sheet intact. Before removing the shading film, be sure the drawing is clean and free of dust and erasures.

3
Remove shading film from backing sheet and directly on drawing, lining up pattern squarely with cartoon. Rub lightly with fingertip or small square of paper to hold temporarily in place. The wax adhesive on the back of the shading film holds the screen to your drawing.

4
Use blade or cutting needle to cut out pattern exactly where you want it-in this case along the outlines of the figure. The surplus film is removed and stored for later use.

5
The pattern may now be bonded permanently with drawing by placing a sheet of paper over the screen and rubbing thoroughly with a bone burnisher or the back of a spoon. The more you burnish, the more permanent the bond.

Cartoonerama ®

PERMISSION FROM LEO STOUTSENBERGER · CARTOONS FOR ADVERTISIN

MISCELLANEOUS
SCREENS & PATTERNS

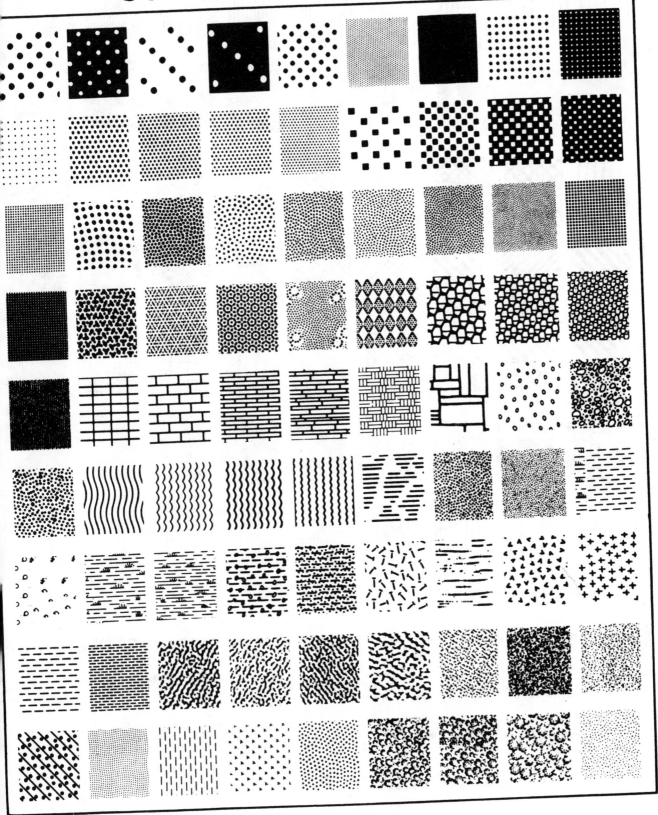

MORE SCREENS AND PATTERNS!

AMONG THE MANY COMPANIES THAT MAKE PATTERN SCREENS ARE

MICOTYPE · ZIPATONE · FORMATT · ARTYPE
CHARTPAK · LETRATONE · PRESFILM
AND NORMATONE

HERE ARE SOME ADDITIONAL PATTERNS THAT I'VE USED WHEN I WAS DRAWING A COMIC STRIP.

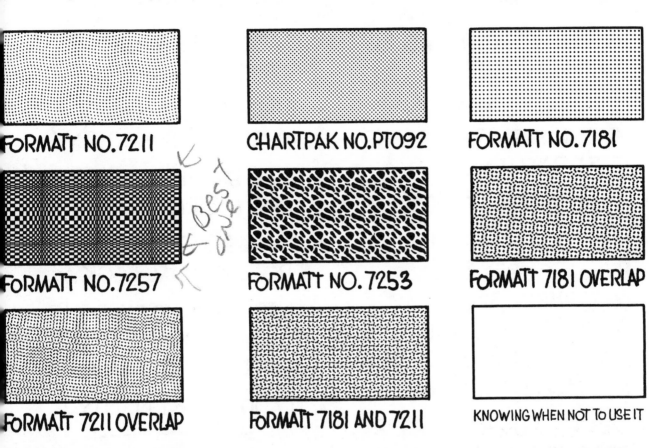

FORMATT NO. 7211

CHARTPAK NO. PT092

FORMATT NO. 7181

← Best one ←

FORMATT NO. 7257

FORMATT NO. 7253

FORMATT 7181 OVERLAP

FORMATT 7211 OVERLAP

FORMATT 7181 AND 7211

KNOWING WHEN NOT TO USE IT

LAST BIT OF ADVICE ON USING PATTERN SCREENS:

I HAVEN'T HAD ANY LUCK WITH THE HIGH GLOSS PATTERN SCREENS. THEY ARE CALLED "MYLAR GLOSS", AND THE PROBLEM IS WHEN IT'S LAID OVER YOUR CARTOON IT STICKS TOO WELL. AFTER YOU CUT OFF WHAT YOU DON'T NEED AND TRY TO PEEL IT OFF, IT TAKES SOME OF THE INK OFF YOUR DRAWING. THAT'S MY EXPERIENCE. PLAN AHEAD WHERE YOU'RE GOING TO ADD THE SCREEN.... DON'T JUST PUT IT DOWN ANYWHERE. YOU'LL GET A CHECKERBOARD EFFECT... AND IT WILL TAKE A LOT OF TIME! USE A SHARP BLADE AND DON'T USE TOO MUCH PRESSURE OR YOU'LL CUT-OUT THE ART.

STICK WITH ONE OR TWO PATTERNS.

DISADVANTAGES TO ZIP SCREEN

- WHEN IT GETS OLD IT WON'T STICK ANYMORE!

- IT TURNS YOUR ART WORK YELLOW WHEN IT AGES, AND IT STAYS YELLOW!

- IT'S RELATIVELY EXPENSIVE!

- IF IT'S USED EXTENSIVELY, IT CAN BE VERY TIME CONSUMING, ADDING AS MUCH AS ONE THIRD, AND EVEN TAKING AS MUCH TIME AS DRAWING THE STRIP!

- THERE'S A DANGER OF ZIP BECOMING A "CRUTCH"... WHERE YOU *DEPEND ON IT!*

- BEWARE OF HEAT FOR LONG PERIODS OF TIME...IT WILL NEVER STICK AGAIN!

- BEWARE OF REDUCTION!

ADVANTAGES TO ZIP SCREEN

- IT ADDS "COLOR" TO YOUR STRIP, GIVING IT A SHADED EFFECT!

- THERE ARE DOZENS OF SCREENS FOR VARIETY!

- USED SPARINGLY, IT DOESN'T TAKE A LOT OF TIME!

- IT GIVES THE STRIP THAT PROFESSIONAL LOOK!

- IT STILL WORKS OVER THE TOUCH-UP PAINT YOU USED TO CORRECT MISTAKES!

- IT ADDS PERSONALITY!

BESIDES, IT'S FUN TO USE!

GRAFIX

HADING MEDIUMS

DUO-SHADE STIPPLE TONE NO. 260

- ■ UNI-SHADE
- ■ UNI-SHADE STIPPLE TONE
- ■ DUO-SHADE
- ■ DUO-SHADE STIPPLE TONE
- ■ TOP SHADE
- ■ COLOR SHADE

GRAFIX is the new system of improved drawing aids which accommodates the basic needs of the graphic arts for a wide range of shadings in black and white and in color.

UNI-SHADE, DUO-SHADE, TOP-SHADE and COLOR-SHADE Shading Mediums are excellent for every kind of illustration requiring various degrees of tone, dimension and color separation.

GRAFIX meets the most exacting professional standards for quality, performance and dependability and at no increase in price.

GRAFIX Shading Mediums, in fact, afford appreciable savings in labor, time and money. All sheets are printed from new plates, assuring sharp, intense patterns consistently. Revolutionary GRAFIX Developers permit long use of brushes and pens. Improved COLOR-SHADE is simpler to reproduce, less costly. All GRAFIX-produced artwork is far more stable, lasts much longer without fading whether used often or stored.

For the finest, most rewarding results at the greatest economy, always use new GRAFIX Shading Mediums. They will give you a new experience in graphic arts excellence.

OHIO GRAPHIC ARTS SYSTEMS, INC.
1037 Ivanhoe Road
Cleveland, Ohio 44110
(216) 761-5861

GRAFIX SHADING MEDIUMS

UNI-SHADE

Each sheet is processed with a single, invisible dot or line pattern for straight line shadings. Patterns are made visible by improved GRAFIX Developer. Draw directly on UNI-SHADE. Apply GRAFIX Developer over desired shaded areas. Do not expose to direct sunlight. **Also available in stipple tone.** * 17½" x 24" sheet . . . .

DUO-SHADE

Available in 3 ply drawing board and translucent tracing vellum.

Each sheet is processed with two invisible patterns for light tone and dark tone, plus black and white. Draw directly on DUO-SHADE. Apply GRAFIX Developers with brush or pen to bring up shadings where desired. Developed art reproduces as straight line work.

Either the light tone or dark tone developer may be applied first. Make sure your brush or pen is clean. It is advisable to use a different brush or pen for each chemical. Blot one developer and be sure it is completely dry before applying the other.

Do not expose DUO-SHADE to direct sunlight. Follow these instructions carefully, and your artwork will remain fresh and sharp for repeated use. **Also available in stipple tone.** * 17½" x 24" sheet . . . .

<u>An **introductory kit**</u> containing 2 Student Size Sheets Duo Shade Drawing Board 1 each, Duo Shade Vellum and Duo Shade Stipple Tone and 1 set of Developer is available for . . . .

TOP-SHADE

This is a transparent overlay film processed with a visible, removable black or white dot or line pattern. Place film over artwork for desired shadings or to break up solids. Remove unwanted shaded areas with a stump. TOP-SHADE is available in the same patterns as Uni-Shade. 17½" x 24" sheet . . . .

COLOR-SHADE

This is a newly developed transparent film processed with hidden screens properly angled for full fidelity color reproduction. Revolutionary COLOR-SHADE may be processed either by camera or direct contact. Write for further details. 17½" x 24" sheet . . .

The patterns listed below are available on a special rough finish 3 ply drawing paper.
UNI-SHADE pattern numbers 32L-24L-42L and 32D . . . .
DUO-SHADE pattern numbers 240-232. . . . .

*UNI-SHADE and DUO-SHADE stipple tone patterns are processed on coquille board. Additional shadings and gradations can be achieved with litho crayon or grease pencil.

1. Drawing is penciled and then inked on Grafix Duo-Shade board in the normal manner.

2. Light or dark tone developer is liberally brushed over the areas where the pattern is desired and the tone appears instantly. Blot excess developer dry.

3. The other developer is brushed on the same way to make the crosshatch pattern visible. tones may be developed in any sequence. Blot excess developer dry.

ACTUAL SIZE

UNI-SHADE, 32 LINE SCREEN, NO. 32D

THE SINGLE SHADE IS ABOUT A DOLLAR LESS THAN THE DOUBLE SHADE. EACH SHEET IS 17½" x 24", AND IS VERY EASY TO USE FOR PEN OR BRUSH. WRITE FOR INTRODUCTORY KIT...AND USE A LIGHT-BOX FOR BEST RESULTS!

50% REDUCTION

I PREFER UNI-SHADE FOR AREAS IN THE CARTOON THAT WOULD BE TOO TIME CONSUMING TO CUT-AROUND...LIKE THE "COLORING" PAGE.

DUO-SHADE NO.232

ACTUAL SIZE

HERE'S A TOTAL WASTE OF PERFECTLY GOOD, AND EXPENSIVE DUO-SHADE DRAWING BOARD. THE EFFECT COULD HAVE BEEN ACCOMPLISHED BY USING ZIP SCREEN...... AND IT'S CHEAPER.!

50% REDUCTION

THIS PATTERN NUMBER (232), CAN'T TAKE A REDUCTION OF MORE THAN FIFTY PERCENT WITHOUT BLOCKING.!

DUO-SHADE NO. 232

ACTUAL SIZE

NOTICE HOW MUCH FUN YOU CAN HAVE WHEN IT'S USED CREATIVELY! THERE IS A TENDENCY TO OVER-USE THE TONE AND GO TOO FAR ...... YOU'LL HAVE TO PLAN AHEAD! PLAN YOUR AREAS IN BLUE PENCIL.

50% REDUCTION

DUO-SHADE IS USED BY POLITICAL CARTOONISTS AND STRIP ARTISTS! IT IS ALSO USED IN COMMERCIAL ART AND IN FASHION ILLUSTRATION.

UNI-SHADE DRAWING PAPERS
TOP-SHADE BLACK AND WHITE SHADING FILMS

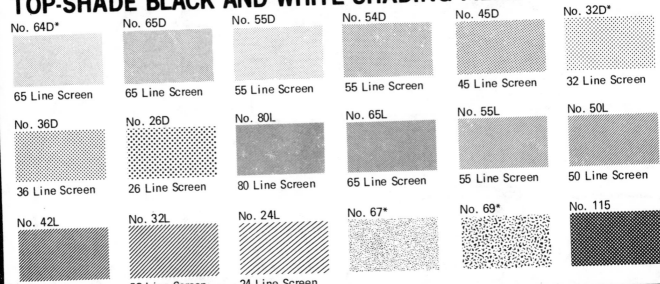

No. 64D* — 65 Line Screen
No. 65D — 65 Line Screen
No. 55D — 55 Line Screen
No. 54D — 55 Line Screen
No. 45D — 45 Line Screen
No. 32D* — 32 Line Screen

No. 36D — 36 Line Screen
No. 26D — 26 Line Screen
No. 80L — 80 Line Screen
No. 65L — 65 Line Screen
No. 55L — 55 Line Screen
No. 50L — 50 Line Screen

No. 42L — 42 Line Screen
No. 32L — 32 Line Screen
No. 24L — 24 Line Screen
No. 67*
No. 69*
No. 115

DUO-SHADE DRAWING BOARDS AND TRACING VELLUMS

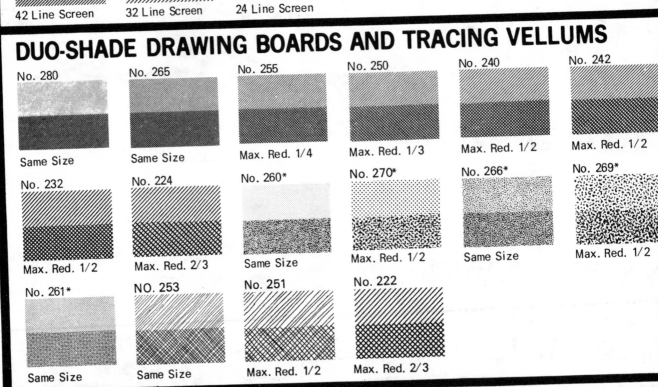

No. 280 — Same Size
No. 265 — Same Size
No. 255 — Max. Red. 1/4
No. 250 — Max. Red. 1/3
No. 240 — Max. Red. 1/2
No. 242 — Max. Red. 1/2

No. 232 — Max. Red. 1/2
No. 224 — Max. Red. 2/3
No. 260* — Same Size
No. 270* — Max. Red. 1/2
No. 266* — Same Size
No. 269* — Max. Red. 1/2

No. 261* — Same Size
NO. 253 — Same Size
No. 251 — Max. Red. 1/2
No. 222 — Max. Red. 2/3

DOUBLE DOT COLOR-SHADE FILMS AND BOARDS

65 Line Screen _____   _____ 85 Line Screen _____

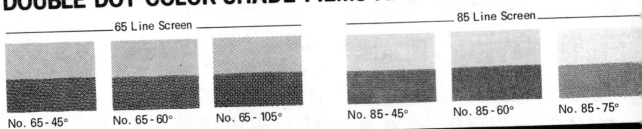

No. 65 - 45°
No. 65 - 60°
No. 65 - 105°
No. 85 - 45°
No. 85 - 60°
No. 85 - 75°

*Also available in stipple tone

DISADVANTAGES TO GRAFIX UNI-SHADE AND DUO-SHADE BRISTOL !

- THE PATTERN WILL NOT SHOW THROUGH THE MISTAKES THAT HAVE BEEN *"WHITED-OUT!"*

- IT TURNS YELLOW WITH AGE !

- IT'S MORE DIFFICULT TO PURCHASE THAN ZIP SCREEN !... TRY BUYING SOME WHILE TRAVELING AND SEE !

ADVANTAGES

- IT'S EASIER TO USE AND IS NOT AS TIME CONSUMING AS ZIP !

- AND ALL THE OTHER ADVANTAGES OF ZIP SCREEN !

NOTE: GRAFIX DUO-SHADE DRAWING BRISTOL IS USED CONSISTENTLY IN COMIC BOOK ART !

ABCDEFGHIJKLMNOPQRSTUVWXYZ

KARTOON LETTERING

GHIJKLMNOPQRST

I REALLY THINK MOST CARTOONISTS HATE TO LETTER WITH A PASSION, BECAUSE MORE TIME IS SPENT MASTERING THE DRAWING SKILLS THAN LETTERING. THOSE WHO SPEND MORE TIME MASTERING THE ART OF LETTERING ARE CALLED DESIGNERS, OR LETTERING MEN! GOOD LETTERING TAKES A LOT OF PRACTICE, AND YOU HAVE TO LOVE IT! INKING THE LETTERING REQUIRES AN ADDITIONAL SKILL THAT WILL ALSO TAKE A LOT OF PRACTICE... AND YOU HAVE TO LOVE IT! THINK OF ALL THE DIFFERENT PEN POINTS THERE ARE AND THE EFFECTS THEY HAVE ON THE LETTERING, AND HOW LONG IT TAKES TO FIND ONE YOU FEEL COMFORTABLE WITH. ADD TO THIS THE FACT THAT IN TIME, WITH A LOT OF INKING, THE PEN POINT WEARS INTO A DIFFERENT SHAPE... AND THEY DO! THIS WILL ALTER THE FLOW OF INK. IT'S NO WONDER A LOT OF PROFESSIONALS WILL HAVE NOTHING TO DO WITH IT, AND WILL HIRE AN ASSISTANT FOR THEIR LETTERING, AMONG OTHER DUTIES, FOR THEIR STRIP! MAKE IT SIMPLE FOR YOURSELF, PICK A PEN POINT FOR LETTERING AND STICK WITH IT UNTIL YOU MASTER IT! THERE ARE A FEW POINTERS THAT I HOPE I CAN HELP YOU WITH. AT LEAST THE ONES I KNOW ABOUT!

MOST THINGS YOU'LL FIND OUT THE HARD WAY!

HOW DOES THE CARTOONIST LETTER?

HERE'S A TYPICAL CARTOONIST'S ALPHABET

A B C D E F G H I J K L M N O P
Q R S T U V W X Y Z 1 2 3 4 5 6 7 8 9 0

... AND ANOTHER ONE

A B C D E F G H I J K L M N O
P Q R S T U V W X Y Z

THE IMPORTANT THING TO REMEMBER ABOUT LETTERING IS THE SINGLE ONE THING THAT MAKES IT LOOK PROFESSIONAL:

KERNING IS WHEN LETTERS FORMING WORDS ARE FIT INTO EACH OTHER LIKE THIS:

KERNED	PORTFOLIO	GETTING	LETTERING
MECHANICAL	PORTFOLIO	getting	LETTERING

NOTICE IN THIS SENTENCE SOME LETTERS ARE NOT ONLY KERNED ... BUT ALSO DIFFERENT SIZES!

IF YOUR CARTOON LETTERING IS NOT KERNED, IT WILL TAKE UP MORE SPACE!

BUT IF YOUR CARTOON LETTERING IS KERNED, IT WILL USE LESS SPACE!

ANOTHER SECRET IS TO PICK A BUNCH OF LETTERS AND MAKE THEM DIFFERENT SIZES OR SHAPES! NOTICE MY "O's ARE LARGE JUST LIKE MY C's, AND I EXTEND THE CENTER-LINE THROUGH THE E's SOMETIMES. ALSO MY R's DO NOT CONNECT, AND THE W's ARE NOT UP-SIDE DOWN M's! HERE IS MY ALPHABET: ABCDEFGHIJKL MNOPQRSTUV WXYZ!

OF COURSE, OTHER CARTOONISTS PRINT IN THEIR OWN STYLE.

WHY NOT YOU?

THE CARTOONIST'S ALPHABET

THIS IS THE TYPICAL HAND-LETTERED ALPHABET:

ABCDEFGHIJKLMNOPQRSTU
VWXYZ   1 2 3 4 5 6 7 8 9 0

...AND IF YOU LETTERED A BALLOON
IT WOULD LOOK LIKE THIS:

THE ONLY PERSON THAT IS GOING TO BELIEVE THAT I CAN FLOAT IN THE AIR IS THE IDIOT CARTOONIST WHO DREW ME!

OK, SO YOU SAY IT LOOKS GREAT AND IS REAL EASY TO READ. SO IT IS, BUT IT IS TOO MECHANICAL! IN OTHER WORDS, IT HAS NO CHARACTER.

WHERE THE GOOD TIMES ARE

HERE IS A TYPICAL FREE-LANCE JOB FOR A CARTOONIST!

THE LOCAL CBS DETROIT AFFILIATE NEEDED A FUNNY LOGO FOR THEIR NEW TV SEASON SOME YEARS AGO. THEY WANTED SOMETHING TO ATTRACT ATTENTION TO A NEW BATCH OF COMEDY SHOWS!

OF COURSE IT WASN'T THIS EASY. THERE WERE A LOT OF MEETINGS WITH TIM ROCHA, THE PROMOTION MANAGER, WHO IS ALSO A VERY TALENTED ARTIST.

THIS IS AN EXAMPLE OF HOW THE JOB EVOLVED FROM SCRATCH.

THE TV2 LOGO WAS ALREADY IN USE, SO WAS ADDED WITH THE CARTOON!

203

HERE'S THE ORIGINAL SIZE!

THE CARTOON WAS DRAWN WITH BRUSH...
A NO.2 WINSOR–NEWTON, SERIES 7

THE LETTERING WAS WORKED-OUT WITH
TRACING PAPER, VIA LIGHT-BOX, FOR SPACING!

SOME PROFESSIONAL TIPS ON BALLOON LETTERING

DO NOT LEFT MARGIN YOUR LETTERING BECAUSE IT IS OUT OF BALANCE.!

LETTERED WITH A SPEEDBALL A5

INSTEAD, CENTER THE LINES UNDER EACH OTHER SO IT WILL BE ALOT EASIER TO READ.. AND LOOK PROFESSIONAL.!

LETTERED WITH A SPEEDBALL C5

YOUR LINES OF LETTERS HAVE TO BE THE SAME DISTANCE APART OR IT WILL BE HARD TO READ.!

GILLOTT'S 170

AND DON'T GET IT TOO CLOSE TOGETHER.!

SPEEDBALL A5

PRINTING THIS SMALL WILL GIVE YOU MORE ROOM TO DRAW, BUT WHEN YOUR STRIP IS REDUCED YOU WON'T BE ABLE TO READ IT!

LETTERED WITH A HUNT 107 QUILL

IF YOU DON'T PRACTICE, YOU'LL BE A LOUSY LETTERER.!

MORE TIPS
ON BALLOON LETTERING

THE LETTERING IS SO CLOSE TO THE TOP OF THE PANEL, IT'S PAINFUL!

LETTERED WITH A SPEEDBALL A5

GOOD LETTERING, BUT SOME OF IT MAY VANISH IN REPRODUCTION, AND SO WILL THE BALLOON!

LETTERED WITH A GILLOTT 170

THE LESS SAID THE BETTER

LETTERED WITH A GILLOTT 1290

THE MORE AIR AROUND THE LETTERING, THE *BETTER IT LOOKS!*

LETTERED WITH A SPEEDBALL A5

LETTER WITH THE PEN POINT THAT IS THE EASIEST FOR YOU, AND PRACTICE INKING ON YOUR SCRAP BRISTOL

AND MORE...

IF YOU'RE GOING TO BE SLOPPY AND NOT USE GUIDELINES, KEEP IT READABLE!

LETTERED WITH A HUNT 107 QUILL

OR DO SOMETHING SPECIAL!

HUNT 107 QUILL

OUTLINED AND THEN FILLED-IN

ITALIC, OR SLANTED LETTERING IS USED IN A LOT OF COMIC BOOKS!

LETTERED WITH A SPEEDBALL C5

Or you might have the patience to do Upper and Lower case!

LETTERED WITH A SPEEDBALL A5

IF YOU LETTER PROFESSIONALLY, YOUR COMIC STRIPS WILL COMMAND ATTENTION. PLAN YOUR LETTERING VERY CAREFULLY, PENCIL-IN FIRST, AND THEN INK! ABOVE ALL, LETTER OPTICALLY, NOT MECHANICALLY, FOR BEST RESULTS!

IT IS ABSOLUTELY UNBELIEVABLE THE NUMBER OF WELL DRAWN COMIC STRIPS THAT ARE RUINED BY POOR LETTERING!

HERE'S A TERRIFIC LETTERING GUIDE YOU CAN MAKE FROM SOME SCRAP BRISTOL ... JUST PLACE IT ON YOUR STRIP AND WITH A T-SQUARE YOU CAN RULE THE LINES ALL THE WAY ACROSS THE STRIP.

AND KEEP YOUR LETTERS INSIDE THOSE GUIDE LINES!

ABCDEFGH
IJKLMNOP
QRSTUVW
XYZ 123
4567890

ABCDEFGHIJKLMNOPQRSTU
VWXYZ 1234567890.!?""
(THIS ONE WAS LETTERED WITH A C6)
18 PT. BIGDEAL

ABCDEFGHI
JKLMNOPQR
STUVWXYZ
1234567890

ABCDEFGHIJKL
MNOPQRSTUVW
XYZ 12345678

ABCDEFGHIJ
KLMNOPQRST
UVWXYZ
1234567890

ABCDEFGHIJKLMNO
PQRSTUVWXYZ!""?-
1234567890

72 PT. BLOCKHEAD

ABCDEFG
IJKLMNOP
QRSTUVW
XYZ 123
4567890

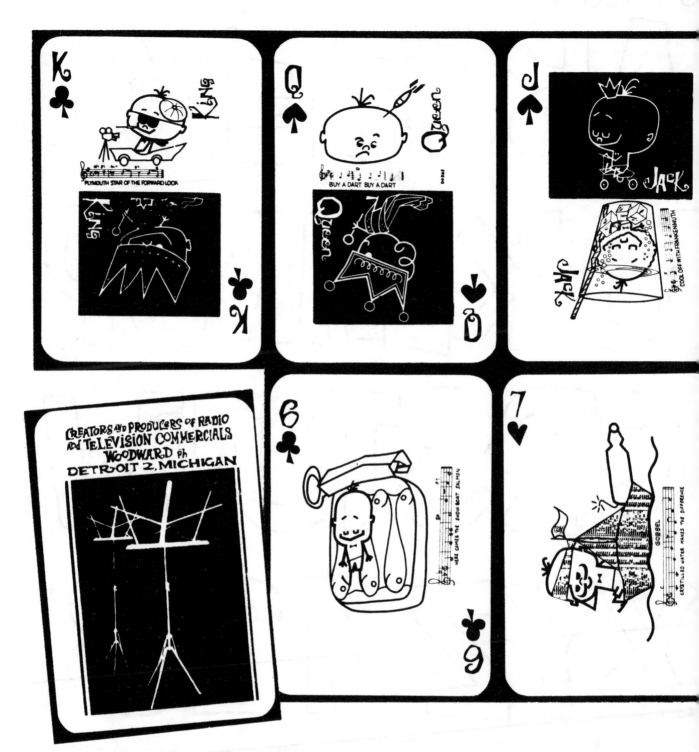

AN EXAMPLE OF THE TYPES OF FREE LANCE THAT
CARTOONISTS ARE CALLED UPON TO DO! THIS
WAS A CARD DECK WITH THE CLIENT'S SONGS
ON THE FRONT! THE BOTTOM LEFT WAS THE BACK

NOTICE THAT *EVERYTHING* IS DRAWN AND HAND-
LETTERED! I DID THIS JOB MANY YEARS AGO...
AND I REMEMBER IT TOOK TWO WEEKS TO DO!

HOW TO DRAW AND SELL A COMIC STRIP!

STEP ONE

WHAT KIND OF COMIC STRIP WOULD YOU LIKE TO "DRAW."... NOT WHAT KIND OF A COMIC STRIP AM I GOING TO "COPY." IF YOU CAN'T BE ORIGINAL YOU'L NEVER TAKE PRIDE IN YOUR WORK, AND ALL THE MONEY YOU MAKE WILL NEVER MAKE YOU HAPPY!

LET'S ASSUME YOU DECIDE TO DRAW A *FUNNY* COMIC STRIP... AFTER ALL, THE BULK OF THE WORLD'S POPULATION IS MUCH TOO SERIOUS.....THERE ARE ENOUGH OF THOSE PEOPLE AROUND, SO WE NEED MORE CARTOONISTS TO CHEER THEM UP!

THE FIRST SECRET IS TO WRITE GAGS ABOUT THINGS AND EVENTS YOU ARE FAMILIAR WITH. FOR EXAMPLE, IF YOU WORK IN AN OFFICE THEN JOKES ABOUT OFFICE LIFE WOULD BE RIGHT DOWN YOUR ALLEY

IT WOULD BE FOOLISH TO DO A COMIC STRIP ABOUT THE ARMY IF YOU HAD NEVER SERVED A HITCH, BE-CAUSE YOU WOULD HAVE NO FIRST HAND KNOWLEDGE

I'M ASSUMING THAT BY NOW YOU HAVE A GOOD IDEA WHAT KIND OF A COMIC STRIP YOU WOULD LIKE TO CREATE AND SELL...SO LET'S TAKE IT FROM THERE!

ONWARD

NEXT

DECIDE HOW YOUR MAIN CHARACTER IS GOING TO LOOK AND DRESS!

MAKE THE HAIR SIMPLE!

A5 SPEEDBALL

GILLOTT'S 290

GILLOTT'S 290

TRY DIFFERENT PEN POINTS

DON'T BE AFRAID OF BLACKS

GILLOTT'S 1290

A5 SPEEDBALL

GILLOTT'S 290

NEXT

HOW MANY HEADS TALL IS YOUR MAIN CHARACTER?

MAIN CHARACTERS ARE NOT THAT EASY TO CREATE BECAUSE IT'S HARD TO DECIDE.!

REMEMBER WHEN YOU DECIDE, YOU'LL HAVE TO LIVE WITH IT.!

GILLOTT'S 290

1

2

3

4 HEADS

4

EXAGGERATE PROPORTIONS

1

2

3

4

4¾

THIS ONE IS 4¾ HEADS.!

GILLOTT'S 1290

YOU DON'T WANT THE STAR TO BE 5 HEADS IN ONE PANEL AND SIX HEADS IN ANOTHER PANEL.!

AND THIS ONE IS 5¼ HEADS

A5 SPEEDBALL

THE NEXT THING IS TO FIGURE OUT THE DOODLE ON YOUR CHARACTER SO IT CAN BE EASILY REDRAWN!

ALL YOU'RE DOING IS MAKING A PATTERN TO BUILD ON!

ALL CARTOONISTS DRAW THIS WAY!

AN EXAMPLE OF USING THE DOODLE TO BUILD A CARTOON CHARACTER!

START OFF WITH HEAD AND BODY DRAWN IN PENCIL

SUGGEST POSITION OF LEGS AND FEET

ARMS AND HANDS ARE ADDED

JACKET AND TROUSERS DRAWN IN

STRUCTURE LINES OF ARMS & LEGS ARE TAKEN OUT

DRAWING IS CARRIED FARTHER

NOW BEGIN THE INKING-IN

SOLID BLACK AREAS BEGUN

FINAL INKING. ERASE PENCIL LINES

Cartoonerama

PLATE 31 · LESSON 5

ANOTHER WELL DONE PLATE FROM "CARTOONERAMA" CARTOON COURSE!

222

COMIC FIGURES PLATE 3.
THE CIRCLE SYSTEM OF DRAWING

GROUP 1.

GROUP 2.

GROUP 3.

GROUP 4.

GROUP 5.

GROUP 6.

LESSON ON HOW TO CONSTRUCT COMIC FIGURES

223

SAMPLE PLATE • HERSHBERGER HOME-STUDY COURSE • 1924–1970

SHADING COMIC FIGURES

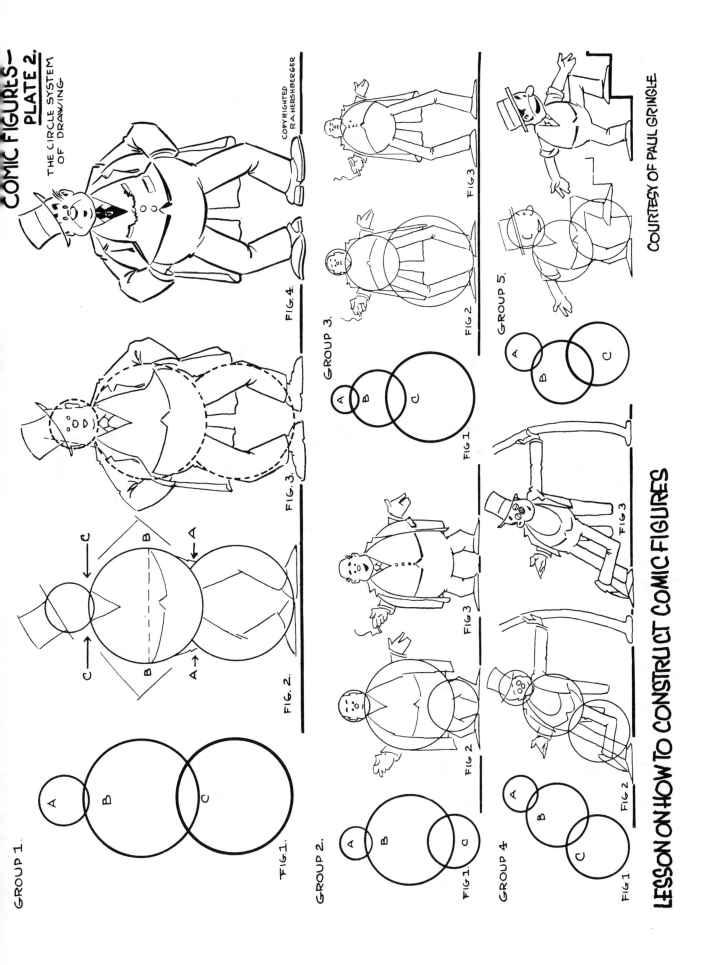

COMIC FIGURES—
PLATE 2.
THE CIRCLE SYSTEM
OF DRAWING

COPYRIGHTED
R.A.HERSHBERGER

GROUP 1.

FIG.1.

FIG.2.

FIG.3.

FIG.4.

GROUP 2.

FIG.1.

FIG.3.

GROUP 3.

FIG.1.

FIG2

FIG3

GROUP 4

FIG1

FIG.2

FIG.3

GROUP 5.

FIG1

FIG2

FIG3

COURTESY OF PAUL GRINGLE

LESSON ON HOW TO CONSTRUCT COMIC FIGURES

225

TRY DIFFERENT PEN POINTS, EVEN TRY A BRUSH! WHATEVER IS EASIEST!

GILLOTT 1290   A5 SPEEDBALL   GILLOTT QUILL #659   No.1 BRUSH   GILLOTT 290

YOU HAVE TO FEEL COMFORTABLE WORKING WITH YOUR TOOLS, ESPECIALLY IF YOU'RE LUCKY ENOUGH TO DRAW A STRIP FOR TEN OR TWENTY YEARS!

IT WOULDN'T BE A VERY WISE DECISION TO CHANGE YOUR PEN POINT AFTER YOUR CHARACTER HAS BEEN ESTABLISHED...... ALTHOUGH, A SKILLFUL CARTOONIST *MIGHT* PULL IT OFF!

SWITCHING FROM A PEN TO A BRUSH, OR FROM A BRUSH TO A PEN WOULD BE NOTICEABLE!

STUDY THE DIFFERENCE ABOVE, NOTICE HOW EACH PEN POINT AFFECTS THE CARTOON...ESPECIALLY THE ONE IN *BRUSH*!!

KEEP THESE POINTS IN MIND WHEN DEVELOPING YOUR MAIN CHARACTER:

DON'T MAKE CLOTHING TOO INVOLVED. FOR EXAMPLE, BY PUTTING THIS FELLOW IN A TRENCH COAT... IT MAY BE FUN TO DRAW AND MAY LOOK TERRIFIC, BUT IF IT'S ON ALL THE TIME YOU'LL CURSE THE DAY YOU DREW IT! YOU'LL HAVE ALL KINDS OF PROBLEMS AND HARD WORK DRAWING ALL THOSE FOLDS AND WRINKLES FOR AS LONG AS THE STRIP RUNS, BECAUSE IT'S THE CHARACTER'S TRADE MARK!

INSTEAD, ONLY HAVE HIM WEAR THE TRENCH COAT ONCE IN AWHILE! THAT GOES FOR INVOLVED CLOTHING PATTERNS TOO!

UNLESS YOU WANT TO DRIVE YOURSELF UP THE WALL!

AND MOST IMPORTANT: DEVELOP YOUR HERO WELL ENOUGH SO YOU CAN DRAW HIM OR HER DOING **EVERYTHING.**

DRAWN WITH GILLOTT'S 290

AND I MEAN EVERYTHING!

ALL OF THESE CARTOONS RETRACED FROM TRACING PAPER TO BRISTOL USING A LIGHTBOX!

THIS CAR WAS TRACED FROM A MAGAZINE AD, AND THEN RETRACED TO BRISTOL VIA A LIGHTBOX!

DRAWN WITH GILLOTT'S 290

DURING INKING, THE BRISTOL WAS <u>TURNED</u>!

ONE MORE LAST THING.....
HOW DOES YOUR HERO LOOK WITH OTHER PEOPLE?

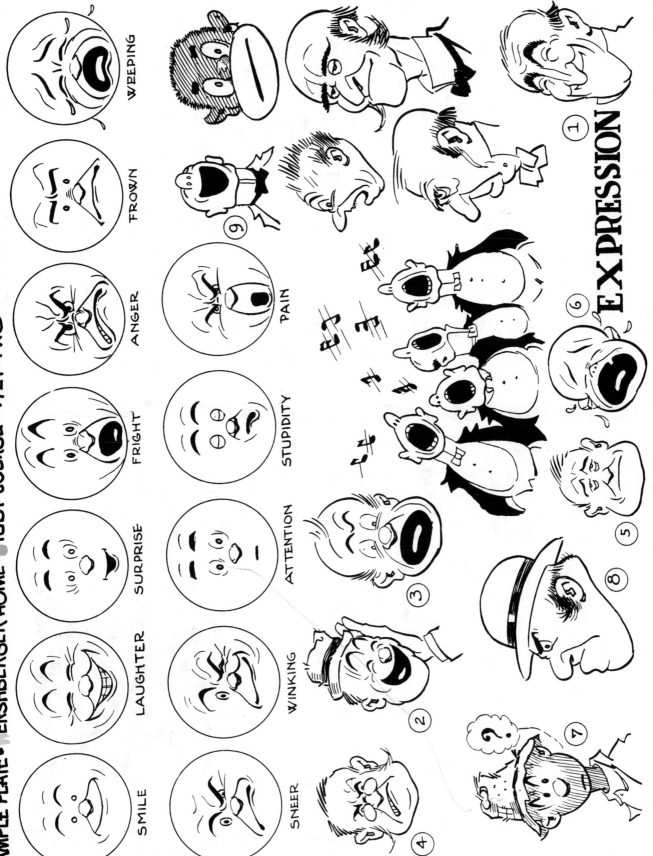

EXPRESSION

COURTESY OF PAUL GRINGLE

LESSON ON CARTOON EXPRESSION

AND REMEMBER THE RULE OF THUMB:

USE PEN AND INK ON HIGH SURFACE BRISTOL
OTHER NAMES: *PLATE, SMOOTH, **HOT** PRESSED*

USE BRUSH AND INK, OR TEXTURED PENCILS
ON MEDIUM SURFACE BRISTOL
OTHER NAMES: *GRAINED, TEXTURED, **COLD** PRESSED*

YOU CAN CERTAINLY IGNORE THESE RULES IF YOU WISH ... YOU MIGHT BE THE SORT OF PERSON WHO ENJOYS A CHALLENGE!

YOU WOULD SOON DISCOVER THE DIFFERENCE OF CONTROL FROM EACH SURFACE THAT THE PEN AND BRUSH PRODUCE! HOWEVER, IT'S YOUR BAG!

A SAMPLE PLATE FROM R.A. HERSHBERGER'S HOME-STUDY COURSE IN CARTOONING! THE CORRESPONDENCE SCHOOL OPERATED FROM 1924 TO 1970!

HERSHBERGER'S COURSE WAS RESPONSIBLE FOR THE CAREERS OF MANY PROFESSIONAL CARTOONISTS! HIS TEACHING TECHNIQUE IS STILL SOUND!

SAMPLE PLATE · HERSHBERGER HOME-STUDY COURSE · 1924-1970

COMIC HANDS

GROUP 1.

GROUP 2

GROUP 3.

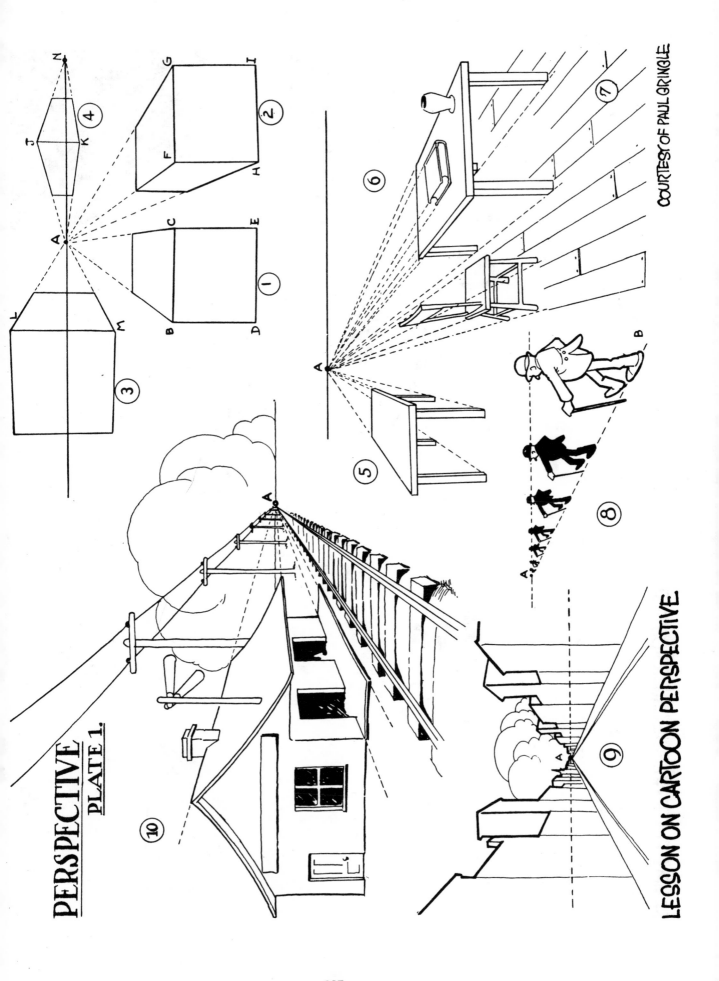

PERSPECTIVE
PLATE 1.

COURTESY OF PAUL GRINGLE

LESSON ON CARTOON PERSPECTIVE

235

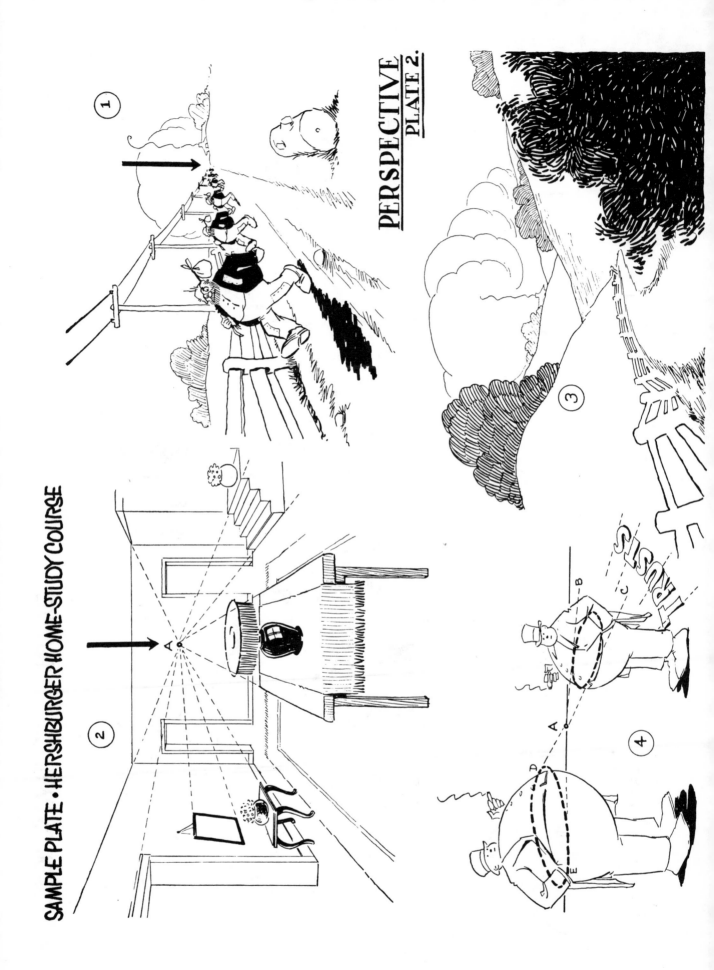

SAMPLE PLATE • HERSHBURGER HOME-STUDY COURSE

PERSPECTIVE
PLATE 2.

NEXT

WHAT KIND OF BRISTOL AND WHAT SIZE ARE YOUR STRIPS?

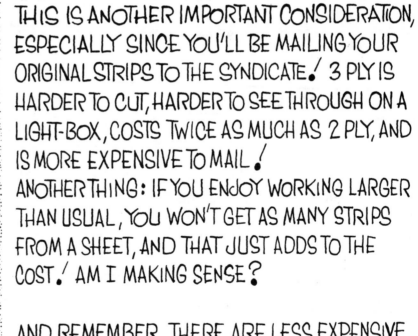

THIS IS ANOTHER IMPORTANT CONSIDERATION, ESPECIALLY SINCE YOU'LL BE MAILING YOUR ORIGINAL STRIPS TO THE SYNDICATE! 3 PLY IS HARDER TO CUT, HARDER TO SEE THROUGH ON A LIGHT-BOX, COSTS TWICE AS MUCH AS 2 PLY, AND IS MORE EXPENSIVE TO MAIL!

ANOTHER THING: IF YOU ENJOY WORKING LARGER THAN USUAL, YOU WON'T GET AS MANY STRIPS FROM A SHEET, AND THAT JUST ADDS TO THE COST! AM I MAKING SENSE?

AND REMEMBER, THERE ARE LESS EXPENSIVE BRANDS OF DRAWING BRISTOL THAT HAVE EX-CELLENT SURFACES FOR PEN POINTS AND BRUSH!

TAKE A TRIP TO YOUR LOCAL ART STORE AND CHECK-OUT EVERYTHING. AND GET ALL THE ART CATALOGS YOU CAN GET YOUR HANDS ON!

NEXT

WHAT SIZE ARE YOU DRAWING YOUR STRIP?

CHECK THE CHAPTER ON COMIC STRIPS AND YOU'LL FIND DIFFERENT SIZES FOR DAILY STRIPS. THIS DOESN'T MEAN THE CARTOONIST CAN DRAW ANY SIZE HE WANTS! ALL OF THESE DIFFERENT SIZES ARE THE SAME RATIO WHEN THEY ARE REDUCED TO 4 COLUMN BY 2 INCHES, OR ROUGHLY 40 PICAS BY 12 PICAS. (6⅝ X 2)

SIZES WILL VARY IN DIFFERENT NEWSPAPERS, DE-PENDING ON SPACE LIMITATIONS! SOME PRINT 3 COLUMN WIDE! WILL YOUR LINES HOLD-UP?

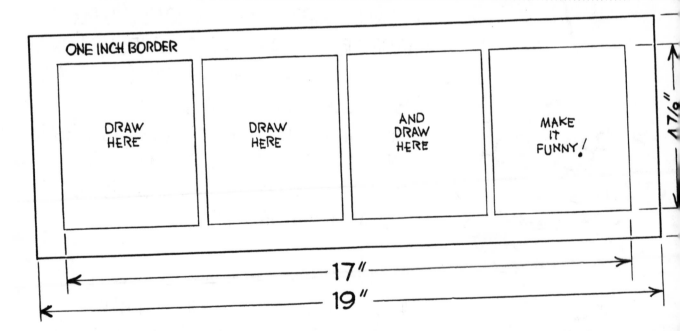

THIS IS A GOOD SIZE TO WORK A STRIP. THE ACTUAL DRAWING AREA BEING 17 X 4⅞ INCHES, WITH A ONE INCH BORDER ALL THE WAY AROUND, SO THAT WHEN IT'S CUT, THE WHOLE THING IS 19" X 6⅞"!

THE SIZE IS IMPORTANT WHEN YOU'RE TRYING TO GET THE MOST STRIPS FROM A SHEET OF BRISTOL

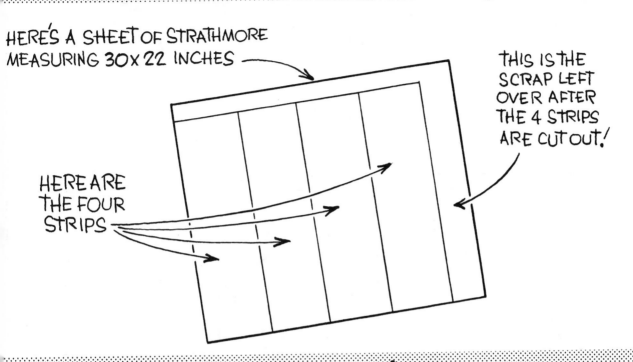

HERE'S A SHEET OF STRATHMORE MEASURING 30 x 22 INCHES

THIS IS THE SCRAP LEFT OVER AFTER THE 4 STRIPS ARE CUT OUT!

HERE ARE THE FOUR STRIPS

YOU CAN USE THE SCRAP THAT'S LEFT OVER FOR A LOT OF THINGS, SUCH AS CHRISTMAS CARDS, SIGNS, KIDS TO DRAW ON, TESTING NEW PEN POINTS, ETC., AND BELIEVE ME, AFTER JUST ONE YEAR OF DOING A STRIP, YOU'RE GOING TO HAVE A LOT OF SCRAP!

KEEP THESE POINTS IN MIND WHEN DECIDING ON SIZE: IF YOU DRAW TOO BIG, IT'S GOING TO BE HARDER TO HOLD YOUR FINE LINES IN REDUCTION. THE REDUCTION IS ABOUT 43%. THAT'S MORE THAN HALF SIZE, AND THE BIGGER YOU DRAW THE MORE REDUCTION IS USED TO BRING THE STRIP DOWN TO 4 COLUMNS...AND IF YOU'RE ADDING ZIP-SCREEN, IT MAY BLOCK-UP FROM BEING REDUCED TOO MUCH!

PLUS, THE ADDED PROBLEM OF NOT BEING ABLE TO GET AS MANY STRIPS FROM A SHEET OF BRISTOL. THAT MEANS YOU'LL HAVE TO BUY MORE!

THE SUNDAY PAGE!

USUALLY, THE DAILY STRIP BECOMES A SUNDAY STRIP! THERE ARE EXCEPTIONS, LIKE PRINCE VALIANT, OR PUZZLE PAGES....AND THE SPECIAL FEATURES THAT ARE *JUST* SUNDAY STRIPS. USING THE IDEAL FORMAT OF 20X16, YOU CAN RATIO TO ANY ORIGINAL SIZE YOU WISH, WITH WHATEVER ARRANGEMENT AND SIZE PANELS YOU LIKE! IT'S A GOOD IDEA TO CREATE THE GAG SO THE TOP ROW OF PANELS CAN BE EXCLUDED WITHOUT AFFECTING THE OUTCOME!
NOTE: DO NOT COLOR THE ORIGINAL...
HAVE A STAT MADE TO NEWSPAPER SIZE AND COLOR THAT!

THERE ARE SYSTEMS FOR FIGURING THE
SIZE STRIP YOU WANT FOR ANY
RATIO! THE PROPORTIONAL DIAL IS
ONE OF THEM!

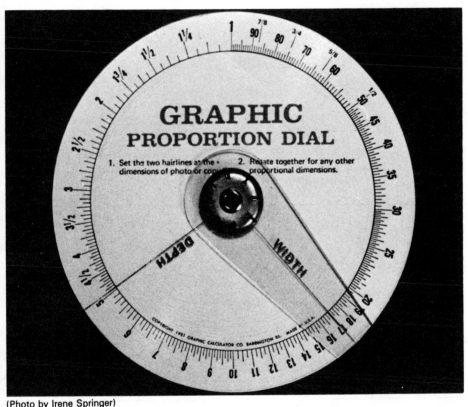

(Photo by Irene Springer)

THE DEPTH LINE
IS ON THE CELL
COVERING THE
WHOLE DIAL, AND
THE WIDTH LINE
IS ON ANOTHER
MOVING CELL. BY
TURNING THE
DEPTH CELL, THE
WIDTH MOVES
CHANGING SIZES
BUT NOT RATIOS!

TO GIVE YOU AN EXAMPLE, I'VE SET THE DEPTH
TO 4⅞, AND THE WIDTH TO 17... THAT'S THE
DRAWING AREA SIZE FOR YOUR COMIC STRIP,
AND BY TURNING THE PLASTIC DIAL THAT COVERS
THE GUIDE I CAN GET THE FOLLOWING, AMONG
MANY DIFFERENT SIZES... ALL THE CORRECT RATIO:
19 x 5½... 17 x 4⅞... 15½ x 4½... 14 x 4⅛...
12 x 3½... 8½ x 2½... 6⅞ x 2... 4¼ x 1¼!

THE OTHER WAY IS JUST AS GOOD!

LET'S SAY THIS IS THE CORRECT SIZE OF THE ORIGINAL COMIC STRIP! FIRST, SQUARE IT WITH A T-SQUARE!

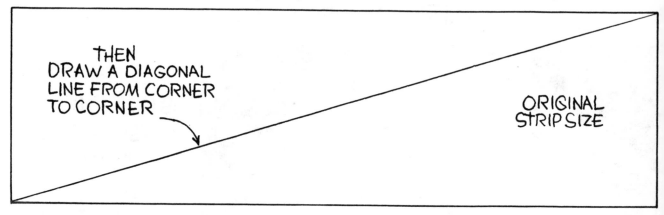

THEN
DRAW A DIAGONAL
LINE FROM CORNER
TO CORNER

ORIGINAL
STRIP SIZE

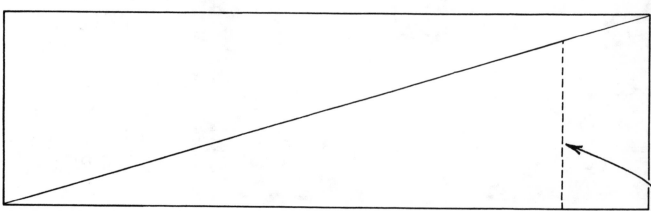

THEN DECIDE HOW WIDE YOU WANT IT, TAKE AN ANGLE AND DRAW IT IN

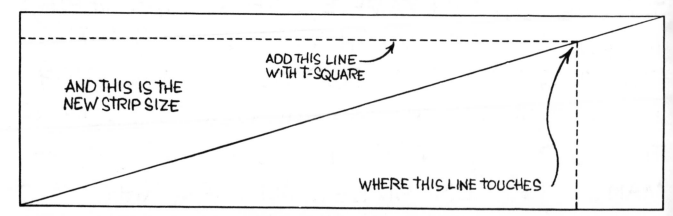

ADD THIS LINE
WITH T-SQUARE

AND THIS IS THE
NEW STRIP SIZE

WHERE THIS LINE TOUCHES

AND THE NEW STRIP SIZE IS $6\frac{5}{16}$ X $1\frac{7}{8}$"....YOU MAKE IT BIGGER BY EXTENDING THE DIAGONAL LINE!

 **WHAT WILL BE THE THICKNESS OF YOUR SQUARES?**

OK, SO YOU THINK IT'S A DUMB QUESTION! BUT THAT LITTLE DECISION, AND I DON'T CONSIDER IT LITTLE, IS WHAT WILL HOLD YOUR ART WORK TOGETHER. BEFORE WE GET INTO EXAMPLES & COMPARISONS, YOU SHOULD CHECK-OUT THE COMIC STRIP SECTION AND THEN ASK YOURSELF THIS QUESTION:

IF THE THICKNESS OF LINES AROUND THE ART IS NO BIG DEAL......HOW COME THEY'RE NOT THE SAME AROUND ALL THE STRIPS?

I'LL TELL YOU WHY... BECAUSE IT'S _PART_ OF THE _ART WORK_!

THERE ARE CERTAIN RULES THAT BECOME OBVIOUS WHEN YOU BECOME INVOLVED IN THE BUSINESS OF DRAWING CARTOONS: VERY THIN LINES AROUND ART WORK MAKE THE DRAWING STAND-OUT, AND VERY THICK LINES TURN THE ART INTO A _DESIGN_! MOST CARTOONISTS FALL SOMEWHERE IN THE MIDDLE!

FORMATT 27.50 LINE SCREEN 10-90% NO.7056

HERE ARE FOUR ORIGINAL PANELS WITH VARIOUS THICKNESSES OF LINE
TO DEMONSTRATE THE EFFECT IT HAS ON THE CARTOONIST'S FINAL ART!
THESE PANELS ARE RATIO FOR A STRIP SIZE OF 14 X 4⅛"!

FREE-HAND MEDIUM   GILLOTT #1290

THICK LINE   FB5 SPEEDBALL

MEDIUM LINE   A5 SPEEDBALL

VERY THIN LINE   GILLOTT #290

HERE ARE SOME MORE EXAMPLES OF DIFFERENT LINE THICKNESSES IN THE ACTUAL SIZE THE NEWSPAPER PRINTS THEM!

ORIGINAL LINE THICKNESS IN FREE STYLE

VERY HEAVY LINE THICKNESS

VERY THIN LINE THICKNESS

OF COURSE YOUR DRAWING STYLE AND THE TYPE OF PEN OR BRUSH YOU USE WILL DETERMINE THE THICKNESS OF YOUR LINES ... *EXPERIMENT!*

AVERAGE THICKNESS RULED LINE

AVERAGE THICKNESS SHAG LINE

HEAVY RULED LINE

ME IDEAS FOR LINES AROUND COMIC STRIPS!

VE EQUAL SQUARES AND NO SPACE BETWEEN. THE OLD STRIPS DID THIS!

HREE EQUAL SQUARES, BUT STAGGERED. MODERN APPROACH!

TWO EQUAL RECTANGLES WITH ROUNDED CORNERS. THE OLD STRIPS DID THIS TOO!

S EQUAL SQUARES. MODERN IDEA, BUT YOU HAVE TO DRAW TOO SMALL. EFFECTIVE!

SOME MORE IDEAS ON LINES AROUND COMIC STRIPS!

TWO RECTANGLES WITH ONE OPEN. DRAWS ALOT OF ATTENTION. USED OFTEN!

EQUAL SQUARES WITH SPACES AND ROUNDED CORNERS. GOOD DESIGN FEELING.

TWO THIRDS OF STRIP IN RECTANGLE AND THE LAST THIRD OPEN. USED OFTEN!

COMBINATION. 4 EQUAL SQUARES, ONE OPEN, AND THE LAST ONE A DIFFERENT SIZ

HERE ARE SOME EXAMPLES!

GILLOTT 170 FOR LETTERING

THIS ONE USES THE EDGES OF THE PANEL.!

THIS ONE USES BOTH SIDES AND THE TOP OF THE PANEL, BUT LEAVES THAT PART OUT!

SPEEDBALL A5 FOR PANELS

AND THIS ONE USES THE SHAPE OF THE PANEL TO FORM THE BALLOON, LEAVING THE PANEL LINES OUT!

THERE ARE A LOT OF MODIFICATIONS ON THIS TYPE! STUDY THE COMIC AND NOTICE HOW MODERN THIS LOOKS. IT'S ALSO GOOD DESIGN!

THEN THERE'S THE STRAIGHT-SIDED BALLOON, EVEN THOUGH IT BEARS NO RELATIONSHIP TO A BALLOON!

GILLOTT 170

HERE'S A FREE STYLE TYPE!

GILLOTT 170

TALK FROM A PHONE.!

GILLOTT 170

THOUGHT BALLOON.!

GILLOTT 170

SPEEDBALL A5

SLOPPY BALLOONS FOR SLOPPY LETTERING AND CARTOONS!

INTERESTING!

SPEEDBALL A5

THESE BALLOONS CAN HAVE DIFFERENT FEELINGS BY JUST USING DIFFERENT PEN POINTS, AND THICKNESSES OF LINE.. *THERE'S MOR*

SPEEDBALL A5

IT'S APPARENT, IN THOSE DAYS, THE CARTOONISTS DIDN'T USE GUIDE LINES FOR THEIR LETTERING — AND LETTERED WITH THE SAME PEN THEY DREW WITH!

HERE ARE BALLOONS FROM THE PAST

HUNT GLOBE 513

GRAFIX UNI-SHADE BOARD NO. 32D • DRAWN WITH NO.3 BRUSH

NEXT

RULE A RECTANGLE ON EACH CUT-OUT PIECE LEAVING AN INCH MARGIN ON ALL SIDES

LET'S ASSUME YOU ARE DOING YOUR STRIP TO 17"X4⅞" SIZE. IN THAT CASE THE BRISTOL WOULD BE CUT TO 19"X6⅞". NO NEED TO ADD THE PANELS YET BECAUSE YOU MIGHT HAVE DIFFERENT SIZES DEPENDING ON YOUR GAG. I ALWAYS HAVE MY RECTANGLES DIVIDED IN HALF, BUT IT'S NOT REALLY NECESSARY

WHY NOT MAKE A MONTH'S SUPPLY?

BE SURE YOU DO IT IN PENCIL!

GRAFIX UNI-SHADE BOARD NO.32D

ONE

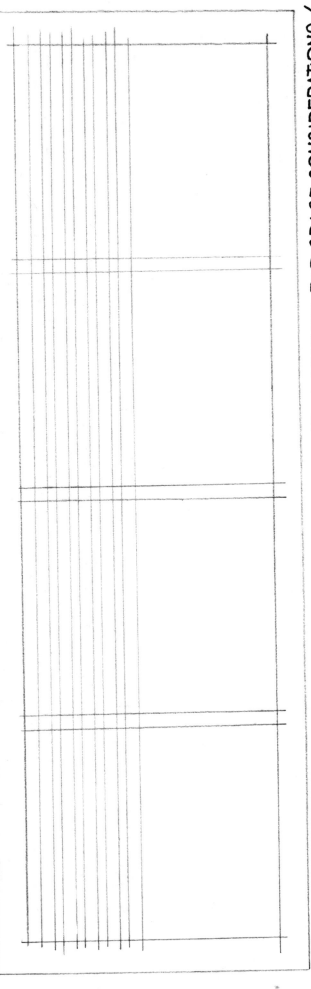

DIVIDE YOUR STRIP IN HALF SO NEWSPAPERS CAN TURN IT INTO A SQUARE, FOR SPACE CONSIDERATIONS!

- ALLOW AT LEAST 1/2" BORDER AROUND YOUR PANELS!

- YOU CAN LETTER ANY SIZE YOU WANT. A GOOD DEPTH IS 3/16" WITH 1/8" BETWEEN LINES!

- A GOOD SIZE IS 4 7/8" X 17" WITH 1/4" BETWEEN PANELS...AND DO 12 STRIPS AT A TIME... LIKE A PRODUCTION LINE!

TWO

LEAVE ABOUT ½" HERE, IN CASE NEWSPAPER WANTS TO PUT IN NAME OF THE STRIP!

- AT THIS POINT THE STRIP IS ROUGHED-IN SO THE CARTOONIST CAN SET THE GENERAL FEELING FOR HIS LAYOUT AND COMPOSITION!

- SOME CARTOONISTS WOULD INK-IN THE LETTERING AT THIS POINT, SO THEY'LL KNOW HOW MUCH SPACE IS LEFT FOR THE DRAWING!

- TAKE IT EASY WITH THAT PENCIL...DON'T BEAR DOWN TOO HARD!

- BREAK DOWN THE WORDING....KEEP IT DIRECT AND SIMPLE!

THREE

- INK THE LETTERING. I USED A GILLOTT 1290. DON'T LETTER WITH A LEFT MARGIN. CENTER THE WORDS OVER EACH OTHER FOR BALANCE!

- NOW TIGHTEN-UP THE ART. THIS IS WHERE ALL THE WORK IS!

- NOW YOU CAN MAKE CHANGES, EXPRESSIONS, BACKGROUNDS, ETC.

- DECIDE THE SHAPE OF YOUR BALLOONS, AND THE EXTENDERS!

FOUR

- INK THE CARTOONS WITH A PEN OR BRUSH. I USED A GILLOTT 1290 FOR BOTH DRAWING AND LETTERING!

- INK THE BALLOONS AND THE EXTENDERS. TURN BRISTOL WHEN INKING!

- IT'S A GOOD IDEA TO INK THE MAIN CHARACTER ON ALL THE 12 STRIPS FIRST... THAT GOES FOR THE LETTERING TOO!

- DO NOT ADD BLACKS YET!

FIVE

- ERASE ALL THE PENCIL MARKS WITH A *"KNEADED"* ERASER!

- GO BACK AND CHECK YOUR LINES FOR REPRODUCTION... SOME MIGHT NEED STRENGHENING BECAUSE OF THE 43% REDUCTION!

- ALL 12 STRIPS SHOULD BE AT THE SAME STAGE!

- IF YOU'RE USING A PEN TO INK, TRY A HIGH SURFACE BRISTOL FIRST!

- *REMEMBER*, IT TAKES TIME TO WARM-UP TO INKING!

- FILL-IN YOUR BLACKS... USE A BRUSH FOR THE LARGE AREAS AND A PEN FOR THE SMALL AREAS—WORK FROM LEFT TO RIGHT!

- NOW IS WHEN YOU CORRECT MISTAKES AND INK SMEARS BY USING A BRUSH (NO.1 IS GOOD) AND "PRO-WHITE" TOUCH-UP PAINT!

- THIS IS ALSO THE TIME TO DECIDE IF YOU'RE GOING TO ADD ZIP-SCREEN TO THE STRIP...OR IF YOU'RE GOING TO LEAVE IT LIKE IT IS!

SEVEN

IT'S NOT NECESSARY TO ADD THE NAME OF THE STRIP ON THE ORIGINAL ... THE SYNDICATE TAKES CARE OF THAT!

AND JEOPARDIZE OUR MARRIAGE?

YOU DIDN'T TELL ME YOU HAD ANOTHER WIFE AND FAMILY!

WHAT DID I DO NOW?

I'M GETTING A DIVORCE, JOHN!

KEN MUSE

- I'VE ADDED A ZIP-SCREEN. FIRST PANEL: FORMATT NO. 7000, WHICH DIDN'T TAKE THE REDUCTION TOO WELL (ONLY 59%), AND FORMATT NO. 7002, WHICH DID, IN PANEL 4! WATCH OUT FOR THESE THINGS.

- AT THIS POINT YOUR STRIP IS FINISHED, EXCEPT FOR THE SYNDICATE STICKERS. MISTAKES IN SPELLING ARE CORRECTED IN STEP FOUR!

- EACH STEP IS COMPLETED ON ALL 12 STRIPS, SO THAT YOUR TWO WEEKS SUPPLY IS FINISHED AT THE SAME TIME ... YOU HOPE!

ACTUALLY, I DON'T DRAW A STRIP USING THE SEVEN STEP METHOD!

I JUST WORK-OUT THE FINISHED CARTOONS ON TRACING PAPER, LIKE THIS! I LIKE TO DO THIS BECAUSE I MAKE DOZENS OF CHANGES BEFORE I DECIDE ON THE FINAL DRAWING.

IF I WERE TO MAKE ALL THOSE CHANGES ON THE BRISTOL BOARD, THERE WOULD BE NO MORE TEXTURE LEFT TO DRAW ON!

REPRINTED WITH PERMISSION OF LEO STOUTSENBERGER

NEXT

THE TIME HAS NOW ARRIVED TO MAIL IN YOUR STRIP TO THE SYNDICATE!

EXAMINE THE 12 STRIPS VERY CAREFULLY FOR MISTAKES IN SPELLING, POOR WORDING, BAD JOKES, (IF IT'S A HUMOR STRIP), AND CLEANLINESS! YOU'D BE SURPRISED HOW IMPORTANT THAT IS...YOU'D BE SURPRISED HOW UN-IMPORTANT THAT IS TO A LOT OF "WOULD BE" CARTOONISTS! THAT ART WORK YOU SEND IN IS TELLING A LOT OF THINGS ABOUT YOU: CAN YOU DRAW? ARE YOU FUNNY? CAN YOU COMMUNICATE? ARE YOU NEAT? IF YOU WANT TO BE A PROFESSIONAL, ACT LIKE ONE ... *CLEAN IT UP!*

DO THIS

PICK OUT A SYNDICATE FROM THE EDITOR & PUBLISHER, OR THE ARTIST'S MARKET. THE SYNDICATE YOU DECIDE ON IS YOUR CHOICE. IT CAN BE ONE CLOSE-BY, (IN THAT EVENT, YOU CAN TAKE IT), A BIG SYNDICATE OR A SMALL ONE. IT'S REALLY NOT THAT IMPORTANT...THE IMPORTANT THING IS: *IS IT SALEABLE ?* BE SURE TO READ CAREFULLY, SOME SYNDICATES DO NOT WANT COMIC STRIPS, SOME, ONLY CARTOON PANELS!

SOME SYNDICATES WANT ONLY ORIGINAL ART, PROBABLY BECAUSE THEY WOULD LIKE TO SEE THE WAY YOU WORK!

GILLOTT 1290

IF I WERE THE SYNDICATE, AND RECEIVED A REALLY GOOD STRIP, I'D BE HAPPY TO KNOW I HAD THE ORIGINALS, AND NOT MY COMPETITION!

OTHERS PREFER PHOTO-STATS, AND WILL STATE SO!

SPEEDBALL A5

DO YOU WANT MY ADVICE?
STAT TO NEWSPAPER SIZE AND SEND ALONG WITH ORIGINALS!

THIS IS WHAT I DID...

ENVELOPE WITH
LETTER AND STAMPS
OR CHECK FOR
RETURN POSTAGE

KEN MUSE
BIG CITY

BILL MEADOR
MANAGING EDITOR
GREAT LAKES SYNDICATE
STERLING HGTS, MICH. 48077

AIR MAIL

PAPER
TAPE

IT'S DIFFICULT TO KNOW THE RETURN POSTAGE COST, AND ENCLOSE IT INSIDE! BUT THIS WAY, YOU CAN TAKE THE LETTER AND TAKE TO THE POST OFFICE, AND WHEN YOU FIND OUT, WRITE THE CHECK, OR PUT IN THE STAMPS.......TAPE IT AND MAIL IT!

I KNOW THIS IS GOING TO SOUND STRANGE, BUT NOW IS A GOOD TIME TO START DRAWING ANOTHER COMIC STRIP!

AND HE AIN'T KIDDIN'!

INK

IF YOU WANT TO REACH ALL THE POSSIBLE MARKETS IN THE STRIP BUSINESS... YOU'RE NOT GOING TO DO IT WITH JUST ONE STRIP!

JUST ONE COMIC STRIP IDEA WILL NOT APPEAL TO EVERYONE... OF COURSE NONE OF THEM DO, *BUT YOU DON'T KNOW WHAT THE SYNDICATES WANT*... SO YOU'VE GOT TO TRY DIFFERENT KINDS, LIKE KID STRIPS, SPACE STRIPS, DOCTOR STRIPS, GAG STRIPS, FAMILY STRIPS, GIRL STRIPS, ANIMAL STRIPS, SCIENCE FICTION, ETC.

OF COURSE YOU CAN'T DO THEM ALL, BUT IF YOU CAN'T THINK-UP ANY MORE THAN ONE STRIP... *FORGET IT, YOU'RE IN THE WRONG BUSINESS!*

DOING TWO OTHER DIFFERENT **STRIPS**, WHILE THE FIRST ONE IS IN THE MAIL WILL KEEP YOU ACTIVE, KEEP THE GAGS FLOWING, FORCE YOU TO THINK, AND GIVE YOU SOMETHING TO LOOK FORWARD TO EVERY DAY! ALL OF THESE STRIPS WILL BE GOING BACK AND FORTH IN THE MAIL TO VARIOUS CARTOON SYNDICATES!

ZIP-A-TONE, NO. 220, 12 LINES PER INCH

DURING ALL THIS TIME, ALL YOUR COMIC STRIPS ARE GOING BACK AND FORTH IN THE MAIL! NOW, EVERY TIME ONE COMES BACK YOU CAN ADD A FUNNIER STRIP (WHICH YOU WILL BE WORKING ON WHILE IT'S IN THE MAIL), AND SEND IT OFF AGAIN!

I'LL GUARANTEE YOU ONE THING FROM ALL THIS: THE SYNDICATES WILL KNOW WHO YOU ARE!

NAME OF FEATURE	SYNDICATE	SENT	BACK
BIG SHOT	KING	2/7/75	2/23/75
WAYOUT	UNITED	3/8/75	4/2/75
DR. WIGGLE	MCNAUGHT	5/7/75	5/27/75
PRIVATE EYES	GENERAL	8/9/75	8/20/75
WAYOUT	GENERAL	9/3/75	9/27/75
MR. FUNNY	NEA	11/1/75	12/29/75
BIG SHOT	UNITED	12/12/75	1/12/76
DR. WIGGLE	KING	1/18/76	2/1/76
MR. PENNY	FIELD	2/20/76	3/12/76
WAYOUT	CHRONICLE	3/8/76	4/14/76
PRIVATE EYES	L.A. TIMES	5/5/76	5/31/76
JIMMY'S	MCNAUGHT	6/18/76	7/3/76
BIG SHOT	GENERAL	9/3/76	10/18/76
DR. WIGGLE	UNITED	11/2/76	11/24/76
PRIVATE EYES	KING	11/18/76	12/19/76
JIMMY'S	NEA	12/1/76	1/7/77
WAYOUT	NEA	1/23/77	2/2/77

SAMPLE CHART FOR MAILING COMIC STRIPS!

WITH A BUNCH OF COMIC STRIPS GOING BACK AND FORTH, YOU'LL NEED THE SAME SYSTEM THAT GAG CARTOONISTS USE TO KEEP TRACK OF THEIR PANELS, SO THE SAME SYNDICATE WON'T GET THE SAME STRIP AGAIN!

IF YOU FIND TIME TO CUT THE GRASS, TAKE OUT THE GARBAGE, SHOVEL THE SNOW, ETC., ETC., AFTER ALL THIS... YOU'LL GET SOME KIND OF MEDAL!

AND REMEMBER... NOTHING IS AS IMPRESSIVE AS WELL RENDERED ORIGINAL COMIC STRIPS!

WHEN YOU MAIL ORIGINALS, PACK THEM BETWEEN TWO PIECES OF CORRUGATED CARDBOARD, CUT TO THE SAME SIZE AS THE STRIPS AND TAPE THE SIDES WITH PAPER TAPE. PRINT YOUR NAME, ADDRESS, AND PHONE NUMBER ON THE BACK OF EACH STRIP. IN THE EVENT THEY GET SEPARATED, THEY'LL KNOW WHO THEY BELONG TO!

LETTERED WITH A SPEEDBALL C6

ENCLOSE A LETTER SOMETHING LIKE THIS:

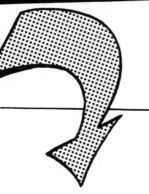

JANUARY 2, 1990

BILL MEADOR
MANAGING EDITOR
GREAT LAKES SYNDICATE
STERLING HGTS., MICH., 48077

DEAR MR. MEADOR:

ENCLOSED FIND 12 ORIGINAL COMIC STRIPS, TITLED: "BIG SHOT," FOR YOUR CONSIDERATION.
IF THEY DO NOT MEET YOUR NEEDS, I AM ENCLOSING POSTAGE FOR THEIR RETURN.

THANK YOU FOR YOUR TIME.

SINCERELY,
Ken Muse
BIG CITY, MICH.
(313) 000-0000

LETTERED WITH A GILLOTT 1066

SAMPLE LETTER... KEEP IT SIMPLE!

IT'S NOT NECESSARY TO TELL THEM YOUR FATHER IS AN ENGINEER, YOUR MOTHER IS A PIANO TEACHER, AND YOUR SISTER IS A NURSE. THEY DON'T CARE WHAT KIND OF A CAR YOU DRIVE, WHERE YOU WORK, WHAT SCHOOL YOU FAILED, TO WHAT POLITICAL PARTY YOU BELONG, IF YOU ARE MARRIED OR SINGLE... OR WHAT COLOR YOU ARE! THESE HAVE NOTHING TO DO WITH YOUR ABILITY AS A CARTOONIST!

LETTERED WITH A GILLOTT 1066

HOW DOES THE SYNDICATE WORK?

JUST LIKE ANY OTHER BUSINESS. IF THE PUBLIC LIKES A PRODUCT A COMPANY MAKES, THE BUSINESS IS SUCCESSFUL! THE SYNDICATE IS NO DIFFERENT. IF THEY RECEIVE A REALLY GREAT COMIC STRIP, THEY'LL PASS IT AROUND THE OFFICE TO GET THE REACTION. THEY'LL TAKE IT HOME, SHOW IT TO NEIGHBORS, FRIENDS, AND ALL KINDS OF PEOPLE. IF EVERYONE LIKES IT, THEY MAY SEND OUT PHOTO-STATS WITH THEIR SALESMEN TO SHOW THE NEWSPAPER FEATURE EDITORS. SOME SMALLER SYNDICATES USE THE MAILS FOR THIS PURPOSE!

IF ENOUGH EDITORS LIKE IT, AND PROMISE TO RUN IT FOR SIX WEEKS OR SO, THE SYNDICATE WILL TAKE A *GAMBLE* AND DECIDE ON A DATE TO LAUNCH THE STRIP. YOU WILL THEN BE ASKED TO FLY-IN, (AT THEIR EXPENSE), AND SIGN YOUR CONTRACT. SOMETIMES, DURING THE TESTING OF THE STRIP, YOU'RE ASKED TO SIGN A TEMPORARY ONE!

SO THE CARTOONIST STARTS DRAWING STRIPS LIKE MAD SO THERE WILL BE PLENTY AHEAD – USUALLY 6 WEEKS!

THE CARTOONIST NOW THINKS HE'S MADE IT TO THE TOP!

AFTER THE SHORT RUN IN ALL THOSE NEWS-
PAPERS, SOME OF THE EDITORS WILL DROP
THE STRIP, FOR VARIOUS REASONS THAT ARE
TOO NUMEROUS TO MENTION. *HOPEFULLY NOT
TOO MANY BIG PAPERS – BECAUSE THEY PAY MORE!*

THE CARTOONIST, OF COURSE, IS NOT AWARE OF ALL THIS . . . . . HE
JUST KEEPS ON DRAWING HIS STRIP, THINKING HE'LL KEEP THOSE
NEWSPAPERS FOREVER. IN THE MEANTIME, THE SYNDICATE IS NOW
TRYING TO GET THE FEATURE EDITORS TO RENEW FOR A LONGER
PERIOD OF TIME, LIKE 3 OR 4 YEARS, OR MORE. MANY SYNDICATES
WILL START RIGHT-OFF WITH A YEAR, OR LONGER CONTRACT!

WHEN A COMIC STRIP SALESMAN IS TRYING TO
SELL A NEW STRIP, THE NEWSPAPER USUALLY
HAS TO DROP ONE IN ITS PLACE. THIS IS NOT
AN EASY DECISION FOR THE FEATURE EDITOR
BECAUSE THERE MAY NOT BE ENOUGH SPACE
TO JUST ADD A NEW STRIP. WHICH ONE GOES?

IF THE CARTOONIST'S STRIP
IS GOOD, THINGS TURN OUT OK!
FROM THEN ON, ONLY HIS
SENSE OF HUMOR AND HIS
ABILITY AS A CARTOONIST
KEEP IT GOING!

WHEN A NEWSPAPER BUYS THE RIGHTS TO PRINT A COMIC STRIP FOR A CERTAIN LENGTH OF TIME, LIKE 3 OR 4 YEARS, OR WHAT EVER, THE PAPER ALSO GETS TERRITORIAL RIGHTS. FOR EXAMPLE, A PAPER WITH A LARGE CIRCULATION GETS A GUARANTEE THAT THE STRIP WON'T BE SEEN WITHIN A CERTAIN RADIUS. THERE IS NOTHING STRANGE IN THIS. IF YOU BOUGHT INTO A FRANCHISE HAMBURGER CHAIN, YOU CERTAINLY WOULDN'T WANT THE SAME FRANCHISE TO OPEN-UP ANOTHER CHAIN ACROSS THE STREET WOULD YOU?

BUT A NEWSPAPER, FOR VARIOUS REASONS CAN BUY A STRIP AND NOT PRINT IT, THUS TAKING IT OUT OF CIRCULATION IN THAT AREA, AND PREVENTING OTHER PAPERS FROM USING IT! PERHAPS AT THE TIME THERE WASN'T SPACE FOR AN ADDITIONAL STRIP AT THAT TIME, BUT THERE WOULD BE IN THE FUTURE!

I'VE KNOWN SOME CARTOONISTS WHO WERE BEING PAID BY CERTAIN NEWSPAPERS FOR THEIR STRIPS, WHICH HADN'T APPEARED FOR YEARS IN THAT PAPER!

NOTE: THERE ARE OVER 300 CARTOON FEATURES UNDER SYNDICATION IN THIS COUNTRY, AND NO ONE NEWSPAPER COULD POSSIBLY PRINT THEM ALL!

By Ken Muse

MOST SYNDICATES GIVE THE CARTOONIST A LIST OF THE PAPERS USING HIS STRIP....

...EVERY MONTH WITH HIS CHECK! AFTER EACH PAPER IS LISTED THE AMOUNT....

...PAID FOR THE MONTH! IT'S A SIMPLE MATTER TO SEND FOR A COPY OF THE PAPER...

...AND SEE IF YOUR COMIC STRIP IS RUNNING!

IF YOU'RE INTERESTED IN SELF-SYNDICATION, THERE IS A GREAT BOOK THAT'S PACKED WITH INFORMATION. I DON'T KNOW IF IT'S STILL IN PRINT... IT CAME OUT IN 1967:

**THE ROAD TO SYNDICATION
EDITED BY W.H. THOMAS
TALENT INFORMATION PRESS
NEW YORK**

CLIFF WIRTH, IN THE COMIC STRIP SECTION, SYNDICATES HIS OWN STRIP, JUST FOR MICHIGAN PAPERS... AND IT'S DOING VERY WELL!

ONCE OR TWICE A MONTH, THE SYNDICATED CARTOONIST RECEIVES THESE FROM HIS SYNDICATE!

THEY ARE PROOF SHEETS OF THE STRIPS TWO WEEKS, OR A MONTH AHEAD OF PUBLICATION! THEY ARE ALSO SENT TO THE SUBSCRIBING NEWSPAPERS WHO USE ONE-A-DAY FROM THE SHEET! THESE STRIPS ARE 7⅜ X 2 ¼".

SOME CLOSING THOUGHTS ON BEING A SYNDICATED CARTOONIST....
EVERY DAY, ALL THE NEWSPAPERS ARE BOMBARDED WITH COMIC
STRIP SALESMEN FROM OTHER SYNDICATES WHO WANT TO RE-
PLACE YOUR LOUSY STRIP, OR PANEL, WITH ONE OF THEIR LOUSY
STRIPS OR PANELS. AND SOMETIMES, IF YOUR STRIP DOES NOT
DELIVER WHAT IT PROMISED, IT *IS* REPLACED! IF ENOUGH *BIG*
PAPERS DROP YOUR STRIP YOU'RE IN BIG TROUBLE, BECAUSE
YOUR CHECKS WILL GET SMALLER... AND IF THIS KEEPS GOING,
THE PROFIT DROPS FOR THE SYNDICATE TOO... AND ONE DAY YOU'LL
WAKE UP AND FIND A REGISTERED LETTER FROM YOUR SYNDI-
CATE, AND IT WILL BE ALL OVER!
SO.... UNLIKE ANY OTHER PROFESSION... YOUR JOB IS
ON THE LINE EVERYDAY!

THE PAPER PAID ME, BUT NEVER RAN IT!

ONE COMIC STRIP 1964-1970

ONE COMIC STRIP 1970-1971

WHAT'S IT LIKE TO DRAW A SYNDICATED COMIC STRIP?

WHAT'S IT LIKE TO DRAW A SYNDICATED COMIC STRIP? THAT DEPENDS!

IF YOU CAN AFFORD AN ASSISTANT TO CUT THE BRISTOL TO STRIP-SIZE, RULE THE SQUARES, HELP YOU WITH IDEAS, DO THE LETTERING, DRAW THE BACKGROUNDS, INK YOUR PENCIL LINES, LAY ON YOUR ZIP SCREEN, AND EVEN GHOST THE WHOLE COMIC STRIP... *THEN YOU'RE A BUSINESSMAN!*

IT WOULD BE ENTIRELY DIFFERENT IF YOU DID ALL THOSE THINGS YOURSELF!
OF COURSE IF YOU CAN AFFORD IT, WHY NOT?

AFTER ALL, THE STRIP WAS YOUR ORIGINAL IDEA IN THE FIRST PLACE, AND YOU'RE THE ONE WHO SLAVED OVER IT... *AND SOLD IT!* SINCE ALL STRIPS START OUT THIS WAY, LET'S ASSUME YOU'RE DOIN' THIS ALL BY YOURSELF!... AND IT'S GOING TO BE A LOT OF HARD WORK.

THERE ARE TIMES, AND THEY COME AROUND OFTEN, WHEN YOU BARELY MAKE IT FROM DEADLINE TO DEAD-LINE... AND EVEN WHEN YOU GET A LITTLE AHEAD, AND TAKE A FEW DAYS OFF... YOU WORRY ABOUT IT!

TAKING A TWO WEEK VACATION UNDER THESE CONDITIONS IS DIFFICULT, EVEN IF YOU DRAW YOURSELF INTO A STUPOR JUST TO GET TWO WEEKS AHEAD...IT'S STILL WITH YOU. IT SEEMS LIKE A BIG WASTE TO LET A DAY GO BY ON VACATION WITHOUT GETTING AT LEAST *ONE GAG!* THE SAD THING IS, TO CREATE THE GOOD GAGS, YOU HAVE TO KEEP AT IT. IT'S SORT OF LIKE PLAYING A MUSICAL INSTRUMENT, IF YOU DON'T PRACTICE EVERY DAY...... *YOU GET RUSTY!*

FINALLY, IT'S NO EASY TRICK GETTING BACK TO THE DRAWING BOARD AFTER THAT LONG VACATION...*IT'S AGONY!*

YOU SOON ENVY THOSE LUCKY PEOPL WHO LEAVE THEIR WORK AND GO HOM

SO WHY DO CARTOONISTS WANT TO DR COMIC STRIPS IF IT'S SO MUCH WORK THAT'S A GREAT QUESTION!

THERE ARE *THREE REASONS!*

SO WHY DO SO MANY CARTOONISTS LIVE FOR THE DAY THEY CAN DRAW THEIR OWN COMIC STRIP?

INDEPENDENCE, FINANCIAL REWARD, AND THE CHANCE OF BECOMING WELL KNOWN!

BUT ISN'T THIS TRUE OF A LOT OF PROFESSIONS, LIKE MUSIC, DANCING, WRITING, ACTING, PAINTING, PHOTOGRAPHY, ETC.?

A TYPICAL DAY

IN THE LIFE OF A COMIC STRIP CARTOONIST
(ONE DAY AT A TIME)

SO WHAT'S A TYPICAL DAY LIKE TO A NATIONALLY SYNDICATED CARTOONIST? OF COURSE, I CAN ONLY SPEAK FOR MYSELF, AND FOR THE FRIENDS I HAVE IN THE BUSINESS. SO, FROM MY OWN EXPERIENCE I'LL MAKE UP A TYPICAL DAY. ARE YOU READY?

FIRST DAY

YOU'VE JUST SENT YOUR TWO WEEKS SUPPLY OF STRIPS TO THE SYNDICATE BY AIR MAIL BECAUSE YOU FELL BEHIND YOUR SCHEDULE WHEN YOU RAN-OUT OF ZIP SCREEN AND BRISTOL, AND DROVE TO THE ART STORE FOR IT. THERE YOU MET TWO GUYS YOU USED TO WORK WITH AT THE AGENCY... AND YOU WENT OUT FOR DINNER! YOU COULD HAVE WORKED INTO THE NIGHT TO GET BACK SOME OF THE LOST TIME, BUT YOU WERE TIRED!

SECOND DAY

TODAY YOU'RE SPEAKING AT YOUR LOCAL HIGHSCHOOL, ALONG WITH QUESTIONS AND ANSWERS. FINISHED ABOUT 11:30, AND THEN HAD LUNCH IN THE SCHOOL CAFETERIA WITH THE SCHOOL ART TEACHER. YOU'VE BEEN THINKING-UP GAGS ALL MORNING, AND HAVE BEEN MAKING NOTES. GOT HOME, AND BACK ON THE DRAWING BOARD ABOUT 1:30! SINCE YOU'RE DRAWING HUMOR STRIPS, YOU'LL NEED 12 REALLY TERRIFIC GAGS. THAT MEANS YOU'LL HAVE TO CREATE TWICE THAT MANY, AND PICK THE BEST TWELVE... UNLESS YOU'RE LUCKY AND GET TWELVE GOOD ONES. GAGS COME INTO YOUR MIND ALL THE TIME, BUT THEY HAVE TO BE REFINED FOR YOUR STRIP. YOU GOT TWO REALLY GOOD ONES WHILE WORKING ON ONE OF YOUR STRIPS... THAT LEAVES 10 MORE! THE WORST WAY TO GET IDEAS IS A LOT OF TIME STARING AT WHITE PAPER! GOD, I'LL NEVER MAKE THE NEXT BATCH OF STRIPS!

THIRD DAY

DURING BREAKFAST GOT ANOTHER TWO GOOD ONES READING THE MORNING PAPER. CAN'T TRY TOO HARD, GUESS I'LL CUT-UP SOME STRATHMORE AND SQUARE-IT OFF. FINISHED WITH ABOUT 4 WEEKS WORTH OF SQUARED AND CUT-UP BRISTOL... WON'T HAVE TO WORRY ABOUT THE NEXT TIME! TIME FOR LUNCH. AFTER LUNCH CLEANED STUDIO..... SO YOU COULD FIND THINGS. STILL NO NEW GAGS! SPENT HALF HOUR LOOKING THROUGH YELLOW PAGES FOR IDEAS. DREW-UP SOME SITUATIONS ON BOND PAPER TO STIMULATE PUNCH LINES. GOT 4 MORE! I WAS OFF MY ROCKER TO GET INTO THIS STRIP BUSINESS. DECIDED TO WORK AT IT UNTIL I COULD GET AT LEAST 6 MORE... IT WORKED ... AT ABOUT 11:30 IN THE EVENING I HAD THE REST. THOSE LUCKY PEOPLE COMING HOME FROM WORK!

# FOURTH DAY

AFTER A GOOD BREAKFAST AND THAT SECOND CUP OF COFFEE, IT'S TIME TO GET DOWN TO DRAWING COMIC STRIPS, AND THE FIRST THING IS PENCILING THE LETTERING FIRST, FOR THE GAGS. FOR MOST CARTOONISTS, THE PRODUCTION METHOD OF DRAWING STRIPS IS THE ONE THAT WORKS THE BEST. SO, PENCILING-IN ALL THE LETTERING ON ALL 12 STRIPS IS DONE FIRST, FOLLOWED BY DRAWING THE BALLOONS AROUND ALL THE LETTERING IN PENCIL VERY LIGHTLY, AND DON'T ADD THE TALK POINTERS UNTIL DRAWING IS ROUGHED-IN!

GOT TO STOP... THERE'S THE MAIL! GOOD TIME FOR COFFEE!

BACK TO THE DRAWING BOARD. THE BALLOONS ARE ADDED BEFORE THE CARTOONS SO YOU'LL KNOW HOW MUCH SPACE YOU'LL HAVE FOR DRAWING. THAT'S WHY IT'S IMPORTANT TO KEEP YOUR DIALOG TO A MINIMUM. NO INKING YET! NOW COMES THE CARTOONING.

A NICE HOT CUP OF COFFEE HELPS AT THIS POINT... AND SINCE YOU'RE GOING TO JUST DRAW ON BOND PAPER THE REST OF THE DAY... SOME STEREO IS NICE. MOST CARTOONISTS DRAW THE CARTOONS RIGHT ON THE BRISTOL, LIGHTLY, WITH A MEDIUM LEAD, AND THEN A SOFTER LEAD FOR FINISHING. I DON'T! I PREFER TO TRACE FROM THE BOND PAPER TO TRACING PAPER, AND THEN FROM THE TRACING PAPER, VIA A LIGHTBOX, TO THE STRATHMORE! IT TAKES A LITTLE LONGER, BUT IT GIVES ME MORE CONTROL IN PUTTING MY CHARACTERS IN RELATION TO EACH OTHER. IN OTHER WORDS, I CAN FOOL AROUND WITH THE COMPOSITION!

HOLY MACKEREL, IT'S 12:30 AND I MISSED THE 11:00 NEWS, GUESS I'LL WATCH A LATE MOVIE TO UNWIND!

FIFTH DAY

UP BRIGHT AND EARLY. LAST NIGHT FINISHED TRACING FROM THE BOND TO THE TRACING PAPER. TODAY I TRACE FROM THE TRACING PAPER TO THE STRATHMORE. SOUNDS LIKE ALOT OF WORK, BUT IT'S A NICE FEELING KNOWING THEY'RE GOING TO BE THE BEST I CAN DO. I CAN EVEN REFINE THE DRAWINGS EVEN MORE WHEN TRANSFERING ON TO THE BRISTOL! USED TO DO IT THE OTHER WAY, BY DRAWING DIRECTLY ON THE BRISTOL, UNTIL SPENDING TWO YEARS IN ANIMATION... IT WAS THERE I LEARNED ABOUT THE REFINEMENT OF ART WORK, AND CARTOONING!

SPENT THE REST OF THE DAY TRACING ON TO MY STRATHMORE!

SIXTH DAY

GOT A LATE START BECAUSE MY CAR NEEDED SERVICING. STOPPED BY THE TV STATION, WHERE I USED TO WORK, TO VISIT WITH THE GUYS IN THE ART DEPARTMENT. PICKED UP SOME NEW GAGS. BACK TO THE DRAWING BOARD ABOUT 2:00! NOW READY FOR INKING! THIS IS THE PART I REALLY ENJOY. SOMETIMES I CAN EVEN WATCH TV, OR EVEN TALK TO A VISITOR. FINISHED UP THE DAY BY INKING ALL THE LETTERING, BALLOONS, AND POINTERS. (THE POINTERS ARE THOSE LINES FROM THE BALLOONS THAT GO TO THE PERSON TALKING). AT 7:30 I WENT TO THE MOVIES!

SEVENTH DAY

SUNDAY IS A GOOD DAY TO REST. MOST OF THE TIMES I TAKE OFF SATURDAY TOO. CLEANED OFF THE DRAWING BOARD, CHECKED MY PEN POINTS, AND GOT READY FOR MONDAY'S INKING!

EIGHTH DAY

RIGHT AFTER BREAKFAST, AND THE MORNING PAPER, I WAS READY TO INK THE STRIPS. MY FAVORITE THING TO DO! FIRST I INKED THE MAIN CHARACTER... THAT WAY HE LOOKS THE SAME IN ALL THE PANELS THROUGHOUT THE 12 STRIPS. A LITTLE TRICK I PICKED UP IN ANIMATION WHEN I INKED CELLS! NEXT, INK EVERYTHING ELSE. BREAK FOR LUNCH. READ MAIL. MAKE A FEW PHONE CALLS. PAY SOME BILLS! BACK TO INKING. FINISHED ALL THE INKING ABOUT 5:30. HAD DINNER. WATCHED THE NEWS. NEXT THING IS TO ERASE ALL THE PENCIL LINES. THAT TOOK ABOUT HALF AN HOUR. NOW WITH A PEN, FILL IN SMALL BLACK AREAS, AND WITH A BRUSH, FILL IN THE LARGE BLACK AREAS. NOT FINISHED YET! IT'S 9:30.

NINTH DAY

IF YOU DIDN'T ADD ZIP SCREEN TO YOUR STRIPS, YOU'D BE DONE BY NOW. GONNA' HAVE TO STOP USING THAT STUFF, TAKES TOO LONG. FINISHED PUTTING ON ZIP BY NOON. LAST THING TO BE DONE IS TO STICK-ON SYNDICATE LABELS. WRAPPED STRIPS FOR MAILING!

TENTH DAY

HAD BREAKFAST AND DROVE DOWN TO POST OFFICE WITH STRIPS! HEY, I'M TWO DAYS AHEAD OF THE GAME, AND IF I'D WORKED ON SUNDAY, I WOULD BE THREE DAYS AHEAD OF THE GAME! ACTUALLY, WHEN THE STRIP WAS LAUNCHED, I HAD ABOUT 6 WEEK SUPPLY AHEAD OF ME ALL FINISHED, AND THE SYNDICATE WOULD LIKE TO KEEP IT THAT WAY! FINISHED THE DAY THINKING-UP GAGS

ELEVENTH DAY

SYNDICATE SENT BACK TEN STRIPS... SAID THEY WEREN'T FUNNY

WORKING AT HOME

WHEN YOU DO YOUR ART WORK AT HOME, YOU HAVE TO ADJUST TO A DIFFERENT WORLD. YOUR FRIENDS AND RELATIVES DON'T THINK OF YOU AS WORKING LIKE *THEY* DO, BECAUSE YOU ARE HOME ALL DAY, AND YOU HAVE ALL THE TIME IN THE WORLD TO DO WHATEVER YOU WANT. THE BEST METHOD OF WORKING AT HOME IS TO SET-UP DEFINITE HOURS FOR DRAWING YOUR STRIP, AND STICKING TO IT. EVERYTHING ELSE MUST WAIT. ...WOULD YOU COME HOME FROM WORK TO CUT YOUR LAWN, AND THEN GO BACK TO WORK AGAIN?

ONE THING YOU WILL MISS IS THE DAY-TO-DAY CONTACT WITH PEOPLE THAT YOU ENJOYED ON THE JOB. I'M SURE IN MANY WAYS YOU MAY WELCOME THIS, AND IN OTHER WAYS YOU MAY NOT! CERTAINLY BEING AROUND PEOPLE STIMULATES NEW IDEAS. OF COURSE YOU'RE NOT TOTALLY OUT OF CONTACT WITH PEOPLE, IT JUST MEANS YOU'LL HAVE TO USE OTHER METHODS OF GETTING FRESH IDEAS. LISTEN TO RADIO, WATCH TV, READ NEWSPAPERS, GO TO PARTIES, THE MOVIES, READ MAGAZINES, ETC., ETC., ETC., ETC., ETC., ETC., ETC., ETC.

FORMATT 7081

ADVANTAGES OF DRAWING A COMIC STRIP:

YOU ARE YOUR OWN BOSS!

YOU WORK AT YOUR OWN PACE!

ALL THE MONEY IS YOURS, THERE ARE NO DEDUCTIONS!

YOU CAN LIVE ANYWHERE IN THE WORLD YOU WISH!

YOU CAN VACATION WHENEVER AND WHEREVER YOU WANT, FOR AS LONG AS YOU WANT... BUT YOU HAVE TO KEEP DRAWING!

YOU ARE A MEMBER OF A RELATIVELY SELECT GROUP OF PROFESSIONALS!

BIG CHECKS EVERY MONTH!

YOU BECOME A CELEBRITY!

NO MORE FIGHTING TRAFFIC.

YOU CAN SLEEP-IN!

A COMPLETE FEELING OF FREEDOM!

LOTS OF FAN MAIL!

PEOPLE YOU HAVEN'T SEEN IN YEARS, CONTACT YOU!

GILLOTT'S 1290

SPEEDBALL A5

DISADVANTAGES OF DRAWING A COMIC STRIP:

DEADLINES!

YOU PAY YOUR OWN SOCIAL SECURITY, HOSPITALIZATION, AND ALL THE OTHER FRINGE BENEFITS YOU HAD ON THE JOB!

THE IRS OWNS YOU!

DURING SYNDICATION, YOUR SYNDICATE OWNS THE STRIP, YOU'RE ONLY A VENDOR!

PEOPLE WILL TELL YOU THAT YOU WERE JUST LUCKY!

EVERYONE THINKS YOU'RE RICH!

NOT ENOUGH HOURS IN THE DAY!

RELATIVES THINK YOU'RE UNEMPLOYED!

ALWAYS RUNNING OUT OF IDEAS!

NO ONE AROUND TO TALK TO!

YOU COULD START GETTING NEWSPAPER CANCELLATIONS!

IT'S HARD WORK!

ORMATT 7002

GILLOTT'S 1290

IF YOU THINK ONE OR TWO GAGS ARE EASY TO COME BY... TRY CREATING SIX ORIGINAL, AND FUNNY GAGS EVERY WEEK FOR JUST THREE YEARS...

... AND ALL OF THEM TOP QUALITY... GOOD ENOUGH TO COMPETE WITH THE BEST OF THEM! NO ONE CAN DO THAT, OF COURSE! SOME COME CLOSE...

...THAT'S WHY THEY'RE TOP CARTOONISTS! YOU COULD BUY YOUR GAGS FROM PROFESSIONAL GAG WRITERS. NOTHING THE MATTER WITH THAT... MANY DO!...

HOW ARE ALL THOSE GAGS CREATED? EVERYONE IN THE BUSINESS DOES IT HIS OWN WAY OF COURSE, BUT THERE IS ONE BASIC PRINCIPLE INVOLVED:

ASSOCIATION!

ARE YOU READY?

WHEN I WAS A KID, I WAS ALWAYS LOOKING FOR A WAY TO THINK-UP JOKES FOR MY CARTOONS! THEN ONE DAY, WHILE LOOKING THROUGH THE PHONE BOOK YELLOW PAGES, IT HIT ME! HERE IN THIS BOOK WAS JUST ABOUT EVERY OCCUPATION IN THE WORLD, PLUS EVERYTHING THAT'S MANUFACTURED!

WOW! ALL IT TAKES IS GETTING THE PERFECT COMBINATION OF THINGS TOGETHER TO FORM AN ASSOCIATION FOR A FUNNY GAG!

THIS IS WHAT I DID: I CUT-UP SMALL PIECES OF CARD-BOARD AND PRINTED A DIFFERENT OCCUPATION ON EACH ONE... FROM THE YELLOW PAGES...LIKE THIS:

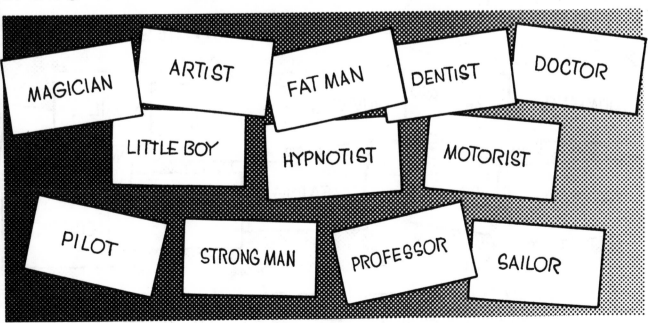

MAGICIAN ARTIST FAT MAN DENTIST DOCTOR

LITTLE BOY HYPNOTIST MOTORIST

PILOT STRONG MAN PROFESSOR SAILOR

THEN ON ANOTHER BATCH OF CARDS I PRINTED THE ACCESSORIES, OR THINGS, LIKE THIS:

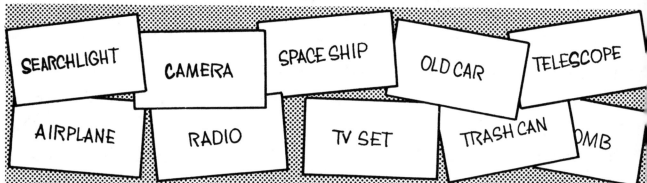

THEN ON ANOTHER BATCH OF CARDS I PRINTED DIFFEREN[T] PLACES, LIKE THIS:

AND THEN ANOTHER BATCH FOR ACTIVITIES, LIKE THIS:

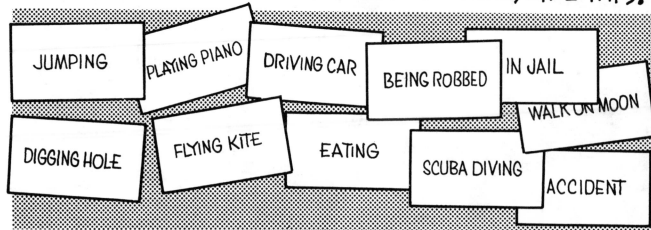

KEEP GOING, THERE'S MORE ⟹

THEN THE LAST BATCH OF CARDS WITH ALL THE EMOTIONS...... LIKE THIS:

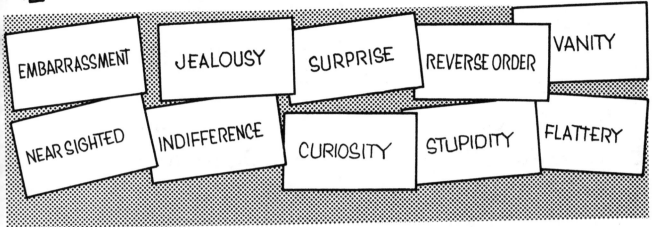

EMBARRASSMENT JEALOUSY SURPRISE REVERSE ORDER VANITY

NEAR SIGHTED INDIFFERENCE CURIOSITY STUPIDITY FLATTERY

THEN I MADE FIVE PILES OF CARDS, FACE DOWN, AND DREW ONE OFF EACH PILE ... AND GOT THIS:

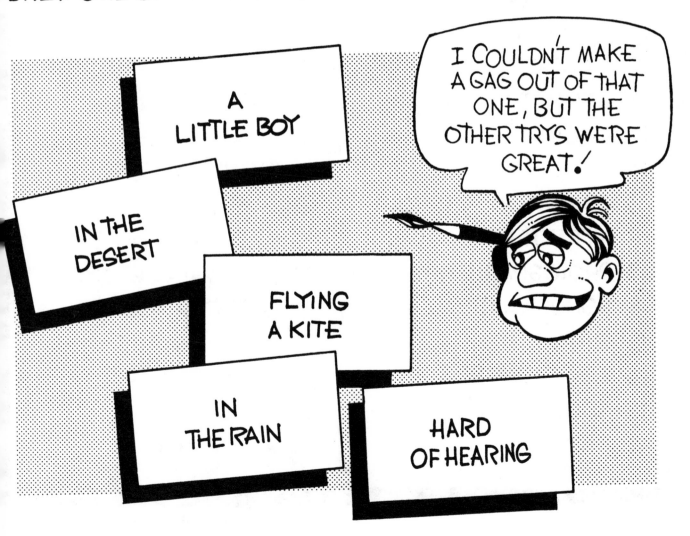

A LITTLE BOY

IN THE DESERT

FLYING A KITE

IN THE RAIN

HARD OF HEARING

I COULDN'T MAKE A GAG OUT OF THAT ONE, BUT THE OTHER TRYS WERE GREAT!

PEOPLE

1 MAGICIAN
2 ARTIST
3 FAT MAN
4 PROFESSOR
5 TV NEWSMAN
6 TV REPAIRMAN
7 POLICE WOMAN
8 BEAUTIFUL GIRL
9 STRONG MAN
10 LITTLE BOY
11 WEATHERMAN
12 DENTIST
13 DOCTOR
14 ASTRONAUT
15 COMPUTER OPERATOR
16 HYPNOTIST
17 PHOTOGRAPHER
18 HOUSE PAINTER
19 MOTORIST
20 BUS DRIVER
21 SOLDIER
22 PILOT

PLACES

1 TV STUDIO
2 THE MOON
3 NUDIST CAMP
4 CASTING OFFICE
5 DOG SHOW
6 THE BEACH
7 GOLF COURSE
8 BOWLING ALLEY
9 BEAUTY PARLOR
10 SPORTING EVENT
11 DOCTOR'S OFFICE
12 GAS STATION
13 TRAFFIC COURT
14 MOUNTAIN TOP
15 UNDER WATER
16 AT THE NORTH POLE
17 HARDWARE STORE
18 OUTER SPACE
19 A BANK VAULT
20 AIRPORT
21 THE DESERT
22 AT THE ZOO

SPEEDBALL A5   ZIP-A-TONE 27½ LINE   10 PERCE

THINGS

1 FLYING SAUCER
2 BIG DOG
3 AIRPLANE
4 PIANO
5 A FLOOD
6 A FIRE
7 BOMB
8 MONEY
9 RADIO
10 TV SET
11 CAMERA
12 TELESCOPE
13 TAPE RECORDER
14 OLD CAR
15 ROCKET SHIP
16 SNOW
17 CREDIT CARD
18 LITTLE DOG
19 SNAKE
20 SEARCHLIGHT
21 TRASH
22 RAIN

ACTIVITIES

1 JUMPING
2 CRAWLING
3 RUNNING
4 PLAYING THE PIANO
5 DIVING
6 CLIMBING
7 DIGGING
8 ACTING
9 FLYING A KITE
10 PAINTING A HOUSE
11 SLIDING
12 CAMPING
13 DRIVING
14 SLEEPING
15 WALKING ON THE MOON
16 EATING
17 BEING ROBBED
18 IN JAIL
19 WATCHING TV
20 DEEP SEA DIVING
21 GETTING MARRIED
22 A CAR ACCIDENT

ZIP-A-TONE 27½ LINE 10 PERCENT   SPEEDBALL A5

AND OF COURSE THESE CAN BE COMBINED WITH SOME OF THE EMOTIONS BELOW:

1 EMBARRASSMENT
2 NEAR SIGHTED
3 HARD OF HEARING
4 JEALOUSY
5 INDIFFERENCE
6 SURPRISE
7 REVERSED ORDER
8 CURIOSITY
9 VANITY
10 FLATTERY
11 ARROGANCE
12 EXAGGERATION
13 STUPIDITY
14 COYNESS
15 ANGER
AND ON, AND ON, AND ON!

TURN TO THE NEXT PAGE FOR AN EXAMPLE OF TWO STRIPS USING THIS METHOD!

ZIP-A-TONE 27½ LINE   10 PERCENT

USING THE YELLOW PAGES FOR MY ASSOCIATION TECHNIQUE FOR THE GAGS... HERE ARE THE RESULTS:

MOTORIST, WITH A TELESCOPE, IN A NUDIST COLONY. EMOTION: ANTICIPATION!

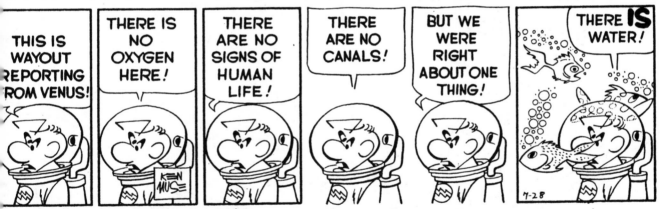

AN ASTRONAUT, ON VENUS, WITH A FISHBOWL. EMOTION: SURPRISE!

YOUR CHARACTER, OFFICE SUPPLY CO., MAKING A CHOICE. EMOTION: CONFUSION.
OF COURSE THE ORIGINAL IDEAS ARE CHANGED ABOUT FOR THE GAG!

THE CHANCE METHOD!

PLAN AHEAD

WHAT MAKES THINGS FUNNY?

ARE YOU KIDDING? NO ONE HAS BEEN ABLE TO ANSWER THAT ONE. YOU CAN'T DEFINE HUMOR BECAUSE IT DEPENDS ON WHO IS LISTENING!

YOU COULD DEFINE HUMOR AS CONTRAST, SURPRISE, CURIOSITY, EXAGGERATION, MISUNDERSTANDING... YOU NAME IT!

IF THERE WERE A TRUE DEFINITION FOR HUMOR, WE'D ALL LAUGH AT THE SAME JOKES! WE DON'T.

ONE TRICK THAT HAS ALWAYS WORKED FOR ME: BY STARTING TO DO A STRIP WITH NO INTENTION OF FINISHING... LIKE THIS:

KEN MUSE
6-3c

FINALLY LEFT THE FIRST 3 BALLOONS BLANK, AND THE LAST ONE SAID: "THAT LANGUAGE IS UNFIT TO PRINT."

HERE ARE TWO MORE THAT CAN INSPIRE
SOME IDEAS JUST BY LOOKING AT THEM:

THE GUY IN THE CAPSULE COULD SAY ALMOST ANYTHING AND IT WOULD
BE FUNNY. IT'S WORTH DRAWING BECAUSE YOU'RE BOUND TO GET A GAG.

IT MIGHT SOUND LIKE A WASTE OF TIME TO GO TO ALL THIS KIND
OF TROUBLE WITH NO PUNCH LINE IN MIND. BUT IT WORKS. THE
ONES YOU CAN'T WORK OUT ARE PUT ASIDE AND LOOKED ON....
ANOTHER DAY... *AND PRESTO!* IT JUST COMES TO YOU. THIS IS
WHAT'S CALLED *ASSOCIATION!* OF COURSE YOU WOULDN'T
DO A FINISHED STRIP... JUST A _ROUGH_!

ANOTHER TECHNIQUE IS TO BUY A BUNCH OF GAG BOOKS
FULL OF CARTOON PANELS AND CUT-OFF THE PUNCH LINES.
THE SITUATIONS WILL THEN CREATE _NEW_ GAG IDEAS!

WITH THE PHRASE METHOD OF CREATING GAGS, THE PUNCH LINES GIVE YOU THE IDEAS!

"YOU AND WHO ELSE?"

"I'M SORRY, HAVE YOU BEEN WAITING LONG?"

"THIS PERSON SAYS HE KNOWS YOU."

"IF YOU EVER NEED ADVICE, JUST ASK ME."

"IT'S JUST A DOLLAR DOWN AND A DOLLAR A WEEK."

"THEY COULDN'T AFFORD A NEW CAR."

"YOU'RE WASTING YOUR TIME, I ALREADY HAVE ONE."

"I CAN ALWAYS TELL WHEN YOU'RE MAD."

"WHERE IS EVERYONE?"

"SORRY, BUT THAT ONE'S NOT FOR SALE."

"WHAT AM I SUPPOSED TO DO NOW?"

"EVER HAD ONE OF THOSE DAYS WHEN EVERYTHING GOES WRONG?"

"DON'T YOU FEEL BETTER LOSING THAT WEIGHT?"

"THERE HAS TO BE ANOTHER ROUTE."

"IT WON'T DO YOU ANY GOOD TO RUN AWAY."

"HOW MANY TIMES DO I HAVE TO TELL YOU?"

"SORRY, BUT WE'RE CLOSED TODAY."

"I CAN SEE YOU'VE NEVER BEEN MARRIED."

"NOW THAT'S FUNNY."

"CAN'T YOU FIND A BETTER WAY TO SPEND YOUR MONEY?"

"WRAP IT UP—I'LL TAKE IT."

"WHAT DO YOU MEAN YOU DON'T WORK HERE?"

"I TRY TO KEEP IT A SECRET."

AND HERE ARE THREE STRIPS USING THE PHRASE METHOD!

OCK PHRASE: "I'M SORRY, HAVE YOU BEEN WAITING LONG?"

OCK PHRASE: "IT WON'T DO YOU ANY GOOD TO RUN AWAY!"

OCK PHRASE: "THERE HAS TO BE ANOTHER ROUTE!"

EE IF YOU CAN CREATE THREE NEW SITUATIONS FOR THESE PHRASES!

STOCK PHRASE METHOD

IF THIS ONE DOESN'T GIVE YOU IDEAS FOR A GAG, YOU ARE JUST TOO NORMAL! SOMETHING RIDICULOUS!

JUST THE PICTURE ON THIS ONE IS FUNNY!

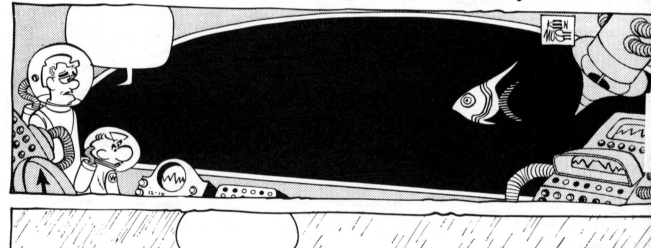

COLLECT ALL THE STOCK PHRASES FOR FUTURE USE TO PUT TO YOUR CARTOON SITUATIONS! WHEN YOU GET PHRASES FOR THESE THREE.... SWITCH THEM!

HERE ARE THREE SITUATIONS.... SEE IF THEY GIVE YOU ANY IDEAS!

HIS IS THE OLDEST SITUATION IN THE WORLD, BUT IT GOES ON AND ON!

T SHOULDN'T TAKE LONG TO COME UP WITH A GOOD ONE FOR THIS BABY!

THIS MIGHT BE A LITTLE TOUGHER! YOU COULD USE STOCK PHRASES LIKE: "THERE'S NO ONE HERE BY THAT NAME!" IF THIS ASSOCIATION TECHNIQUE DOESN'T WORK FOR YOU, YOU NEED *PRACTICE!*

IN THE ASSOCIATION METHOD, YOU SIT DOWN IN A RELAXED MOOD— MUSIC IF YOU WANT, AND THUMB THROUGH NEWSPAPERS, MAGAZINES, CATALOGS, ETC...

ALLOW YOUR MIND TO WANDER!

THE FREE ASSOCIATION OF PICTURES, WORDS, AND DRAWINGS, WILL STIMULATE GAG IDEAS.... BELIEVE IT OR NOT, BUT THE GAGS AND THE IDEAS DEVELOPED THIS WAY WILL BE YOUR MOST ORIGINAL, BECAUSE OF NO RULES!

IT TAKES PRACTICE.

MANY TIMES THIS METHOD WORKS AFTER THE READING IS OVER AND YOU'RE DOING SOMETHING ELSE... ALL OF A SUDDEN... POW...YOU GOT ONE!

OF COURSE ALL THESE METHODS ARE TYPES OF ASSOCIATION!

DRAWN WITH A GILLOTT 1290

CARTOONIST PUBLICATIONS

NOMINEES FOR THE REUBEN AWARDS

Dick Hodgins, Jr.

Roy Doty

Harry Devlin

Wallace Wood

Al Williamson

John Fischetti

Bill Crawford

Bill Mauldin

Murray Olderman

Bruce Stark

SION OF NATIONAL CARTOONISTS SOCIETY

ANNIVERSARY ISSUE OF THE MONTHLY PUBLICATION OF "THE CARTOONIST", AND COMES OUT ON THE NIGHT OF THE REUBEN AWARDS! ALL THE CARTOONISTS MEET IN ONE BIG ROOM, EAT, DRINK AND DANCE, AND STEAL EACH OTHER'S JOKES!

STORY STRIPS

John Prentice 'Rip Kirby'

Stan Drake 'Heart of Juliet Jones'

Alex Kotsky 'Apartment 3-G'

HUMOR STRIPS

Otto Soglow 'The Little King'

George Gately 'Hapless Harry'

Mort Walker 'Beetle Bailey'

SYNDICATED PANELS

Bil Keane

BERRY'S WORLD

Bob Dunn

TODAY I AM 21!

NCS

PRINTED BY PERMISSION OF NATIONAL CARTOONISTS SOCIETY

CARTOONIST PUBLICATIONS

invariably hold different meanings. These meanings emerge as discussion continues, as the two parties place the words into action, or as they try to write jointly a definition.

Freedom to *The Star* and to Sanders was defined by each, when *The Star* granted it and when Sanders tried to exercise it. It's obvious they hold different views and it's not surprising that they do.

The important divergence stems from how Sanders conceives his role as an editorial cartoonist—and *The Star's* conception of this role.

Sander's view can most easily be seen by looking at who he admires, those who fulfill his views of what he wishes to be himself. Herblock of *The Washington Post*, Conrad of *The Los Angeles Times*, and Jules Feiffer with *Hall's Syndicate* are three who represent to Sanders the men, if not to beat, at least to equal. The most important characteristic these three share is absolute freedom. Herblock, for example, was vehemently for Stevenson when everyone else on *The Washington Post* was for Eisenhower. Conrad was for Johnson while his paper, *The L. A. Times*, was foursquare behind Goldwater.

Herblock, Conrad, Feiffer, and Sanders belong to a New Wave of cartoonists who see themselves as independent editorialists speaking for themselves and themselves only, as do columnists. They feel that the libel laws of America are restraint enough and anything more than this is a restriction of freedom.

The Star, and most papers west of the Appalachians, take a much narrower view. Their view holds that Sanders, for example, speaks for *The Star*, that his every statement should be taken for *The Star's* point of view. They believe that a cartoonist may speak for himself if it is clear that he does so. Mauldin is frequently printed in *The Star*, but *The Star* doesn't feel identified with Mauldin's views since the readers accept him as a personality speaking for himself through syndication.

Sanders's morning begins when he rough sketches his ideas for cartoons on newsprint with a soft pencil. The sketches are submitted to the editors who approve, modify, or reject. The process is informal and discussion is free, but once the discussion ends, the editorial decision rules. By noon the decision is made. Sanders goes to lunch and starts the approved cartoon when he returns. It takes him most of the afternoon and appears in the following day's *Star* edition. He works a five day week which means two cartoons must be created on Friday, one for the Saturday issue and one for the Monday issue.

He draws with a water color brush and black ink. His talent has been seen by Kansas Citians for almost four years. There is no question that he [is na]tional and that [his reputa]

Collection. President Johnson has some Sanders originals in his office.

Sanders has been reprinted in *The New York Times*, *The London Observer*, *Izvestia*, *Time*, *Newsweek*, and in newspapers throughout Europe and South America. He is reprinted in two encyclopedias: Americana and World Book.

He holds the highest honor the 150 members of the Association of Ameri-can Editorial Cartoonists [can award:] is their [great] Cartoonist [award.]

to out-of-town offers he receives, whereas six months ago he ignored them. His loss to Kansas City would be serious.

He won't comment on rumors of his disagreements with The Star and refuses to say even 'No comment'. In the [motion] that two [papers]

No tellin' wut kind of characters will come in here if they pass that public accommodations law!

George (SWAN) Swanson

RELEASE TUESDAY, FEBRUARY 8, 1927

SALESMAN SAM
(Reg. U. S. Pat. Off.)
By Swa[n]

PERMISSION OF NATIONAL CARTOONISTS SOCIETY

The Cartoonist
MAY 1967

OTTO SOGLOW, winner of this year's National Cartoonists Society REUBEN AWARD, is congratulated by our new NCS President, JERRY ROBINSON.

PERMISSION OF NATIONAL CARTOONISTS SOCIETY

THIS IS THE OFFICIAL MAGAZINE OF THE NATIONAL CARTOONISTS SOCIETY, SENT TO EACH MEMBER ONCE A MONTH. IT CONTAINS SOCIAL GET-TOGETHERS, NOSTALGIA DEPT., ADVICE, STORIES ON CARTOONISTS' LIVES, THE STRIP BUSINESS, PROFILES, ETC., ETC.! NOT FOR SALE!

THIS IS THE DIRECTORY OF THE NATIONAL CARTOONISTS SOCIETY! IT LISTS ALL MEMBERS IN GOOD STANDING, WITH A SAMPLE OF THEIR ART AND A SHORT HISTORY OF THEIR CAREERS! EACH MEMBER BUYS A COPY. THEY GO FAST! NOT ON NEWSSTANDS!

HEY! WHAT'S 'DIS?!

SAY WHAT

IT'S A...

HEY! WE'RE GONNA HIT THE —

-ZIP

ALBUM
OF THE NATIONAL CARTOONISTS SOCIETY

WITH OVER 350 BIOGRAPHIES, PHOTOS AND DRAWINGS BY AMERICA'S BEST-LOVED CARTOONISTS, DONE BY THEIR OWN HAND

PRODUCED BY MORT WALKER

$7.00 A COPY

FOR THE BENEFIT OF THE MILT GROSS FUND

WITH AN EDITORIAL ASSIST BY BOB GUSTAFSON

"WE'D LIKE A POUND OF BACON, PLEASE — AND WOULD YOU TRIM OFF ALL THE FAT?"

BORN IN FRANKLIN, OHIO, SEPT. 14, 1902... FAMILY MOVED TO COAST AND, AFTER L.A. HIGH, JOINED THE L.A. HERALD ON NEW YEARS DAY, 1923. WENT TO FORT WORTH, TEXAS AS HEAD OF ART DEPARTMENT IN 1925... MOST IMPORTANT DATE WAS JULY 29 WHEN I MARRIED HELEN TOUSLEY... SECOND MOST IMPORTANT WAS SUMMONS FROM SCRIPPS-HOWARD SPORTS COLUMNIST JOE WILLIAMS TO MEET HIM IN FLORIDA IN SPRING OF '35. JOINED WORLD-TELEGRAM IN THAT YEAR TO COVER

SPORTS IN A CITY I'D NEVER SEEN - ON A WEEK'S TRIAL... HAVE BEEN THERE DRAWING SPORTS EVER SINCE. HAVE CONTRIBUTED WORK TO MANY MAGAZINES, SUCH AS LOOK, AMERICAN, COLLIERS, SATURDAY EVENING POST, ETC... MANY WORLD-TELEGRAM CARTOONS ALSO RUN IN J.G. TAYLOR SPINK'S SPORTING NEWS. HAVE BEEN A MEMBER OF THE NATIONAL CARTOONISTS SOCIETY SINCE ITS FOUNDING, SERVED AS FIRST VICE-PRESIDENT IN 1956, SECOND V-P IN 1959 (GOT DEMOTED)... OVERWHELMED BY BEING CHOSEN CARTOONIST OF THE YEAR FOR THE REUBEN AWARD IN 1954... HELPED FORM NATIONAL CARTOONISTS SCHOOL WITH FAMOUS ARTISTS SCHOOL IN WESTPORT, CONN...

KATE MURTAH

I WAS BORN IN LOS ANGELES, OCT. 29,1920— AND AM STILL HERE, AT 15146 MOORPARK, SHERMAN OAKS. STATE 4-7503. UNTIL 1947, MY TWO SISTERS AND I WERE A COMEDY SINGING TRIO— PLAYING TOP SPOTS IN THE COUNTRY. — LATER, I DID A SINGLE ACT. MY FIRST CARTOON SALE WAS "ANNIE AND FANNIE"— WITH UNITED FEATURES. MISGUIDED SOULS BUY MY OIL PAINTINGS___ MY SISTER ONRIETT AND I ARE PROFESSIONAL THEATRICAL PHOTOGRAPHERS___ OCCASIONALLY I ACT ON T.V.___ NO LONGER AM I A GIRL SCOUT LEADER!—'TWAS TOO RUGGED !!!

BEN BOLT

WAYOUT

IT SAYS REST ROOM

JOHN CULLEN MURPHY
BORN-N.Y.C.-1919. LIVED IN CHICAGO, STUDIED ART AT ART INSTITUTE THERE, LATER IN N.Y. AT PHOENIX ART INST., GRAND CENTRAL AND STUDENTS LEAGUE... STUDIED WITH NORMAN ROCKWELL IN NEW ROCHELLE. PAINTED COVERS FOR MAG-(LIBERTY, COLUMBIA) THEN JOINED IN '41. SERVED IN ANTI-AIRCRAFT ALL

OVER THE STATES AND IN AUSTRALIA, NEW GUINEA, PHILIPPINES AND JAPAN WITH MACARTHUR'S HQS. DEPARTED ARMY IN '46 AS MAJOR, BECAME ILLUSTRATOR FOR ADS AND 'HOLIDAY', 'LOOK', 'ESQUIRE', 'SPORT' 'COLLIER'S', ETC. STARTED BEN BOLT IN '50. I LOVE DOING WATER COLORS AND PORTRAITS. HAD EXHIBIT IN GREENWICH, CONN. IN '64. I MARRIED JOAN BYRNE IN '51, HAVE 7 WONDERFUL CHILDREN. WE ARE NOW LIVING IN IRELAND, WILL RETURN HOME IN '66. BUSY DRAWING 'BEN' AND PAINTING LOCAL COLOR. HOPE TO HAVE A SHOW WHEN I GET HOME....

116

KEN MUSE

I was born in Detroit, Michigan on April 28, 1925. I started drawing at the age of five, already hoping to someday draw a comic strip. At the age of thirteen, I took a correspondence course with the Landon School of Cartooning. By fifteen, I was working in art studios, learning paste-up and keyline. I graduated from Southeastern High and went into the Army Medics for four years, where I served with the 99th General Hospital in Verdun, France.

After the War, I went to the Meinzinger Art School in Detroit on the G. I. Bill, earning extra funds playing piano in combos. After art school, I was on live television in Detroit for eight years, drawing cartoons and caricatures for various childrens' shows. I was then behind the scenes for five years in TV art. This was followed by two years in animation, and two years of free-lance work.

I then felt that I had enough background to break into the comic strip biz. Every night, after a full days' work in the TV art department at WJBK-TV CBS, Detroit, I spent another 6 to 8 hours working on comic strips. This took four years of rejection slugs, and when McNaught bought my strip in 1964 I had

many gray hairs!

I am grateful to my wife, Irene, who taught music in the public schools to help me out.

I received no awards, and knew no one personally in the comic strip business, except those who encouraged me through the mail: Lank Leonard, Morris Weiss, Chick Young, Mort Walker, Milt Caniff, Bob Montana, Merrill Blosser, Bud Sagendorf, and Al Smith.

In a sense, I work backward: I draw the strip first in pencil—without any gag in mind—and let the drawing inspire the idea. This gives me more freedom to draw what I want. It also gives me a filing cabinet full of unfinished strips!

I use a quill pen, Artone extra dense ink, 2-ply plate finish Strathmore, HB pencils, and an A-5 Speedball for lettering.

My hobbies are astronomy and music. My only ambitions are to contribute what little talent I have to making people laugh, and to improve my drawing.

I live at 18506 Westmoreland on Detroit, with my ex-school teacher wife and two children, David and Ardith, aged twelve and nine respectively. If I had to do over again, nothing would be different.

117

CARTOONIST PROfiles

When we interviewed cartoonist Stan Drake, about his new syndicated panel "Pop Idols", and about his upcoming portrait show featuring 50 famous cartoonists, we said we'd like to feature one of the portraits on our cover. But Stan didn't want to appear to favor one cartoonist over another, so he suggested we solve the problem by using his portrait of your editor, Jud Hurd.

No. 42, JUNE 1979

$ 3.50

WITH PERMISSION OF JUD HURD

CARTOONIST PROFILES, EDITED BY JUD HURD, THE GENTLEMAN CARTOONIST ON THE COVER, IS A SLICK, FIRST CLASS MAGAZINE, FOR AND BY CARTOONISTS!

JUD DOES TWO CARTOON PANELS FOR UNITED FEATURE SYNDICATE CALLED "HEALTH CAPSULES" AND "TICKER TOONS."
IF I DON'T GET MY COPY OF "CARTOON PROFILES" IN MARCH, JUNE, SEPTEMBER, AND DECEMBER, I FEEL TOTALLY LEFT OUT!

IN OTHER WORDS, IF YOU WANT TO KNOW WHAT'S GOING ON IN THE PROFESSION... THIS IS IT!

ART POINIER, who does 6 political cartoons each week, distributed by the United Feature Syndicate, has had a long and distinguished career in this field, including service as editorial cartoonist on three major American newspapers. He also produced a comic strip for a number of years, at the same time he was doing his political cartoons. He's a Past President of the Association of American Editorial Cartoonists. And another side of his varied career has to do with his apple orchard business which he talks about here. Art lives in Ann Arbor, Michigan.

Poinier

HOME SWEET HOME?

NUCLEAR HAZZARDS

Q: There's a lapse of two or three days between the time you do your cartoon in the Ann Arbor and its appearance in the papers to which The United Feature ... distributes it 6 times a week.

... handled the ...

... never had any trouble with ... had on, such as The ... or with

subject matters which the papers will be dealing with on a continuing basis. Nowadays I'm drawing in straight black and white, eliminating screens and crayon shading effects, simplifying things so that a paper can reduce the cartoon as much as they want to. If a paper wants to pull it down to two columns, that's perfectly possible.

LATIGO
BY STAN LYNDE

STAN LYNDE was born, brought up, and continues to live in the western atmosphere which he portrays so excitingly in the new strip 'LATIGO' which he is doing for the Field Newspaper Syndicate. Over twenty years ago he created the 'Rick O'Shay' strip and he accumulated countless fans during the many years he continued to produce it. We featured the story of that strip in our first issue, over ten years ago. When we heard that Stan, a longtime friend, had turned his hand to a new strip, we quickly asked him to talk about it.

Red Lodge, Montana

It's late at night here in my home-studio as I put the finishing touches to a daily LATIGO strip scheduled for publication in August. As I've done with some six thousand other daily strips, I give it a final check before placing it with the other finished work.

Not a great strip, I tell myself, but good . . . pretty damn good.

This time is always a favorite time for

© FIELD ENTERPRISES, INC. 1979

1

the drawing board, nowadays you're successful apple ay, often doing

s work is done, the it's a good time both ck-trail to see where ng ahead to see where

go, I was just completr of producing RICK Chicago Tribune-New ndicate. Tonight, I'm e first year of my new), for Field Newspaper d I'm a little surprised, d, to find the excitement is

gallons of ink, I wonder? pen points and brushes? be well over a mile or two of in daily strips and Sunday nty years of deadlines met ed. Successes, disappointnds made, time shared — ugh time — and now, with t less hair and somewhat more , to find that after all the this feeling of excitement hasn't . This cartooning trade is really ing else.

good condition. As far as the diabetic condition was concerned would burn ..

Claudius Max, the meanest, vilest, most treacherous robber baron around.

Dark Star—Crow medicine woman, as beautiful as she is wise.

© Field Enterprises, Inc. 1979

Cole "Latigo" Cantrell—His word is the only law he knows

"Duke" Sateen— Professional gambler and cold-hearted cynic

Justin Fair—Old-fashioned lawman wears a heart of gold behind his silver star

Karin Anders— Tends the home fires for her husband Lars—while she carries a torch for Latigo

I remember some favorite quotes by cartoonists over the years:

Chic Young: "The real danger in this business is falling asleep at the board and putting your eye out with a pen."

Al Capp: "Cartooning is illustration plus a personal point of view."

Gus Edson: "How's business? Liar!"

For them, too, and for all the others who have given life to that blank piece of paper, the magic never failed.

I think back over the years with RICK O'SHAY and find few regrets. I've been able to do the work I've wanted to do the way I wanted to do it, while living in the area — and in the life-style — I've wanted to, as well.

Country singer Waylon Jennings says it in a song: "My heroes have always been cowboys, and they still are today."

Right on, Waylon.

The American West, with its lore, legend, and history, has a hold on me that has never lessened.

My young years growing up on my dad's ranch in southeastern Montana, working — and playing — with cow-

MONTANA TERRITORY—1867

STAN LYNDE

ARTY, STONEWALL... S TIME TOMORROW LL BE IN DRADO GULCH... ON OUR WAY TO A TUNE IN GOLD!

NOT IMPRESSED, EH? WELL...I SUPPOSE GREAT WEALTH DOES MEAN MORE TO MEN THAN TO MULES!

WITH PERMISSION OF JUD HURD

CARTOON PROFILES

POPEYE
On His 50th Birthday

1929 — **1979**

© KPS

Popeye, the world's best-known sailor, celebrated a half-century of bravura and spinach-powered derring-do on April 24th at his 50th birthday party in the Waldorf-Astoria Hotel in New York City.

The ham-armed, jut-jawed hero and his sweet patootie Olive Oyl (statistics 19-19-19) was on hand to greet his guests — over 1000 editors and publishers who were in New York City for the American Newspaper Publishers Association Convention.

Among the Old Salt's special guests was Forrest C. (Bud) Sagendorf, who was a protege of E. C. Segar, the creator of Popeye, and who has written and drawn the comic strip since 1958.

Three rooms of the Waldorf-Astoria were transformed into the Cafe de

22

Rough-House, the famous dock-side meeting place for Popeye and the gang. Miss Oyl, who purchased a large, stylish hat for the occasion, also ordered a six-foot birthday cake — made of what else, but spinach. The Old Salt's 22-ft. boat Olive was moored in the bay outside the cafe. Wimpy was busy cooking spinach hors d'oeuvres and miniature hamburgers to serve to everyone, including a few dozen for himself. Some of Popeye's sailor friends trimmed the sails and others provided the music.

"Popeye is celebrating a lot more than just his 50th birthday," Joe D'Angelo, president of King Features, host of the affair, said. "His popularity has always been high, but now it is booming. The comic strip is syndicated by King to more than 250 newspapers in 20 langu-

ages. 'The All New Popeye Hour' is one of the top-rated Saturday morning television shows; Robin Williams and Shelley Duvall will play Popeye and Olive Oyl in a major live-action motion picture musical; and 'Popeye, The First 50 Years,' an elaborate hardback history, will be published by Workman Press in May."

Popeye appeared originally in Elzie Segar's "Thimble Theatre." The raffish cast was composed of Olive Oyl, her brother, Castor Oyl and Ham Gravy, Olive's boyfriend. "Thimble Theatre" was written in the popular style of vaudeville-skits with blackout gags.

When "Thimble Theatre" was in its tenth year, Segar introduced the characters in a trip to Dice Island with their magic wiffle hen. Bernice, Castor and

t down to the waterfront to / for a boat they had bought, potted an odd-looking swab g on a dock.
'e, are you a sailor," asked

I'm a cowboy?" the sailor t was the debut of Popeye. January 17, 1929.
t grasped the imagination almost before Segar had / to perfect him as a

ie the star of the comic radio and animated ition picture theatres

and later for television. King Features licenses more than 1000 products which bear the sailor's likeness, everything from pencils to pajamas.

Popeye's influence on the spinach industry is legendary — but he's had an equally significant impact on the English language.

Goon (from the character Alice the Goon) passed into the language as a synonym for an unattractive person. Jeep, another Segar invention, became a synonym for a girl who is an expensive date. Eugene the Jeep ate nothing but orchids. G. P., a shortened military abbreviation for General Purpose Ve-

hicle, was modified and a second mea ing for jeep entered the vocabulary.

The phrase, "I yam what I yam became a national cry of vexation, an "I'll gladly pay you Tuesday for hamburger today," became a popul phrase as did, "I yam disgustipated."

Segar got most of the characters' od English from his young daughter' struggles with the language.

When Segar died in 1938 "Popeye was drawn by Bela Zaboly and written by Tom Sims. In 1958 Bud Sagendorf was signed by King to continue the comic. ●

At the 33rd Annual REUBEN AWARDS Dinner of the National Cartoonists Society at the Plaza Hotel in New York City on April 16th, SYLVAN BYCK (L.), recently-retired Comic Art Editor of King Features Syndicate, and for years the most famous man in his field, received the SILVER T-SQUARE award from the Society. He is shown here with J. F. D'ANGELO, the president of King Features Syndicate.

23

SAMPLE OF CONTENTS:

BOOK JACKET

"Successful artists view informative promotion as an essential part of their careers — and Artist's Market is the tool for achieving this goal."

— BOB CORNELL, PRESIDENT
CORNELL GALLERIES
SPRINGFIELD, MASSACHUSETTS

"It's direct, accurate and updated information. Everything you need to help you sell your work is here."

— DONALD JARDINE, Ph.D.
DIRECTOR, ART INSTRUCTION SCHOOLS

"We couldn't possibly function without Artist's Market! Now we look forward to each year's new edition. Thank you!"

— KATHLEEN J. MERO
LIBERTY QUILL ARTS
CONCORD, CALIFORNIA

1980 Artist's Market
where to sell your commercial art

3,000 Places to Sell Your Illustrations, Graphic Design, Cartoons and Animation Art!

Writer's Digest Books

ISBN 0-89879-002-0

PERMISSION FROM WRITER'S DIGEST BOOKS © 1979

THE ARTIST'S MARKET CAN CHANGE YOUR LIFE... IF YOU'RE AN **ARTIST.** IF THAT'S A STRONG STATEMENT IT'S BECAUSE A LOT OF HARD WORK WENT INTO ITS CONTENTS AND INFORMATION, AND IF YOU'RE A CAR-TOONIST, OR A COMMERCIAL ARTIST, OR A FINE ARTIST, YOU'RE GOING TO FIND ALL KINDS OF OPPORTUNTIES WITH THE HELP OF THIS BOOK!

IF YOU'RE AN ARTIST, GET YOURSELF A COPY, *QUICK!*

WRITE:

WRITER'S DIGEST BOOKS, 9933 ALLIANCE BOOKS, CINCINNATI, OHIO • 45242

SAMPLE PAGES

Periodicals

Magazines

AB BOOKMAN PUBLICATIONS MAGAZINE. Box AB. Clifton NJ 07015. Contact: Jacob L. Chernofsky. For book dealers. Offset. Query with resume.
Needs: Buys cartoons on bookselling. books, libraries and book collecting. Also uses artists for ad layout and paste-up.

ABC AMERICAN ROOFER AND BUILDING IMPROVEMENT CONTRACTOR. Shelter Publications. Inc.. 915 Burlington St.. Downers Grove IL 60515. (312)964-6200. Editor-in-Chief: J.C Gudas. For owners of roofing businesses. Monthly; 8½x11; 32 pages. Offset. Estab. 1911. Circ 29,220. Query. SASE. Reports in 1 week. "We want only that which is pertinent to our field, which get a lot of material that is totally irrelevant." Buys all rights. Pays on publication. Free sample cop roofing and exterior improvements. not general construction or interior home improvement. Usually, v
Cartoons: Buys 2-3/year on roofing; single panel. Pays $5-50. line drawings. .
Illustrations: Buys 15/year on the industry. Cover and inside: Pays $5, b&w.

ACCENT. 1720 Washington Blvd.. Box 2315. Ogden UT 84404. (801)394-9446. Senior Editor: L Harris. Editor: Valerie Sagers. Concerns travel. Estab. 1968. Circ. 600,000. Monthly. SASE. Rep in 3 weeks. Pays on acceptance.
Cartoons: Buys 1-2/year on business. sports and everyday life. "in good taste." Pays $15, b&w color. Send roughs.

ACCENT ON LIVING. Box 700. Bloomington IL 61701. Editor: Ray Cheever. Emphasis on s and ideas for better living for the physically handicapped. Send previously published samples. R in 2 weeks. Buys all rights. Pays on acceptance. Sample copy $1.
Cartoons: Pays $15.

ACCENT ON YOUTH. 201 8th Ave. S.. Nashville TN 37202. Editor: Margaret L. Barnhart reading for ages 12-14 in the United Methodist Church." Quarterly. Query with resume. Pr published work OK. Buys all rights; reprint rights on cartoons. Pays on acceptance.
Needs: Uses artists for 2- and 3-color illustrations. full-color cover illustrations, cartoons a design. Sample payment: $75. 4-color cover.

ACCESS. Marketing and Services Information Systems Division of Honeywell, 200 Waltham MA 02154. (617)890-8400, ext. 3736. Contact: Jean Gogolin, editor-in-chie personnel (and their families) of divisions responsible for selling and servicing computer ha software. Estab. 1978. Circ. 9,000. Quarterly; 11x14; 12-16 pages. Offset. SASE. Reports Simultaneous submissions and previously published work OK. Buys various rights. Pays tion. Free sample copy.
Illustrations: Needs b&w line drawings. washes and gray opaques. Negotiates pay. Query and samples or arrange interview to show portfolio.

ACROSS THE BOARD. 845 3rd Ave.. New York NY 10022. (212)759-0900, ext. : Chief: Lewis Bergman. Art Director: Josef Kozlakowski. For corporate executive officer Circ. 50,000. Monthly; 8¼x10⅞; 100 pages. Offset. SASE. Reports in 2 weeks. photocopied submissions. Buys first rights. Pays on acceptance.
Cartoons: Buys 20/year on current events and business-related topics; prefers sir $75-175, b&w; $100-175, color. Query with roughs.
Illustrations: Buys 5/issue on current events. education, environment, politics, edito related topics. Cover: Pays $200-325, color. Inside: Pays $75-175, b&w; $75-200, c samples or arrange interview to show portfolio.

ADAM. 8060 Melrose Ave.. Los Angeles CA 90046. Concerns "human sexuali society." Monthly. SASE. Reports in 2-3 weeks. Pays $20, b&w; $35-100,
Cartoons: Buys 8-12/issue on sexual and erotic themes. Pays $25-100, b&w; $35-1
Illustrations: Buys 1-2/issue on assigned themes. Pays on interview to show portfolio.

Syndicates and Clip Art Firms

Syndicates

ALA, LATIN AMERICAN FEATURE SYNDICATE. 2355 Salzedo St.. Suite 203, Coral Gables 33134. (305)442-2462. Editor: Arturo Villar. Estab. 1949. Syndicates to 120 magazines and newspa pers. Submit work. SASE. Reports in 3 weeks. Buys first Latin American rights. Pays on acceptanc
Needs: Cartoon strips about Latino situations and illustrations for editorial material on the same them single panel. Also buys one-shot material. Negotiates payment.

DANNEY BALL PRODUCTIONS. 1105 E. Florida Ave.. Hemet CA 92343. (714)652-4459 Contact: Robert Righetti. senior editor. Estab. 1973. Syndicates to newspapers; features include Ba Libs. For Pete's Sake. Noodles and Milo. "Until recently all material was produced by our staff. but we are presently looking for material that can be marketable on a syndication level." Submit artwork SASE. Reports in 2 weeks. Buys first rights.
Needs: "Cartoons and spot drawings should be camera-ready. reducible at least by 50% and be presentable to all ages; single. double and multipanel." Pays 50% commission.

BP SINGER FEATURES INC. 3164 Tyler Ave.. Anaheim CA 92801. (714)527-5650. Contact: Eldon Maynard. president. Estab. 1940. Syndicates to 300 magazines. newspapers. book publishers. poster and textile firms; strips include Airhawk. 7 Errors and Fun & Games. Buys several thousand pieces/year; local artists only. Send clips. SASE. Reports in 2-3 weeks. Buys reprint or all rights. Artist's guidelines $1.
Needs: Buys cartoon strips; single, double and multipanel; family. children. sex. juvenile activities and games themes. Pays 50% commission.
To Break In: "Send us cartoons on subjects like inflation. taxes or Christmas; we get thousands on sex."

CHICAGO TRIBUNE-NEW YORK NEWS SYNDICATE INC.. 220 E. 42nd St.. New York NY 10017. Editor: Don Michel. Estab. 1919. Syndicates to newspapers. Submit photocopies. SASE. Buys all rights.
Needs: Comic strips and continuing panel themes.

COMMUNITY AND SUBURBAN PRESS SERVICE. Box 639. Frankfort KY 40602. (502)223-1621. Managing Editor: Michael Bennett. Syndicates to 500 weekly newspapers. Reports in 10 days.
Needs: Pays $15, cartoons.

COMMUNITY FEATURES. 870 Market St.. Suite 920. San Francisco CA 94102. Contact: T. Wise. managing editor. Estab. 1976. Syndicates to 1,000 newspapers. Query with previously published work. SASE. Reports in 4-5 weeks. Buys reprint or all rights. Pays on publication. Provides mail and phone campaigns to clients." Artist's guidelines 50¢ and SASE.
Needs: Cartoons and illustrations; single or double panel. Pays $15-100 for assigned work.

CONTEMPORARY FEATURES SYNDICATE INC.. Box 1258. Jackson TN 38391. Editor: Lloyd Russell. Estab. 1974. Syndicates to newspapers and magazines. Mail b&w originals. SASE. Reports in 4-6 weeks. Buys various rights. Pays on publication.
Needs: Single panel cartoons. Pays $5 minimum flat fee or takes 50% commission.

DICKSON FEATURE SERVICE. 17700 Western.#69. Gardena CA 90248. Contact: Naida Dickson. associate director. Estab. 1977. Syndicates to newspapers; features include conservative political cartoon series by Ron Sanders. I Like You Because, and general humor titled Barbs & Brickbats by Allen & Owen Richardson. "We originally had only puzzles but we've lined up a few artists and columnists. and are interested in expansion." Submit material for consideration. SASE. Reports in 3 weeks. Negotiates rights purchased.
Needs: General interest. politically conservative. family and humorous cartoons and spot drawings; strips or single panels. "Moral values are in with us. We will not use racy. radical. bawdy or ultra-liberal material." Pays 50% commission for all rights; less for reprint rights only.
To Break In: "Send samples. We are a small organization. seeking recognition in the field. An artist must be willing to accept very little pay for his talents. perhaps for a long time. We distribute samples

SAMPLE OF CONTENTS FROM 1980 ARTIST'S MARKET!

CREATING THE SLIDE PORTFOLIO • PRICING YOUR ART • GETTING DOWN TO BUSINESS • COPYRIGHT AND CONTRACTS • BUSINESSES DESIGN STUDIOS • ANIMATION AND AUDIOVISUALS • LANDSCAPE DESIGN • BOOK PUBLISHERS • FASHION • GREETING CARDS AND PAPER PRODUCTS • PERIODICALS • RECORD COMPANIES • CLIP-ART FIRMS • SYNDICATES • ART PUBLISHERS • ETC., ETC., ETC.!

IF YOU'RE REALLY SERIOUS ABOUT SELLING YOUR COMIC STRIP YOU'LL GET YOURSELF A COPY OF *EDITOR & PUBLISHER*! IN IT YOU'LL FIND THE NAMES AND ADDRESSES OF THE SYNDICATES THAT BUY COMIC STRIPS!

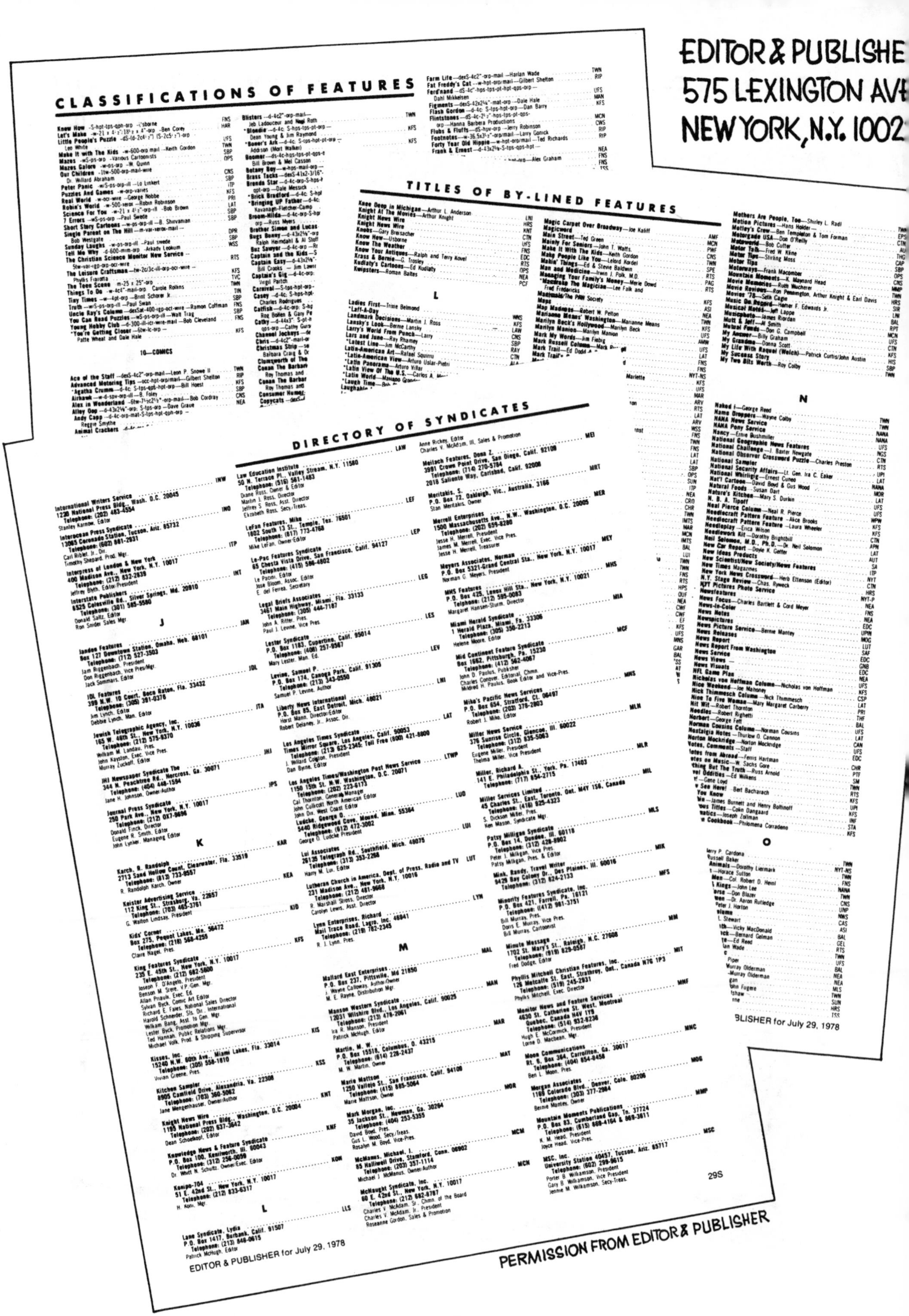

CLASSIFICATIONS OF FEATURES

Know How —S-hpt-tps-qpn-orp —L'sborne
Let's Make —x-21 x 4½"-19"z x 4"-orp —Ben Corey
Little People's Cartoons —dS-td-2c4½"z½ (S-2cS½"z-orp
Leo White
Make It with The Kids —w-600-orp-mail —Keith Gordon
Mares —wS-ps-orp —Various Cartoonists
Mazes Galore —w-os-wp —W. Quinn
Our Children —I'm-500-orp-mail-wre
Dr. Willard Abraham
Peter Panic —wS-4c-orp-ill —Lo Linkert
Puzzles And Games —orp-varies
Real World —w-oc-wire —George Nobbe
Robin's World —w-500-wre —Robin Robinson
Science For You —x-21 x 4½"-orp-ill —Bob Brown
7 Errors —wS-ps-orp —Paul Swede
Short Story Cartoons —w-os-orp-ill —B. Shivraman
Single Parent on The Hill —m-var-vero-mail —
Bob Westgate
Sunday Laughs —w-ps-orp-ill —Paul swede
Tell Me Why —600-mm-orp —Arkady Leokum
The Christian Science Monitor New Service —
Ste-var-gp-orp-oc-wre
The Leisure Craftsman —tw-2c/3c-ill-orp-oc-wre —
Phyllis Fiarotta
The Teen Scene —m-25 x 25"-orp
Things To Do —w-4c4"-maii-orp Carole Rohins
Tiny Times —w-4pt-orp —Brint Schorer Jr.
Truth —wS-ps-orp-ill —Paul Swan
Uncle Ray's Column —desSat-400-gp-oct-wre —Ramon Coffman
You Can Read Puzzles —wS-ps-orp-ill —Walt Trag
Young Hobby Club —o-300-ill-icr-wre-mail —Bob Cleveland
"You're Getting Closer —6tw-lc-wp —
Patte Wheal and Dale Hale

10—COMICS

Ace of the Staff —dexS-4c2"-orp-mail —Leon P. Snowe II
Advanced Motoring Tips —occ-hpt-orp-mail —Gilbert Shelton
Agatha Crumm —d-4c S-tps-qpS-hpt-orp —Bill Hoest
Airhawk —d-4c-orp-ill —B. Foley
Alex in Wonderland —6tw-7½-c2½"-orp-mail —Bob Cordray
Alley Oop —d-43x24"-orp- S-tps-orp —Dave Graue
Andy Capp —d-4c-orp-mat-S-tps-hpt-qpn-orp —
Reggie Smythe
Animal Crackers

Blisters —d-4c2"-orp-mail —
Jeb Ladoucceur and Neal Roth
Bloodie —d-4c S-hps-tps-oh-orp —
Dean Young & Jim Raymond
Boner's Ark —d-4c S-tps-hpt-pt-orp —
Addison (Mort Walker)
Boomer —dS-4c-hps-tps-ot-qps-orp —
Bill Brown & Mel Casson
Botany Bay —w-hps-maii-orp —
Brass Tacks —dexS-41x2-3/16"-
Brenda Star —d-4c-orp-S-hps-t
qps-orp —Dale Messick
Brick Bradford —d-4c- S-hpt
"Bringing UP Father —d-4c-
Kavanage-Fletcher-Camp
Broom Hilda —d-4c-hps-tps-orp
—Russ Myers
Brother Simon and Lucas
Bugs Bunny —d-43x24"-orp
Ralph Heemdahl & Al Stoff
Buz Sawyer —d-4c-orp —Ro
Captain and the Kids —d
Captain Easy —d-43x24½"-
Bill Crooks — Jim Lawr
Captain's Gig —d-4c-orp:
Jingil Patton
Casey —d-4c S-tps-hpt-orp
Casey —d-4c, S-hps-hpt-
Charles Rodrigues
Catfish —d-4c-orp- S-hg
Roe Bollen & Gary Pe
Cathy —d-43x3" S-p-rp
Channel Jockeys —de
Chris —d-4c2"-maii-or
Christmas Strip —w
Barbara Craig & Dc
Clumsworth of The
Conan The Barbar
Roy Thomas and
Conan The Barbar
Roy Thomas and
Consumer Humo
Copycats —dexS

Farm Life —dexS-4c2"-orp-mail —Harlan Wade
Fat Freddy's Cat —w-hpt-orp-mail —Gilbert Shelton
Ferd'nand —dS-4c"-hps-tps-ot-hpt-qps-orp —
Dahi Mikkelsen
Figments —dexS-42x24"-mat-orp —Dale Hale
Flash Gordon —d-4c S-tps-hpt-orp —Dan Barry
Flintstones —dS-4c-2½"-hps-tps-pt-orp —
Hanna Barbera Productions
Flubs & Fluffs —dS-hpr-orp —Jerry Robinson
Footnotes —m-36.5x3½"-orp-maii —Larry Gonick
Forty Year Old Hippie —w-hpt-orp-maii —Ted Richards
Frank & Ernest —d-43x24"-S-tps-orp-hpt —
—orp —Alex Graham

TITLES OF BY-LINED FEATURES

Knee Deep in Michigan —Arthur L. Anderson
Knight At The Movies —Arthur Knight
Knight News Wire
Knight News Wire
Knobs —Gary Breisacher
Know How —Usborne
Know The Weather
Know Your Antiques —Ralph and Terry Kovel
Krass & Bernie —G. Trosley
Kudlaty's Cartoons —Ed Kudlaty
Kwipsitters —Roman Baltes

L

Ladies First —Trixie Belmond
Laff-A-Day
Landman Decisions —Martin J. Ross
Lansky's Look —Bernie Lansky
Larry's World From Punch —Larry
Lars and Jono —Ray Rhumey
"Latest Line —M. Van Rensselaer
Latin-American Art —Rafael Squirru
"Latin-American View —Arturo Uslar-Pietri
"Latin View Of The U.S. —Carlos A. M—
Laugh Time —Bob H—
Laughabl—

Magic Carpet Over Broadway —Joe Kaliff
Magicword
Main Street —Ted Green
Mainly For Seniors —John T. Watts
Make It With The Kids —Keith Gordon
Make People Like You —Lelord Kordel
Makin' Things —Ed & Stevie Baldwin
Man and Medicine —Wren J. Polk, M.D.
Managing Your Family's Money —Merle Dowd
"Mantanna The Magician —Lee Falk and
Fred Fredericks
Manmade/The PNN Society
Map
Map Madness —Robert W. Pelton
Marianne Means' Washington —Marianne Means
Marilyn Beck's Hollywood —Marilyn Beck
Marilyn Manion —Marilyn Manion
Mark My Words —John Fisbig
Mark Russell Column —Mark Ru—
Mark Trail —d-4c Ed Dodd a—
Mark Trail'r—

Mothers Are People, Too —Shirley L. Radl
Motion Pictures —Hans Holder
Motley's Crew —Ben Templeton & Tom Forman
Motorgrade USA —Don O'Reilly
Motorworld —Bob Cutter
Motor Talk —Fred W. Kline
Motor Tips —Striking Moss
Motor Tips
Motorways —Frank Macpmber
Mountain Moments —K. Maynard Head
Movie Memories —Ruth Wucherer
Movie Review —Ron Pennington, Arthur Knight & Earl Davis
Movies '78 —Seth Cagin
Music Be Begged —Hamer F. Edwards Jr.
Musical Notes —Jeff Lappe
Municipets —James Worden
Mutt & Jeff —Al Smith
Mutual Funds —Don G. Campbell
My Answer —Billy Graham
My Grandma —Donna Scott
My Life With Raquel (Welch) —Patrick Curtis/John Austin
My Success Story
My Two Bits Worth —Roy Colby

N

Naked I —George Reed
Name Droppers —Wayne Colby
NANA Service
NANA Pony Service
Nancy —Ernie Bushmiler
National Geographic News Features
National Challenge —Baxter Newgate
National Observer Crossword Puzzle —Charles Preston
National Sampler
National Secy Affairs —Lt. Gen. Ira C. Eaker
National Whirligig —Ernest Cuneo
NAT Cartoon —David Bowl & Gus Wood
Nature's Kitchen —Mary S. Durkin
N. B. A. Tipoff
Neal Pierce Column —Neal R. Pierce
Needlecraft Pattern Feature —Alice Brooks
Needlecraft Pattern Feature —Laura Wheeler
Needleplay —Erica Wilson
Needlework Kit —Dorothy Brightbill
Neil Solomon, M.D. —Dr. Neil Solomon
New Car Report —Dovie K. Getter
New Leader Productions
New Scientist/New Society/News Features
New Times Magazines
New York News Crossword —Herb Ettenson (Editor)
N.Y. Stage Review —Chas. Ryweck
NYT Pictures Photo Service
Newsletters
News Focus —Charles Bartlett & Cord Meyer
News-In-Color
News Notes
News Picture Service —Berne Manley
News Releases
News Report From Washington
News Service
News Views
News Visuals
NFL Game Plan
Nicholas von Hoffman Column —Nicholas von Hoffman
Nice Weekend —Joe Mahoney
Nine Thimmesch Column —Nick Thimmesch
Nine To Five Woman —Mary Margaret Carberry
Hit Wit —Robert Thornton
Needler —Robert Righetti
Norbert —George Fett
Norman Cousins Column —Norman Cousins
Norman Mockridge —Norton Mockridge
Notes, Comments —Staff
Notes from Abroad —Ferris Hartman
Notes on Music —W. Sachs Gore
Nothing But The Truth —Russ Arnold
Novel Oddities —Ed Wilkens
Doctor Low!
See Have! —Bert Bacharach
You Knew
Ws —James Burnett and Henry Boltinoff
bus Titles —Colin Dangaard
Notics —Joseph Zollman
el Cookbook —Philomena Corradeno

O

Jerry P. Cardona
Russell Baker
Animals —Dorothy Liermark
I —Alice Suther
Man —Col. Robert D. Heml
Kings —John Lee
orse —Don Blazer
—T. Aaron Rutledge
Peter J. Horon
slam
L. Stewart
ack —Vicky MacDonald
ack —Bernard Gelman
le —Ed Reed
on Wade
I
Piper
Murray Olderman
—Murray Olderman
gan
John Fugere
N.I.
Jerry Van Time
Joyce Haber

BLISHER for July 29, 1978

DIRECTORY OF SYNDICATES

Law Education Institute .... LAW
50 N. Terrace Pl., Valley Stream, N.Y. 11580
Telephone: (516) 561-1483
Duane Ross, Owner
Marlin J. Ross, Asst. Director
Elizabeth Ross, Gen. Mgr.

LeFan Features, Mike .... LEF
1802 South 13 St., Temple, Tex. 76501
Telephone: (817) 773-4768
Mike LeFan, Owner-Editor

Le-Pac Features Syndicate .... LEP
65 Chestna Vista Drive, San Francisco, Calif. 94127
Telephone: (415) 586-4802
Le Pacini, Editor
Jose Bloom, Pres.
E del Fernea, Secretary

Legal Briefs Associates .... LEG
3461 Main Highway, Miami, Fla. 33133
Telephone: (305) 444-7167
John A. Ritter, Pres.
Paul J. Lewne, Vice Pres.

Lester Syndicate .... LES
P.O. Box 1183, Cupertino, Calif. 95014
Telephone: (406) 257-9567
Mary Lester, Man. Ed.

Levine, Samuel P. .... LEV
P.O. Box 174, Canoga Park, Calif. 91309
Telephone: (213) 343-0550
Samuel P. Levine, Author

Liberty News International .... LNI
P.O. Box 85, East Detroit, Mich. 48021
Horst Mann, Director-Editor
Robert Delaney, Jr., Assoc. Editor

Los Angeles Times Syndicate .... LAT
Times Mirror Square, Los Angeles, Calif. 90053
Telephone: (213) 625-2345; Toll Free (800) 421-8800
J. Willard Colston, President
Dan Byrne, Editor

Los Angeles Times/Washington Post News Service ... LTWP
1999 15th St. N.W., Washington, D.C. 20071
Telephone: (202) 223-6173
Cal Thomson, North American Editor
John Cuthcott North American Editor
John Dos West Coast Editor

Luedke, George .... LUD
5440 Morgan Cove, Mound, Minn. 55364
Telephone: (612) 472-3002
George I. Luedke President

Lui Associates .... LUI
26135 Telegraph Rd, Southfield, Mich. 48075
Telephone: (313) 353-2266
Harry M. Lui, Editor

Lutheran Church in America, Dept. of Press, Radio and TV LUT
231 Madison Ave., New York, N.Y. 10016
Telephone: (212) 481-9668
R. Marshall Stross, Director
Carolyn Lewis, Asst. Director

Lynn Enterprises, Richard .... LYN
Mail Trace Road, Logan, Ind. 46941
Telephone: (219) 762-2345
R. J. Lynn, Pres.

M

Mallard East Enterprises .... MAL
P.O. Box 237, Pittsville, Md 21850
C. Wayne Calloway, Author/Owner
M. E. Rayne, Distribution Mgr.

Manson Western Syndicate .... MAR
12031 Wilshire Blvd., Los Angeles, Calif. 90025
Telephone: (213) 476-2061
Ira R Manson, President
Patrick Murphy

Martin, M. W. .... MAT
P.O. Box 15518, Columbus, O. 43215
Telephone: (614) 228-2437
M. W. Martin, Owner

Marie Mattson .... MGR
1255 Vallejo St., San Francisco, Calif. 94109
Telephone: (415) 885-3064
Marie Mattson, Owner

Mark Morgan, Inc. .... MCM
35 Jackson St., Newnan, Ga. 30264
Telephone: (404) 253-5355
David Bowl, Pres.
Gus L. Wood, Secy./Treas.
Rosalyn M. Boyd, Vice-Pres.

McManus, Michael, J. .... MCN
65 Hallwell Drive, Stamford, Conn. 06902
Telephone: (203) 357-1114
Michael J. McManus, Owner

McKnaught Syndicate, Inc. .... MCN
60 E. 42nd St., New York, N.Y. 10017
Telephone: (212) 682-8787
Charles V. McAdam Sr., Chmn. of the Board
Charles V. McAdam Jr., President
Roseanne Gordon, Sales & Promotion

Anne Rickey, Editor
Charles V. McAdam, III, Sales & Promotion

Meitach Features, Dona Z. .... MRT
3901 Crown Point Drive, San Diego, Calif. 92109
Telephone: (714) 270-3784
2018 Saliento Way, Carlsbad, Calif. 92008

Meritakis, S. .... MER
P.O. Box 72, Oakleigh, Vic., Australia, 3166
Stan Meritakis, Owner

Merrell Syndicate .... MEY
1500 Massachusetts Ave., N.W, Washington, D.C. 20005
Telephone: (202) 955-0280
Jesse H. Merrell, President
James M. Merrell, Exec. Vice Pres.
Jesse H. Merrell, Treasurer

Meyers Associates, Norman .... MHS
P.O. Box 5321-Grand Central Sta., New York, N.Y. 10017
Norman G. Meyers, President

MMS Features .... MIA
P.O. Box 425, Lenox Hill Sta., New York, N.Y. 10021
Telephone: (212) 595-9083
Margaret Harrison-Sturm, Director

Miami Herald Syndicate .... MCF
1 Herald Plaza, Miami, Fa. 33306
Telephone: (305) 350-2213
Helene Moore, Editor

Mid Continent Feature Syndicate .... MHS
Box 1662, Pittsburgh, Pa. 15230
Telephone: (412) 562-4067
John D. Paulus, Publisher
Charles Conover, Editorial Chmn.
Mildred H. Paulus, Book Editor and Vice-Pres.

Mike's Pacific News Services .... MLN
P.O. Box 654, Stratford, Ct. 06497
Telephone: (203) 378-2803
Robert J. Mike, Editor

Miller News Service .... MLR
376 Sunrise Circle, Glencoe, Ill. 60022
Telephone: (312) 835-5063
Eugene Miller, President
Thelma Miller, Vice President

Miller, Richard A. .... MIL
141 E. Philadelphia St., York, Pa. 17403
Telephone: (717) 854-2715

Miller Services Limited .... MLS
45 Charles St., East, Toronto, Ont. M4Y 1S6, Canada
Telephone: (416) 925-4323
Sidney Mason, Pres.
Nan Mason, Syndicate Mgr

Patsy Milligan Syndicate .... MIK
P.O. Box 14, Dundee, Ill. 60118
Telephone: (312) 428-8902
Peter J. Milligan, Vice Pres.
Patsy Milligan, Pres. & Editor

Minn, Randy, Travel Writer .... MFS
9426 Bay Colony Dr., Des Plaines, Ill. 60016
Telephone: (312) 824-2133

Minority Features Syndicate, Inc. .... MM
P.O. Box 421, Farrell, Pa. 16121
Telephone: (412) 981-3751
Bill Murray, Pres.
Doris E. Murray, Vice Pres.
Bill Murray, Cartoonist

Minute Message .... MIT
1702 St. Mary's St., Raleigh, N.C. 27608
Telephone: (919) 829-0587
Fred Dodge, Editor

Phyllis Mitchell Christian Features, Inc. .... MNF
128 Metcalfe St., East, Strathroy, Ont., Canada N7G 1P3
Telephone: (519) 245-2931
Phyllis Mitchell, Exec. Director

Monitor News and Feature Services .... MHC
4630 St. Catherine St. West, Montreal
Quebec, Canada H3z 8236
Telephone: (514) 932-8236
Hugh E. McCormIck, President
Lorne D. Maclman, Mgr.

Moon Communications .... MOG
Rt. 5, Box 364, Carrollton, Ga. 30017
Telephone: (404) 854-8450
Ben I. Moon, Pres.

Morgan Associates .... MMP
1160 Colorado Blvd., Denver, Colo. 80206
Telephone: (303) 377-2984
Bernie Manley, Owner

Mountain Moments Syndicate .... MSC
P.O. Box 83, Cumberland Gap, Tn. 37724
Telephone: (615) 609-4164 & 869-3611
K. M. Head, President
Joyce Head, Vice-Pres.

MSC, Inc. .... MSC
University Station 40457, Tucson, Ariz. 85717
Telephone: (602) 299-9615
Porter B. Williamson, President
Gary B. Williamson, Vice President
Jennie M. Williamson, Secy-Treas.

J

Jandee Features .... JDL
Box 127 Downtown Station, Omaha, Neb. 68101
Telephone: (712) 527-3502
Iam Riggenbach, President
Don Riggenbach, Vice Pres/Mgr.
Jack Sommars, Editor

JDL Features .... JTA
399 N.W. 10 Court, Boca Raton, Fla. 33432
Telephone: (305) 391-0376
Jim Lynch, Jr.
Debbie Lynch, Man. Editor

Jewish Telegraphic Agency, Inc. .... JKI
165 W. 46th St., New York, N.Y. 10036
Telephone: (212) 575-9370
William M Landau, Pres.
John Horan, Exec. Vice Pres.
Murray Luckoff, Editor

JKI Newspaper Syndicate The .... JKL
344 N. Peachtree Rd., Norcross, Ga. 30071
Telephone: (404) 448-1594
Jane H. Johnson, Owner-Author

Journal Press Syndicate .... IPS
250 Park Ave., New York, N.Y. 10017
Telephone: (212) 0X7-9696
Donald Finch, Director
Eugene R. Smith, Editor
John Lytle, Managing Editor

K

Karch, R. Randolph .... KEA
2713 Sand Hollow Court, Clearwater, Fla. 33519
Telephone: (813) 733-9557
R. Randolph Karch, Owner

Keister Advertising Service .... KIO
112 King St., Strasburg, Va. 22657
Telephone: (703) 465-3761
G. Walton Lindsey, President

Kids' Corner .... KFS
Box 275, Pequot Lakes, Mn. 56472
Telephone: (218) 568-4299
Claire Nagel, Pres.

King Features Syndicate .... KIS
235 E. 45th St., New York, N.Y. 10017
Telephone: (212) 682-5600
Joseph D'Angelo, President
Benson M. Srere, v.p. Gen. Mgr.
Allan Priaulx, Exec. Ed.
Sylvan Byck, Comic Art Editor
Richard E. Faxes, National Sales Director
Harold Schneider, Sls. Dir. International
William Brink, Promotion Mgr.
Lester Bock, Promotion Mgr.
Ted Hannah, Public Relations Mgr.
Michael Volk, Prod. & Shipping Supervisor

Kisses, Inc. .... KSS
15240 N.W. 60th Ave., Miami Lakes, Fla. 33014
Telephone: (305) 558-1810
Vivian Greene, Pres.

Kitchen Sampler .... KNT
8905 Camfield Drive, Alexandria, Va. 22308
Telephone: (703) 360-5062
Jane Mengenhauser, Owner/Author

Knight News Wire .... KNF
1195 National Press Bldg., Washington, D.C. 20004
Telephone: (202) 637-3642
Dean Schoelkopf, Editor

Kopuridge News & Feature Syndicate .... KOM
P.O. Box 100, Kenilworth, Ill. 60043
Telephone: (312) 256-0059
Dr. Whitt N. Schultz, Owner/Exec. Editor

Koupo-704 ....
51 E. 42nd St., New York, N.Y. 10017
Telephone: (212) 833-6317
H. Koni, Mgr.

L

Lane Syndicate, Lydia .... LLS
P.O. Box 1417, Burbank, Calif. 91507
Telephone: (213) 848-0615
Patrick McHugh, Editor

International Writers Service .... INW
1228 National Press Bldg., Wash. D.C. 20045
Telephone: (202) 483-4554
Stanley Karnow, Editor

Intercoun Press Station, Tucson, Ariz. 85732 .... INO
13065 Coronado Station, Tucson, Ariz. 85732
Telephone: (602) 861-2931
Carl Riblet Jr., Prod. Mgr.
Timothy Shepard, Prod. Mgr.

Interpress of London & New York .... ITP
400 Madison Ave., New York, N.Y. 10017
Telephone: (212) 832-2639
Jeffrey Blyth, Editor/President

Interstate Publishers .... INT
8525 Colesville Rd., Silver Springs, Md. 20910
Telephone: (301) 585-5580
Donald Saltz, Editor
Ron Snider Sales Mgr.

EDITOR & PUBLISHER for July 29, 1978

29S

PERMISSION FROM EDITOR & PUBLISHER

318

QUESTIONS AND ANSWERS

HERE'S A BUNCH OF QUESTIONS AND ANSWERS TO HELP YOU OVERCOME SOME OF THE MYSTERY ABOUT THE COMIC STRIP BUSINESS!

SOME OF THIS INFORMATION IS ONLY FROM EXPERIENCE!

ABOVE ALL... NEVER GET DISCOURAGED.

THE GREATEST LITTLE COMIC STRIP IN THE WORLD, DRAWN

...AND DRAW, DRAW, DRAW.

QUESTION:

WHY CAN'T I DRAW MY CARTOONS WITH MAGIC MARKER?

ANSWER:

EVERY TIME YOU DRAW WITH A MAGIC MARKER, THE POINT WEARS AND CHANGES THE LINE. WHERE'S THE CONTROL? BESIDES, THEY *SMEAR!* BUT DO WHAT YOU WANT.

QUESTION:

I SEE A LOT OF BADLY DRAWN STRIPS IN THE NEWSPAPERS AND I KNOW I COULD DO BETTER!

ANSWER:

TALK, TALK, TALK!

QUESTION:

INSTEAD OF SENDING A TWO WEEKS SUPPLY OF STRIPS TO THE SYNDICATE, WHY NOT A MONTH'S SUPPLY?

ANSWER:

IF THEY LIKE WHAT THEY SEE, AND WANT TO KNOW IF YOU CAN KEEP UP THE QUALITY, THEY'LL *ASK FOR MORE!* DON'T TRY TO OVERSELL YOURSELF. BESIDES, DO YOU HAVE ANY IDEA WHAT IT COSTS TO MAIL, AND INSURE 24 STRIPS?

QUESTION: HOW ABOUT IF I DRAW AND MY BUDDY DOES GAGS?
ANSWER: OF COURSE, IT'S DONE ALL THE TIME.

QUESTION:

I'VE BEEN SENDING COMIC STRIPS BACK AND FORTH IN THE MAILS FOR TWO YEARS AND ALL I HAVE IS REJECTION SLIPS.!

ANSWER:

WELCOME TO THE CLUB. YOU JUST HAVEN'T FOUND THE RIGHT STRIP YET. START DRAWING NEW ONES. NEVER GIVE UP.

QUESTION:

CAN I GET ORIGINAL STRIPS OR PANELS FROM SOME OF THE FAMOUS CARTOONISTS SO I CAN STUDY THEIR WORK?

ANSWER:

GOOD THINKING.! SOMETIMES YES, SOMETIMES NO. MOST FANS WHO WANTED AN ORIGINAL FROM ME, NEVER BOTHERED TO SEND THE POSTAGE.

QUESTION:

WHERE DO I WRITE?

ANSWER:

TO THE SYNDICATE, AND THEY WILL FORWARD YOUR REQUEST TO THE CARTOONIST.

QUESTION:

BUT WILL HE SEND IT?

ANSWER:

IT'S HARD TO SAY. USUALLY THE SYNDICATE, OR THE ARTIST, REQUESTS A DONATION FOR THE STRIP, FOR THE MILT GROSS FUND, THROUGH THE NATIONAL CARTOONISTS SOCIETY. TRY.!

QUESTION:

DO I HAVE TO DRAW ON EXPENSIVE BRISTOL BOARD?

ANSWER:

OF COURSE NOT, YOU CAN DRAW ON ANYTHING YOU WANT, AS LONG AS YOUR WORK LOOKS PROFESSIONAL!

QUESTION:

DO I HAVE TO DRAW WITH PEN POINTS OR A BRUSH, WHY CAN'T I USE A RAPIDOGRAPH, OR OTHER TYPES OF TECHNICAL PENS?

ANSWER:

YOU CAN DRAW WITH WHAT EVER TOOLS YOU'RE COMFORTABLE WITH. A TECHNICAL PEN MAKES A LINE OF EQUAL THICKNESS FOR DRAWING *MECHANICAL* OBJECTS. A CARTOON IS NOT A MECHANICAL OBJECT, IT HAS PERSONALITY, HUMOR, AND CRAFTSMANSHIP. IT'S HOW YOU LOOK AT LIFE... IT'S <u>YOU</u>! A TECHNICAL PEN IS MONOTONOUS!

QUESTION:

IF MY STRIP IS NOT RETURNED TO ME IN A REASONABLE TIME, SHOULD I WRITE AND DEMAND THEY BE RETURNED?

ANSWER:

THAT WOULD BE STUPID. THEY MIGHT BE CONSIDERING IT FOR SYNDICATION. DON'T BLOW IT. WRITE FIRST AND ASK IF THEY RECEIVED IT, AND IF **NOT**, YOU CAN HAVE IT TRACED! I KNEW OF ONE SYNDICATE READY TO BUY WHEN THE CARTOONIST DEMANDED, AFTER 3 WEEKS, THE STRIPS BE RETURNED. THEY WERE.

QUESTION:

WHAT HAPPENS IF THEY LIKE YOUR COMIC STRIP OR PANEL?

ANSWER:

FIRST THING....THEY'LL ASK YOU TO SEND A COUPLE MORE WEEK'S SUPPLY TO SEE IF YOU'RE CONSISTENT. THEY MAY EVEN ASK FOR A MONTH'S SUPPLY OF ROUGHED-IN GAGS! YOU WON'T GET ANY COMMITMENT UNTIL THEY'RE REALLY SURE!

QUESTION:

HOW CAN THEY BE *REALLY SURE*?

ANSWER:

BY SALESMEN TAKING IT OUT ON THE ROAD AND SHOWING IT TO AS MANY NEWSPAPERS AS POSSIBLE!

QUESTION:

WHAT IF THE NEWSPAPERS LIKE IT?

ANSWER:

WELL, IF THE RESPONSE IS VERY GOOD, THE SYNDICATE MIGHT SEND YOU A TEMPORARY CONTRACT AND TELL YOU TO START DRAWING COMICS!

QUESTION:

HOW FAR AHEAD DOES A CARTOONIST DRAW HIS FEATURE?

ANSWER:

USUALLY SIX WEEKS, BUT THIS VARIES. IT'S A GOOD CUSHION. THE MORE AHEAD THE BETTER!

QUESTION:

HOW LONG DOES IT TAKE A SYNDICATE TO REACT TO A COMIC STRIP SENT THROUGH THE MAIL?

ANSWER:

I'VE HAD STRIPS RETURNED, ALL THE WAY FROM ONE WEEK TO 6 WEEKS. I REMEMBER ONE I ALMOST SOLD, TOOK 3 MONTHS.

QUESTION:

WHAT HAPPENS WHEN THEY DON'T LIKE YOUR STRIP?

ANSWER:

IF YOU INCLUDE POSTAGE, THEY SEND IT BACK. **IT'S NOT THAT THEY DON'T LIKE YOUR STRIP.** MOST OF THE TIME IT DOESN'T FIT THEIR NEEDS. THAT MEANS IT'S THE WRONG STRIP AT THE RIGHT TIME. THOSE ARE THE CHANCES YOU TAKE!

QUESTION:

HOW DO I KNOW THEY WON'T STEAL IT FROM ME?

ANSWER:

THIS HAS ALWAYS BEEN THE EXCUSE OF THE CARTOONISTS WHO ARE TOO LAZY TO PUT FORTH AN EFFORT. LET ME ASK YOU A QUESTION: IF YOU WERE A SYNDICATE, WOULD YOU STEAL SOMEONE ELSE'S STRIP AND HIRE ANOTHER ARTIST TO COPY IT, RISKING A LAW SUIT, WHEN YOU ALREADY HAVE THE ORIGINAL ARTIST... AND AT THE SAME COST? IF IT STILL BOTHERS YOU, SEND PHOTO-STATS!

QUESTION: SHOULD I GO TO AN ART SCHOOL OR A
COLLEGE TO STUDY CARTOONING?
ANSWER: A SCHOOL IS JUST A PILE OF BRICKS.
IF THE TEACHER HAS EARNED A LIVING
AS A CARTOONIST...GO THERE!
QUESTION: HOW ABOUT CORRESPONDENCE SCHOOLS?
ANSWER: THERE ARE GOOD ONES AND BAD ONES,
I'D RECOMMEND "CARTOONERAMA".
QUESTION: CAN A CARTOONIST MAKE A GOOD LIVING?
ANSWER: YOU'D BETTER BELIEVE IT.
QUESTION: CAN A CARTOONIST BECOME WEALTHY?
ANSWER: YOU'DE BETTER BELIEVE IT.
QUESTION: IS IT TRUE THAT ALL CARTOONISTS HAVE
HAD A SERIOUS HEAD INJURY AT ONE TIME?
ANSWER: I'VE HEARD THAT ONE BEFORE. I HAVE!
QUESTION: WHAT IS A CARTOONIST?
ANSWER: A PERSON WHO, WHEN HE RECEIVES GIFTS,
DRAWS ON THE BOXES!

SOME CLOSING REMARKS AND ADVICE!

ALWAYS DRAW SO YOUR LINES CAN
TAKE A **50%** REDUCTION.

KEEP YOUR TOOLS CLEAN!

DISCOVER FOR YOURSELF WHICH DIRECTION
YOU **SHOULD** AND **SHOULDN'T** INK.

EXPERIMENT WITH EVERYTHING YOU
CAN GET YOUR HANDS ON.

WHEN INKING, TURN YOUR BRISTOL.

KEEP YOUR DIALOGUE AS SHORT AND SIMPLE AS POSSIBLE.

DON'T DECEIVE YOURSELF...
IF IT'S BAD, DRAW IT OVER!

DON'T STEAL FROM OTHER CARTOONISTS.

DON'T RUSH YOUR WORK.

DON'T WORK YOUR CARTOON TO DEATH.

SPEND TIME PRACTICING THE THINGS
YOU HAVE DIFFICULTY DRAWING.

GET YOURSELF A CARTOONIST FRIEND!

DRAW EVERYDAY!

WHEN FINISHED, CLEAN-UP YOUR WORK.

WHEN DRAWING,
ERASE AS LITTLE AS POSSIBLE!

MASTER ONE PEN FOR DRAWING, AND ONE FOR
LETTERING.

STUDY THE WORK
OF OTHER CARTOONISTS YOU ADMIRE.

DON'T FILL-IN LARGE BLACK AREAS UNTIL YOU'VE
ERASED YOUR PENCIL LINES.

I'VE KNOWN SOME REAL TALENTED
CARTOONISTS WHO JUST GAVE UP
BECAUSE THEY THOUGHT
TALENT WAS ENOUGH. SOME OF THEM
WERE MY STUDENTS.

THAT DOESN'T BOTHER ME. I DON'T
NEED THE COMPETITION!

BEING SUCCESSFUL IS SIMPLE:

YOU GOTTA WANNA BE SOMETHING
BAD ENOUGH!

A CARTOONIST:

BEGAN STUDYING THE CARTOONS OF OTHERS, AND DRAWING AT A VERY EARLY AGE!

SEES SOMETHING FUNNY IN EVERYTHING!

IS CONSTANTLY EXPERIMENTING AND COMPLAINING ABOUT NOT HAVING ENOUGH TIME TO DRAW!

IS TOLD BY FRIENDS AND RELATIVES TO FORGET IT AND BE A DOCTOR, OR ANYTHING ELSE!

HAS AT LEAST ONE CARTOONIST FRIEND!

HAS A LOT OF COMIC BOOKS .... AND WILL BUY ANYTHING THAT SAYS "CARTOONING" ON IT!

IS ONLY UNDERSTOOD BY OTHER CARTOONISTS!

WILL DRAW ON ANYTHING THAT'S AVAILABLE!

3/13/85

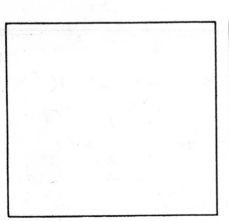
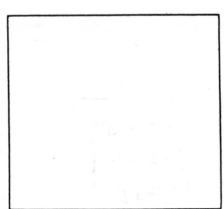